DATE DUE

NOV - 4 1993	MAR 2 3 2000
FEB - 4 1994	APR - 6 2000
FEB 18 1994	FEB 2 4 2001
MAR - 3 1994	MAR 3 0 2002
APR 14 1994	OCT 2 4 2003
OCT 1 3 1994	
JAN 2 5 1995	
MAR 3 1 1995	
JAN 1 7 1997	
FEB 2 8 1997	
MAR 1 2 1997	
APR 1 8 1997	
SEP - 9 1997	
Oct. 9.	
MAR 2 5 1998	
APR - 8 1998	
APR 2 3 1998	

BRODART   Cat. No. 23-221

Feminist Perspectives on Addictions

Nan Van Den Bergh, PhD, serves as the Director of UCLA's employee assistance program (EAP) and previously was tenured faculty in social work at California State University, Fresno. She coedited *Feminist Perspectives on Social Work*, which is one of the major titles in women's issues for social work education. Her interest in addictive behavior as a psychotherapist and EAP professional led her to compile an anthology that would provide a feminist perspective on both the cause and cure of addictive behaviors. She has authored many articles on feminist practice as well as addictions, and is currently doing work in the areas of workplace diversity and mutual aid/self-help groups.

Feminist Perspectives on Addictions

Nan Van Den Bergh, PhD

Editor

SPRINGER PUBLISHING COMPANY
NEW YORK

Springer Publishing Company, Inc.
536 Broadway
New York, NY 10012-3955

91 92 93 94 95 / 5 4 3 2 1

Library of Congress Cataloging-in-Publication Data

Feminist perspectives on addictions / edited by Nan Van Den Bergh.
    p. cm.
  Includes bibliographical references and index.
  ISBN 0-8261-7350-0
  1. Compulsive behavior. 2. Co-dependence (Psychology)
  3. Feminism. I. Van Den Bergh, Nan.
  [DNLM: 1. Compulsive Behavior—psychology. 2. Identification
(Psychology). 3. Social Environment. 4. Substance Dependence—
psychology. 5. Women—psychology. WM 270-F329]
  RC533.F45 1990
  616.86'0082—dc20
  DNLM/DLC
  for Library of Congress   90-10434
                                                                  CIP

Printed in the United States of America

Contents

Part 3 Process Dependencies

Preface

Sometime in 1972 I saw Stanley Kubric's film, *A Clockwork Orange*, and was radicalized—the next day I attended a National Organization for Women meeting dealing with images of women in the media. Having been horrified by the casual way in which women were defiled, raped, and physically brutalized on screen, and as a result of meeting others who shared an interest in taking action against the victimization of women, I became inspired to apply a feminist analysis to the world around me.

That ideological lens has had an impact on the entire course of my adult life; in retrospect, I probably had a feminist view when in kindergarten I chose to build boats with carpenter's tools, rather than to "play house." I am grateful that I have developed a feminist perspective as it is a wholistic, spiritual, energy-creating and life-enhancing philosophy.

Personally and professionally as an educator, therapist, writer and manager, I have tried to conduct my life in such a way that feminist principles, which I will define in the first chapter, such as valuing process (or the ways things are done), reconceptualizing power, believing in the validity of one's own reality and seeing the personal as political, have had an impact on what I do, the way I see the world and how I relate to others. Having used a feminist framework to define social work practice in *Feminist Visions for Social Work*, I saw its value and utility in offering explanations for the cause of some personal and social problems as well as how these problems could be ameliorated. Hence, as I began to work with addictions through my experience with workplace employee assistance and counseling programs, I became intrigued when considering how a feminist paradigm could be used to clarify and define the causes and cures of addictions.

Consonant with a feminist viewpoint, one needed to look at addictions wholistically; hence, I decided to edit an anthology that would include an examination of a broad base of addictive disorders, as well as taking a particular look at certain at-risk-for-addiction population groups, through a feminist lens. As a result, in addition to the topics of drugs and alcohol, the volume also addressed workaholism, eating disorders, gambling, compulsive sexuality, codependent and relationship addiction, and addictive disorders in older women and lesbians. In an attempt to be all-inclusive and broadbased, which is a crucial requirement for a unified feminist perspective, the contributors represent academics and students, as well as practitioners in a wide variety of disciplines. A great deal of energy was expended in searching for someone who could write authoritatively on addiction as it applies to ethnic minority women, and although there were some individuals who showed interest in this topic, it was, unfortunately not possible to include a complete chapter on the subject. This is a significant omission; one that I am unhappy about; and for this reason, some material on addiction as it applies to ethnic minority women is included in the introduction.

This book is one that a broad spectrum of individuals should find useful as most of the contributions are pragmatically oriented, easily generalizable to practice, and several are empirically based and grounded in contemporary theories on addiction. It will be valuable for practitioners and academics since chapters include both an analysis of the addictive disorder as well as a therapeutic perspective focusing on "how it works" when treating clients. Consequently, these chapters should be indispensable for practitioners in a variety of mental health disciplines, employee assistance program professionals, and of great interest to academics and students.

I am grateful for the life experiences that have helped to shape my vision of the world through a feminist lens, and I'm thankful for the experience of my own Twelve Step recovery. In a society which normatively predisposes one to become addicted, because of oppressive societal dynamics and dehumanizing processes, we can begin to empower the planet by empowering ourselves—that is the miracle.

NAN VAN DEN BERGH
University of California, Los Angeles

Acknowledgements

Three women have been particularly helpful to me in bringing this book to fruition; what they all have in common is their superb wordprocessing, editing and manuscript preparation skills. Additionally, a common denominator has been their employment by the higher education institutions where I have worked for the three years that this anthology has been in progress, both California State University, Fresno and the University of California, Los Angeles.

The following kudo is offered to three wonderful women with whom I have truly been blessed—Kathy Haas, Miye Ioki and Jennifer Harper: You're Terrific!

Contributors

Sheila B. Blume, MD, CAC, is Medical Director of the Alcoholism, Chemical Dependency and Complusive Gambling Programs at South Oaks Hospital. Dr. Blume earned her medical degree with honors from Harvard Medical School. She is clinical professor of psychiatry at the State University of New York at Stony Brook, and Director of the South Oak Institute of Alcoholism and Addictive Behavior Studies. Formerly medical director of the National Council on Alcoholism, Dr. Blume was also New York State Commissioner for alcoholism from 1979 to 1983. Dr. Blume was appointed to the National Commission on Alcoholism and Other Alcoholism-Related Problems. An international expert on the topics of chemical dependency, pathological gambling, problems of women, children of addicted parents, and use of psychodrama in the treatment of addictive disorders, Dr. Blume is the author of a large number of papers, chapters and other publications.

Joan C. Chrisler, PhD, is Assistant Professor of Psychology at Connecticut College. She is an experimental psychologist and conducts research on women's health, particularly in the areas of eating behavior and menstrual cycle-related changes. She has post-doctoral training in cognitive and behavior therapy and has led therapy groups for disordered eaters.

Eileen M. Corrigan, DSW, is a Distinguished Professor at the School of Social Work at Rutgers University. Her primary research interest centers around women's alcohol and drug use. She has completed a major study of alcoholic women in treatment in the United States in the mid 1970s and replicated this study in Ireland in the late 1980s. Early findings from this study are to be found in the *International Journal of Addictions* (Corrigan & Butler, "Irish Alcoholic Women in Treatment," in press). Other recent publications are "Women's Combined Use of Alcohol and Other Mind Altering Drugs," in D. Burden & N. Gottlieb (eds.), *Social Work Curriculum for Practice with Women Clients*, London: Tavistock, 1987; and "Gender

Differences in Alcohol and Other Drug Use," Brief Report, *Addictive Behaviors*, 10(3) 1985, 313–318. She is currently consolidating her long standing interest in this area and is working on a book.

Jed Diamond, LCSW, is a licensed psychotherapist and addictionologist. For the past twenty-five years he has been helping people prevent and treat problems associated with sex and "love" addiction, chemical dependency, eating disorders, and other addictive behaviors. A recent book, upon which this chapter is based, is entitled *Looking For Love In All The Wrong Places: Overcoming Romantic and Sexual Addictions*. He will be publishing two additional titles in 1992, *The Acceleration Syndrome* and *The Warrior's Journey Home: Healing Men's Addictions, Healing the Planet*. He received his masters degree in Social Work from the University of California at Berkeley. He has taught classes at the University of California, Berkeley, University of the Pacific, College of Marin, the Merritt-Peralta Institute, and other centers of education throughout the country. He is a nationally recognized educator and trainer in the area of addictions.

Cynthia Downing, MA, CAC, is Director of Earthrise, Inc., a private practice specializing in addictions and self-esteem. She holds a master's degree in Human Services from John Carroll University and is currently a doctoral candidate at Saybrook Institute, San Francisco. Her dissertation research is on core issues in relapse. She has a special interest in long-term recovery and codependency issues. She is a Licensed Professional Counselor in the State of Ohio, a Certified Alcoholism Counselor, and a Certified Relapse Prevention Specialist. She is listed in the private practitioner's section of *The 100 Best Treatment Centers For Alcoholism and Drug Abuse*. She is an author, lecturer, and has conducted training at the local, state, and national levels. Her latest work is *Triad: The Evolution of Treatment for Chemical Dependency*.

Larry Dyer, LMSW, is a research social worker at the Colmery-O'Neil V.A. Medical Center in Topeka, Kansas, and a doctoral student at the University of Kansas in social welfare. He is currently working as a drug and alcoholism counselor and is a consultant on the development of services for older alcoholics.

Diane Fassel, PhD, is an organizational consultant, mediator, and author of *Working Ourselves To Death* and *Growing Up Divorced* and coauthor of *The Addictive Organization*.

Susan G. Hanchey, PhD, is a Licensed Clinical Psychologist and the Clinical Supervisor of the Women's Treatment Center/Eating Disorders Program at Sierra Community Hospital in Fresno, California. In addition, Dr. Hanchey has a private practice specializing in women's issues. She received a doctorate in Clinical Psychology in 1987 from California School of Professional Psychology, Fresno, and has been working as a therapist since 1978.

Sue A. Kuba, PhD, is a licensed psychologist and the founder and former Director of the eating disorders program located at Sierra Community Hospital in Fresno, California. She has been treating anorexic, bulimic and compulsive eating patients for seven years and has pioneered innovative approaches to treatment in the Fresno area. In addition to her work at Sierra Community Hospital, she is currently an associate professor at California School of Professional Psychology and has her own private practice. Dr. Kuba recently coauthored an article about the effects of eating disorder behavior upon the workplace, and presents frequently on the meaning of dream imagery in the eating-disordered population.

Henry R. Lesieur, PhD, received his doctorate in sociology from the University of Massachusetts, Amherst in 1976. Currently, he is an associate professor in the department of sociology and anthropology at St. John's University in Jamaica, New York. Dr. Lesieur is a consultant to the South Oaks Foundation in Amityville, New York, and several state councils on compulsive gambling. He is a member of the Executive Board of the National Council on Problem Gambling, a member of the work group to revise the Diagnostic and Statistical Manual of the American Psychiatric Association, and editor of *Journal of Gambling Studies*. He is the author of *The Chase: Career of the Compulsive Gambler*, book chapters on crime and pathological gambling, and has published many articles in professional journals. Dr. Lesieur has run workshops and given numerous professional presentations in connection with his work on compulsive gambling and addictions. He is currently conducting analyses of surveys of gambling among college students and is writing a book based on interviews with female pathological gamblers.

Nancy V. Minkow, MSW, investigated where women can seek treatment for psychotropic drug dependencies in Los Angeles. Interning in a psychiatric department of a hospital, she completed her graduate program in the School of Social Work at the University of Southern California.

Jo Nol, MSW, is a Smith Doctoral student and has worked in a child and family services agency in Connecticut. She has been involved in both inpatient and outpatient treatment for chemical dependency as well as in substance abuse prevention in communities and schools. Jo has worked with groups both in and out of jail for people convicted of drinking and driving. She has also worked in the area of women's issues such as a battered women's shelter, a rape crisis center, and long-term incest victims' groups where substance use/abuse is also prevalent.

Patricia O'Gorman, PhD, is a psychologist, author, lecturer, and director of Adult Child Counseling Center in East Greenbush, New York. She is the co-author of *12 Steps to Self-Parenting, Self-Parenting 12 Step Workbook, Breaking the Cycle of Addiction,* and *Teaching About Alcohol.*

Jane E. Prather, PhD, has conducted research on women and prescription drugs for over 15 years. The author of papers on pharmaceutical advertising in medical journals, international marketing of drugs, and the prescribing of psychotropics to elderly women, she teaches sociology and women's studies at California State University, Northridge.

Eloise Rathbone-McCuan, PhD, MSW, is Associate Chief of Social Services for Research and Education at the Colmery-O'Neil V.A. Medical Center in Topeka, Kansas, and Research Professor at the School of Social Welfare at the University of Kansas. She has published extensively in the field of alcoholism in aging and older women. She is a Fellow in the Gerontological Society of America, and was Chairperson of the Council on Social Work Education Commission on the Status of Women in Social Work Education.

Anne Wilson Schaef, PhD, is an internationally known lecturer and best-selling author of *Women's Reality, Co-Dependence, When Society Becomes An Addict, Escape From Intimacy, Mediations For Women Who Do Too Much,* and co-author of *The Addictive Organization.*

Chandra Smith, MSW, is the former executive director of Residence XII, an intensive residential treatment center for women. Chandra, who is in private practice in Seattle, specializes in working with women on healing the feminine through therapy, ritual and metaphor. She is currently working on a project that is researching the meaning of work for women in corporate settings.

Brenda Underhill, MS, CAC, is Executive Director of the Alcoholism Center for Women, a community-based agency offering prevention and recovery services to women and other underserved populations. Brenda is a frequent and sought-after speaker, workshop presenter and facilitator with expertise in issues facing those at risk to alcoholism, such as lesbians, incest survivors, and adult daughters of alcoholics.
Drawing on her more than 15 years of practice in the field, Brenda is

a published author, most recently in *Alcohol, Health and Recovery World* as well as *Alcoholism Treatment Quarterly*.

Brenda holds board membership on several national organizations, including the National Association of Lesbian and Gay Alcoholism Professionals (NALGAP) and is on the faculty of the Chemical Dependency Studies Program at the California Family Studies Center in North Hollywood.

Judith A. Wartman, MA, is a research medical sociologist at the Colmery-O'Neil V.A. Medical Center in Topeka, Kansas, and is a doctoral student in social welfare, at the University of Kansas. She has completed extensive research in the fields of health care for the elderly and is interested in the field of aging and mental health.

PART I

Gender Roles, Power, and Addictions

1

Having Bitten the Apple: A Feminist Perspective on Addictions

Nan Van Den Bergh

Having bitten the apple, Eve was banished from Eden with her consort Adam, and both were deemed sinners. But in reaching for the apple, Eve was seeking to discover the world and to become master of her own destiny. The original sin, then, was to question and to define reality through one's own experience.

The development of addictive behavior is in many regards analogous to the message imparted through the "Fall" of Adam and Eve. Feeling a sense of incompleteness and imperfection, humans can reach outside of themselves to an external object, persons or situations which, when ingested, connected to or engaged, provides a sense of wholeness and completion. To the extent that an individual has experienced life situations causing her or him to feel inherently inferior, the propensity is increased to look outside of the self for an experience that will provide a sense of completeness. The obsessional desire for this external experience coupled with compulsive behavior in its pursuit, is the pattern leading to addiction.

A feminist perspective on addiction begins with an acceptance of the premises stated above concerning the relationship between an internal sense of fragility and the pursuit of something external to the self to anesthetize anxiety and fear. However, a feminist perspective also examines societal inequalities that can engender the sense of emptiness and despair, which is present at the genesis of any addictive behavior.

This volume examines a range of addictive behaviors including alcoholism, drug dependence, eating disorders, compulsive gambling, codependence, workaholism, as well as sex and love addiction. For each addiction, authors examine causes and cures through a feminist perspective, which allows for underscoring certain common denominators. Although women

3

are a specific focus of attention within this volume's content, it will also be apparent to the reader that a feminist perspective is broader than a focus specifically on women's issues. An explanation of what constitutes a feminist analysis follows.

WHAT IS A FEMINIST PERSPECTIVE?

A feminist vision is a world view concerned with the elimination of inequality, including dynamics that allow for domination, power over and control of others. Rather than seeing individual men as the "enemy," feminism defines patriarchy as the problem. Feminists have provided varying interpretations of patriarchy as well as its genesis, but it most notably means a system of male domination characterized by a hierarchical dominant-subservient relationship between men and women. Some theorists, dating from Plato, have maintained that patriarchy is the oldest family form. However, discourse begun in the nineteenth century by sociologists and anthropologists such as Briffault, Bacofen and Engels, and continued by many contemporary feminists, maintains that patriarchy arose only after the demise of the original family which was matrilocal and matriarchal (Warren, 1980). Marxist and socialist feminists have concurred with the latter conviction; they believe that patriarchal structures as they exist today, have been affected by the development of private property and subsequently, a capitalist economy. This perspective is perhaps most useful when positing a feminist perspective on addictions; it offers suggestions on how societies motivated by values of conquest, competition and acquisitiveness can engender life conditions that may predispose both men and women to addiction.

Within patriarchal capitalist societies the dynamics of control and acquisition are paramount cultural forces that affect not only the workings of the economic system, but also relationships between the sexes. Ownership and having control becomes a *sine qua non* for status and worth. Hence, people are motivated to look outside of themselves to acquire something that will make them feel important and worthwhile. However, a concomitant of patriarchal capitalism is to control the means by which wealth can be acquired. Women and ethnic minorities, through occupational segregation and poverty, have historically been relegated to positions where they could not easily gain access to the means for acquiring wealth. Hence, an inherent frustration is engendered within capitalist patriarchy as individuals are taught to seek but are not able to acquire that which provides legitimacy and status. Psychologically, over time, that frustration can produce feelings of inferiority and an addiction can develop as a way to numb and deny a sense of powerlessness.

Related to the patriarchal dynamics of power and control is the concomitant techique of dividing and conquering. Some theorists have noted that patriarchal processes are refined during historical periods when there has been much warfare. However, in an examination of the history of western civilization it becomes difficult to locate epochs free from fighting. Military control has frequently been maintained by dividing a country, or precipitating "infighting." In other contexts, essentially the same divide and conquer process is used to view phenomena either in isolation or in a categorized, classicatory way. This deters seeing the interrelatedness and connectedness between things or events and also engenders a short-term rather than long-range view.

Other dynamics associated with capitalist patriarchy include being focused on "ends" rather than "means;" in other words, it makes no difference how you do something, as long as you win. This sets up situations of competition and conquest that reify domination and control, since there will be one winner and many who lose. This focus ultimately can engender feelings of isolation, anomie and despair. It also precludes promotion of values such as cooperation and collective well-being. Meaning and purpose in life are equated with being "the best," and perfection becomes a compelling goal that can ultimately become incapacitating, particularly if one is part of a group systematically precluded from opportunities, resources and rights. Conformity is also a characteristic of patriarchal capitalism as it promotes being able to control and have power over others. Hence, one's personal experience or philosophy is unimportant; what is rewarded is that which conforms to existing beliefs and norms. Consequently, women and ethnic minorities are inherently devalued, since their diversity makes them "other" when compared to those primarily wielding power: white, Anglo-Saxon males.

Feminism, as a mode of analysis, is the antithesis of a patriarchal, capitalist perspective. It is a "liberation" philosophy promoting both nurturance of the self as well as concern with collective well-being. It is concerned with ending domination and resisting oppression, so as to provide equality of opportunity regardless of one's demographics or background. Values consonant with a feminist approach include working collaboratively, collectively and cooperatively; valuing personal experiences; encouraging growth and development; caring for others; building supportive relationships as well as believing in the interconnectedness of people and events.

Although there have been many different definitions of feminism, there are several premises common among them that have relevance to defining a feminist perspective on addictions. Those principles include eliminating false dichotomies and artificial separations; reconceptualizing power; valuing process as equally important to product; validating renaming; and believing that the personal is political (Van Den Bergh & Cooper, 1986).

Eliminating false dichotomies is a reaction to patriarchal dynamics based on a "divide and conquer" model. In a feminist view, interconnectedness and relatedness are valued. For example, health has conventionally been separated into discrete entities (i.e., mental, physical and spiritual). Feminist perspectives on health see one's well-being as the interrelatedness between those domains, whereby dis-ease in one component engenders disease in all others. Reconceptualizing power is a central concern within feminist analysis. As an alternative to the patriarchal notion of power as the ability to control others, a feminist perspective renames power as an energy of influence and responsibility that one uses in order to gain access to rights, resources and opportunities. Valuing process equally to product means that the way in which one pursues a goal is as important as that goal's outcome. Competition and conquest are reinforced when only the ends are rewarded and the means to those ends are ignored (Van Den Bergh & Cooper, 1986). Validating renaming means having the right to define one's own direction, reality or indicators of success rather than conforming to conventional criteria or norms. Finally, to see the personal as political means that experiences in one's personal life can be seen as the individualized outcome of societal inequalities. Additionally, this perspective means that the values and beliefs one holds, the goals one sets and the way one pursues one's life can be considered political statements.

Utilizing a feminist perspective does not mean "add women and stir." Rather, it is a philosophy based on values of individual worth, an inherent connectedness to others, concern with collective well-being as well as a perspective that living is an ongoing process whereby the way in which one addresses each day is actually more important than what one accomplishes.

Having provided a framework for understanding a feminist analysis, it is now appropriate to define what is meant by addictive behavior.

WHAT IS AN ADDICTION?

Addiction is characterized by a mental obsession as well as compulsive behavior related to ingesting a substance (food, alcohol, drugs) or engaging in a process (gambling, sex, work). Schaef (1987) suggests that societal structures can predispose persons to develop addictions; this purview is complementary to a feminist perspective. Living in a patriarchal culture causes people to experience both fear and resentment, since they can be confronted with blocked opportunities, discrimination, poverty, objectification as "others" to be used or abused, and a relentless pursuit of perfection which tends to be equated with money, power and prestige. Because we do not live in a society where individuals believe that they are inherently worthwhile and valuable, women and men engage in lifelong pursuits to acquire "something" external to themselves which will make them feel whole. As Schaef notes in *Women's Reality* (1981) women are continuously confronted with the "original sin" of being born female; hence, inadequate. As a result they cannot expunge themselves of sinfulness and imperfection, even if they engage in good works. Additionally, because one is inherently wrong according to conventional patriarchal religious beliefs, an individual cannot experience spiritual growth on one's own. Rather, it is incumbent for one to affiliate with organized religion (Protestantism, Catholicism, Judaism, etcetera) in order to be ensured of proper spiritual development.

The setup for addiction development, then, is a generalized sense of inadequacy, insecurity and alienation. Additionally, an external locus of control or belief that one's happiness and success is more dependent on other people, situations and events than one's own individual efforts, also sets the stage for addiction onset. Feeling inferior and wishing to escape dealing with feelings of anger, bitterness, frustration, pain and rage that evolve from trying to deal with "life on life's terms" sets up an affective context for the development of addiction.

It has been shown that experiences of abuse, neglect and abandonment are highly related to addiction's development. Those experiences can cause the individual to experience shame in believing that somehow they precipitated the neglectful or abusive behavior. A common denominator throughout discussions of the varying addictions addressed in this book is that individuals had childhood, family or marital experiences with neglect and abuse. Human beings (particularly children) are inherently egocentric and have a need to believe in a "just world" where bad things happen to bad people and good things accrue to the virtuous. As a result, a normal human response to abuse or deprivation is to internalize a sense of either being at fault or having acted wrongly in order to justify experiencing a traumatic event. Consequently, shame can lie at the core of addiction and substances are ingested or processes engaged in so as to anesthetize that "original pain" of believing one is bad, inadequate or unlovable.

Addiction is manifested when a person's attachment to a substance, person or experience causes them to have difficulty either providing for their personal needs or responding to environmental demands. Gradually, there is an increasing mental obsession with acquiring the "high," and engagement in compulsive behavior to get the high-producing substance or process. This is accompanied by unequivocal denial that one has a problem. As the addiction progresses, there is less ability to stop engaging in the behavior; hence, a feeling of powerlessness accompanies an increasingly pathological relationship with the addictive object or person or experience. There are six "d's" associated with addiction, including denial, delusion, dishonesty, defensiveness, distortion and despair (Kellogg, 1989).

Addiction, then, emanates from an internalized sense of powerlessness that is manifested by an obsession to engage in a behavior that is ultimately destructive, but temporarily anesthetizes uncomfortable feelings and fills a sense of internal void. One's propensity to develop an addiction can be directly related to experiences of invalidation, oppression and abuse that can create feelings of shame, inferiority and unworthiness.

Having defined both the meaning of a feminist analysis as well as addiction, it is now appropriate to look at the extent and degree of addictions among women, as an at-risk population within patriarchal systems.

WOMEN AND ADDICTIVE BEHAVIORS: EXTENT AND DEGREE OF THE PROBLEM

Alcoholism

One who abuses alcohol or who has developed alcohol dependence has acquired tolerance (the ability to drink larger quantities), experienced withdrawal symptoms when trying to stop, and used alcohol recurrently despite persistent social, occupational, psychological or physical problems related to drinking. Although estimates on female alcoholism vary, a study undertaken by NIAA in 1985 noted that 2.5 million women were alcohol abusers while more than 3.3 million were alcohol dependent, which represents approximately 6 million women, or 6 percent of the adult female population. In comparison, it is estimated that 12.1 million alcoholics are men, representing 14 percent of the adult male population; hence, it is assumed that there are approximately two males for every female alcoholic. Sixty percent of women over age eighteen drink and the regular use of alcohol is common among high school girls. In a 1983 study, 31 percent of twelfth-grade girls surveyed had consumed at least five or more drinks on one or more occasions in the preceding two weeks (NCA, 1985).

There are demographic differences in female drinking patterns based on age, marital status and ethnicity. Although younger women (under age 25) report more problems related to drinking (i.e., family, occupational, etcetera), women who are older (greater than age 50) are likely to be heavier drinkers. Recent research has suggested that while there has not been a precipitous increase in women's alcoholism, there is an increasing parity in the pattern of alcohol abuse between young men and women (Gomberg & Lisansky, 1984).

There is not a distinct association between marital status and alcoholism propensity, as age becomes a controlling factor. Although the incidence of problem drinking is highest for divorced and separated women under age 35, older women who are married have a higher rate of alcoholism than separated or divorced females. Additionally, for married women, those employed outside the home have higher rates of alcoholism than housewives (Gomberg & Lisansky, 1984). Thus, it seems that other factors; perhaps those related to role strain, ambiguity or loss may be potent predictors to women's alcohol dependence.

There is significant ethnic variation in women's drinking patterns. Heavy drinking has been found to be most prevalent in Blacks (14 percent) and Hispanics (13 percent) but least prevalent among White women (8 percent). What is interesting is that Black women also have the highest rate of female abstainers; Hispanic women have the lowest (Leland, 1984). The most shocking statistics related to ethnicity and women's alcoholism can be seen when comparing alcohol-related death rates among racial and gender groups. It has been estimated that 60 percent of Native American women are alcoholic; and one out of every four Native American female deaths have been attributed to cirrhosis of the liver. This rate is 37 times greater than that for White women (Peluso & Peluso, 1988).

In general, women experience severe health consequences related to alcoholism. It is the third leading cause of death in women between the ages of 35 and 55 (Pope, 1986). Thirty percent more women than men develop cirrhosis within two years of the onset of heavy drinking (Babcock & Connor, 1981). As will be elaborated upon later, this is due to multiple factors including women's increased biochemical susceptibility and decreased likelihood of entering treatment early in the disease process (due to denial, alcoholism's stigma and financial restraints). It is also important to note that among alcoholic women, the incidence of suicide attempts exceeds that of alcoholic men as well as of the female population in general (NCA, 1985).

Although the male to female alcoholism rate appears to be 2:1 (NIAA, 1985; NCA, 1985), that ratio does not carry over to the prevalence of women in treatment programs. Within Alcoholics Anonymous the male to female ratio is 3:1 (NCA, 1990), and in 1978 only 17 of the 578 treatment programs funded by NIAAA were designed specifically for women (Babcock & Connor, 1981). Women constitute less than 20 percent of all clients within alcoholism treatment, nationally; hence, a significant gender disparity exists between prevalence of the problem and access to care (Beckman & Amaro, 1984).

Drug Abuse

Contrary to stereotype, drug abuse is a women's issue; one out of every four patients diagnosed with a drug dependence problem within the United States is female. It is the second most commonly reported mental health disorder for women between the ages of 18 and 24 (Mendelson & Mello, 1986). Of the 200 million prescriptions for psychotropic medications written yearly, as is noted within the Prather chapter, two thirds are for women. Dependence upon psychotropic medications is often found together with alcohol abuse in women entering treatment programs. For example, in one clinical study, tranquilizers and sedatives were used by 43 percent of female patients compared to 20 percent of men (Celentano & McQueen, 1984), which underscores women's significant risk in being poly-addicted. The extent and degree of women's drug abuse have, unfortunately, demonstrated trends toward increases, as noted by the following:

1. In 1984, 42 percent of the callers to 800-COCAINE were women, which was an 18 percent increase over the previous year.
2. Women spend twice as much money per week as men do on cocaine.
3. Heroin addiction has increased faster for women than men.
4. Fifty percent of all drug related suicides occur among women, most of whom are older than age 35.
5. A 1983 survey of Alcoholics Anonymous members showed that 64 percent of the female membership under age 35 were both drug and alcohol dependent.
6. For the first time, the rate at which addiction is being identified is greater among women than men (Peluso & Peluso, 1988).

Consequently, although drug abuse is frequently assumed to be a male problem, the reality is that women are at high risk for drug abuse. The insidious nature of this problem is that the majority of this abuse relates to dependence upon psychotropic medications prescribed by MDs. Consequently, the ostensibly "innocuous" prescription for alleviating anxiety, depression or insomnia may actually be the road to addiction and possibly death.

Eating Disorders

Anorexia, bulimia and compulsive overeating are definitely women's issues as noted by prevalence statistics. One in every four women is a compulsive eater and, as is noted in the Chrisler chapter, 90 percent of participants in weight-loss programs are female. Thinness has become the *sine qua non* of female attractiveness as touted through advertising and media; consequently, it is not surprising that 40 percent of college women believe they are overweight although only 12 percent meet the medical criteria for that condition. Bulimia is a significant problem for young women between the ages of twelve to twenty-four, as discussed in the Kuba and Hanchey article, and it is assumed to affect 5 to 10 percent of that population group. Besides binge and purge behavior, with its health-impairing consequences, bulimics also frequently engage in alcoholism and drug abuse, self-mutilation and shoplifting. Anorexia can be fatal and it is experienced by six in every one thousand women.

Gambling

Although one third of compulsive gamblers are women, they are only 2 percent to 7 percent of participants in Gamblers Anonymous and other treatment programs. It is estimated that nationally there are approximately one million probable compulsive gamblers and two million are assumed to be gambling addicted.

Sex Addicts

As is noted in the Diamond chapter, approximately one in 12 adults is a sex addict; the percent of those who are female is unclear. One important factor is that this population has experienced significant abuse: 72 percent have been physically abused, 83 percent sexually abused, and 97 percent were emotionally abused.

The above data indicate that women are affected in significant ways by a whole range of addictions. Particularly distressing is the imbalance between the extent and degree of the problem and the existence of treatment resources. Clearly, women are not only at risk for the development of an addiction, they seem to be at an even greater risk for going untreated.

Risk, then, is a salient theme when developing a feminist perspective on addictions. Within the next section, a variety of factors that place women at risk for addictive behavior will be examined.

AT-RISK CONDITIONS FOR WOMEN'S DEVELOPMENT OF ADDICTION

Economic Realities

Women have always worked, although not until the last decade have the majority of adult women been in the official labor force. By 1984, 54 percent of all women 16 years of age and older were working. This contributed to more than 62 percent of the total United States civilian labor force growth between 1975 and 1984. One of the most notable trends in women's labor force participation has been the 13 percent rise in the number of working mothers between 1975 and 1984, reaching approximately 20 million, which is nearly 60 percent of all mothers with children under age 18 (Women's Bureau, 1985).

A growth in women's labor force participation has not been paralleled by increased parity with men in salaries. Using year round full-time workers as the basis for comparison, a woman age 25 or older with four or more years of college earns 64 percent as much as a man with comparable job and background. As a matter of fact, such women do not receive as much as men with only a high school education. Gender-based wage disparities can be further noted by the following: (a) for all employed women median annual earnings were $7,222 in 1981, 48 percent of the $15,061 annual earnings of all men and (b) women employed full-time and year round in 1981 had median earnings of $12,000, or 59 percent of the $20,260 received by men. Perhaps most distressing is that among the 5.9 million families maintained by single female workers in 1981, 33 percent had incomes below the poverty level. The figure was 36 percent for the 1.5 million Black families maintained by women workers, (Women's Bureau, 1983).

"The feminization of poverty" is a phrase that was created in the 1980s to describe a distressing phenomenon occurring within the United States: that this country's poor are significantly over-represented by women and their children. Almost half of the poor people in the United States live in female-headed households and such families grew more than 84 percent between 1970 and 1984. That growth is attributed to the high divorce rate as well as to single women deciding to raise children. Female-headed households have a greater likelihood of living in poverty for many reasons, including occupational segregation and failure to receive child support. It is assumed that only 60 percent of women with dependent children are awarded child support; of those awarded support, less than half consistently receive payments. Additionally, most women are clustered in jobs representing only 20 of the approximately 420 possible occupational titles. Those jobs are typically low-paying, such as secretarial or service workers; 70 percent of female heads of households are employed in clerical, food service, nurses aid or household worker capacities. Additionally, the majority of women who have pursued professions are in areas that historically are not high paying, such as teaching, nursing and social work.

Women's economic reality is a significant source of stress; particularly for ethnic minority females. When assessing depression in women, Belle (1982) found that those females experiencing more intractable states of dysphoria were poor, ethnic minorities. Also, studies assessing drug and alcohol treatment success have fairly consistently found that poorer, ethnic women at lower socioeconomic levels did less well than middle or upper class females. One might assume that when an individual does not foresee the ability to raise her standard of living by finding a better paying job, it would engender a state of hopelessness and despair. Consequently, it is easy to see how such a person could become increasingly dependent on drugs, alcohol, gambling or some other "quick fix" in order to escape a feeling of helplessness, despair and powerlessness. Therefore, poverty and the life experiences it engenders can be considered risk factors for addictions.

Physiological Realities

Women are actually at greater risk than men for the development of drinking-related health problems because of innate physiological differences in how alcohol is metabolized. Women have more body fat and less water than men; therefore, alcohol enters a female's system in a less diluted state. As a result, controlling for body weight and height, and given the same quantity of ingested alcohol, a woman's blood alcohol level will rise faster than a man's. Corrigan describes the "telescoping effect" of women's alcoholism in her chapter. She notes that although women may start to drink later than men, they can end up in treatment centers at approximately the same age. Research has shown that women get drunk faster than men, and they are quicker to develop alcohol-related diseases. Alcohol abuse has also been implicated in breast cancer, the second leading cause of cancer deaths in women. A 1987 study found that drinking even moderate amounts of alcohol increased breast cancer potential by 50 percent. Women who had more than eight drinks a week raised their chances of succumbing to breast cancer by 150 percent (Peluso & Peluso, 1988).

Additionally, recent research reported in the *New England Journal of Medicine* found that women have significantly lower amounts of a stomach enzyme that breaks down ethanol before it circulates through the body. Because women have a decrease in the stomach's protective barrier against alcohol, this may explain why they have been found to be at greater risk than men for the development of liver damage and other alcohol-related health problems (Steinbrook, 1990).

The implications of these physiological risks are sobering, particularly when doing a gender comparison of morbidity statistics. Death rates are 50 to 100 times higher for alcoholic women than men; it is estimated that alcoholic women lose as much as 25.9 years of life, the average age of death for a female alcoholic is 51 years and alcoholism is the third leading cause of death in women between the ages of 35 to 55 (Pape, 1986; Johnson, 1989).

Consequently, innate physiological differences between women and men in the body's ability to metabolize alcohol place women at significantly greater health risk. Alcoholism is in many respects a more deadly problem for women than men.

Genetic Predisposition Factors

Research has shown that the rate of alcoholism within the family of origin was significantly greater for female alcoholics than for male alcoholics. Additionally, women's alcoholism has been more linked to the disease's prevalence in their mothers than fathers (Gomberg & Lisansky, 1984). However, women who have an alcoholic father have been shown to be at significantly greater risk for depression than comparison groups of women with no alcoholic father. A study of women in alcoholism treatment by Corrigan (1980) found that 61 percent of respondents had a relative with a drinking problem and 40 percent had an alcoholic parent.

Although alcohol dependence is not completely predictable through genetic inheritance, a greater risk does exist. It has been suggested that the rate of alcoholism for adult children of alcoholics is approximately four times greater than is true for the general population.

Depression

Affective disorders are the primary mental health problem experienced by women; two or three times as many women as men report they are depressed (DeLange, 1982) and one out of every six women will become clinically depressed at some point in her lifetime (Wetzel, 1982). Definite links have been made between depression and the development of a broad range of addictive behaviors, including alcoholism, drug dependence, gambling, compulsive sexual behavior and eating disorders.

When considering why women are at such great risk for depression, there has been considerable agreement that a range of sociocultural and economic factors are causative. The feminization of poverty has already been discussed and its accompanying sense of powerlessness. Poor, nonwhite women who are heads of households and responsible for young children have been shown to be at high risk for depression (Gomberg & Lisansky, 1984). Additionally, cultural beliefs that women should be passive and dependent can engender a sense of learned helplessness. As will be discussed later, both female children and adults sustain a significant amount of sexual and physical abuse; despair is usually associated with victimization.

Research has shown that for women seeking alcoholism treatment, clinical depression has been measured in 20 percent to 25 percent of respondents (Blume, 1985). This phenomenon has led to the categorizations of primary and secondary alcoholism; with the latter alcohol dependence seen as an outcome of "self-medicating" depressive symptomatology. The sense of hopelessness experienced by many alcoholic women was indicated in one study that found that 27 percent of one female treatment sample had attempted suicide at least once (Corrigan, 1980). Depression is related to one's sense of self-esteem and self-concept. There have been numerous studies documenting that women alcoholics have significantly lower self-esteem than women in general, as well as male alcoholics (Braiker, 1984). Additionally, research on women alcoholics seeking treatment has noted that they experienced deprivation and rejection in their childhood; frequently that was related to experiences of neglect and abuse within dysfunctional families (Gomberg, 1980; Corrigan, 1980; Goodwin, Schulsinger, Knop, Mednick, Guze, 1977).

The relationship between depression and the onset of eating disorders has also been substantiated. The Chrisler and Kuba and Hanchey chapters note that a sense of powerlessness and loss is endemic for women who are compulsive eaters, anorexics or bulimics. Frequently, bulimia is treated by prescribing antidepressants along with psychotherapy and that has also been true for compulsive eaters.

Histories of female compulsive gamblers are replete with themes of loss, despair and a sense of hopelessness. As the Lesieur and Blume chapter notes, 26 percent of women in compulsive gambling treatment said they had experienced serious depression and 12 percent had actually attempted suicide.

Attempts to anesthetize the pain of depression are likely at the root of much addictive behavior. The purpose of seeking a "fix" is to dull the feelings associated with disappointment, frustration and despair. However, with the exception of amphetamine and cocaine abuse (which engender excited "hyper" or manic moods), most substances or processes engaged in addictively actually exacerbate a dysphoric mood; therefore, the sought-after solution becomes part of the problem.

Victimization Realities

Rather than being an anomaly, experiencing emotional, physical and sexual abuse is normative for girls and women. A very substantial percentage of the female population, possibly as high as 20 percent, has experienced sexual abuse; 12 percent before the age of fourteen, 16 percent before the age of eighteen and possibly 5 percent of all women have been abused by their fathers (Bass & Davis, 1988). Most child sexual abuse does not involve violence; however, it does involve coercion and misrepresentation of the abusive activity. The primary dynamic within the abusive relationship is unequal power between the child and perpetrator, such that the youth is manipulated. The usual pattern of sexual abuse is such that it begins between the ages of seven and twelve (Courtois, 1988) and becomes repeated, over time.

Those who have had experiences with victimization and abuse are over-represented among women alcoholics and addicts. Research examining the extent of sexual abuse among treatment populations has found that reported experiences of sexual victimization are more the norm than a deviation. In summarizing the literature on this topic, Wilsnack (1984) found that the female alcohol treatment population's experiences with incest or other childhood sexual abuse ranged from 12 percent to 53 percent and up to 74 percent when including all sexual abuse, for example, rape.

In a study of 100 recovering women conducted by Peluso and Peluso (1988) which entailed extensive interviews, 50 percent reported some childhood molestation and 50 percent also reported experiencing sexual battery or rape. Those authors present data suggesting that female incest victims have drug abuse rates seven times higher than nonvictimized females.

Unfortunately, sexual and physical abuse have become commonplace realities for American females. It is estimated that 50 percent of all wives have been physically assaulted by their spouse; but, as little as one third of one percent of such battering comes to the attention of police (Peluso & Peluso, 1988).

Victimization can lead to the development of addictive behavior for a variety of reasons. First, the assumption that the victim is innocent does not usually hold in the case of either incest or rape. Sexist attitudes maintain that the girl or woman somehow "asked for it" through her behavior or appearance. As a result, women and girls can internalize a sense of shame and guilt that may be acted out through a self-destructive addictive behavior. Additionally, experiencing fear and resentment because of victimization may cause females to drink, take drugs, gamble or binge and purge so as to reduce the discomfort of those feelings.

Sex Role Stereotyping

Adherence to conventional notions of femininity and masculinity have significant implications for the development of addictive behavior. The conventional female is subservient, dependent, passive and focused on caring for the needs of others. Serving and affiliating with others are key aspects of a conventional female psyche (Braverman, 1986), which means that women place great emphasis on relationships. The value and worth of a woman, traditionally viewed, are functions of the quality of her relationships with others. Consequently, if a woman has experienced problematic family, marital or couple, friendship or work-related difficulties in getting along with others, it will have a pervasively negative impact on her self-esteem and mental health.

The conventional male is aggressive, competitive and win-oriented. Being sensitive to the needs of others or placing emphasis on developing quality relationships are anathema to the "cult of machismo." Hence, boys and men who do not identify with those values, or feel comfortable in pursuing them, can easily self-disparage and feel inadequate, inferior and "unmanly."

Locus of control is a psychological concept related to the extent with which individuals believe they can influence the events in their lives. Women who are primarily feminine in their sex role self-description have been found to be external in their locus of control, meaning that they see events in their lives as caused by factors outside their control, such as luck or powerful others. On the other hand, men who are conventionally masculine in their sex role definition are internal in locus of control, meaning that they see themselves as the prime movers in determining life outcomes.

It seems tenable to assume that the development of addictive behavior is directly related to having an external locus of control where objects or experiences outside of the self are sought in order to give life a sense of importance, interest and meaning. Consequently, one could argue that if women believe themselves to be innately inferior and if they also believe their role is to be "other-oriented," their locus will be external. Adherence to an external focus could easily lead to the development of dependence on some thing or process outside of the self, to provide a sense of meaning and purpose to one's life. The feminine sex role stereotype, then, can be seen as a "setup" for addiction.

But, how can sex role stereotyping explain addiction in men? It would seem that males who question their ability to conform to traditionally masculine attributes would experience a diminution in an internal sense of control over their life. Hence, it is tenable to assume that they, too, could reach for something external to themselves which could edify a fragile sense of self.

Research undertaken to ascertain the relationship between sex role self-description and addictive behavior has suggested that male and female alcoholics may experience sex role conflict that drinking tends to abate. Studies by both Beckman (1978) and Wilsnack (1973, 1976) found that alcoholic women tend to feel more feminine as a result of drinking. The assumption is that women who have unconscious masculine feelings (which they find disturbing) drink to squelch them so that they can feel more feminine. However, a later study by Wilsnack (1978) found that age was an important control variable; that is, older women drank and felt more feminine while younger women who drank had rejected traditional femininity.

One wonders if findings related to drinking enhancing one's feelings of femininity would apply to lesbians; perhaps not. Many lesbians, particularly those who have been politically active, have consciously rejected traditional feminine norms. It seems unlikely that they drink to feel more in conformity with sex role stereotypes; their drinking may relate more to an attempt to anesthetize the pain of internalized homophobia or their experiences with discrimination and rebuke based on being gay, female, and possibly, an ethnic minority.

Studies on alcoholic men have produced differing results. Some research has suggested that men drink to fulfill unmet dependency needs while other work has suggested that males engage in alcohol use in order to feel more powerful.

Although direction varies, it seems plausible that both men and women could engage in addictive behavior because they seek release from tension caused by believing that they do not conform to conventional male and female norms. Concerns with conformity could manifest in appearance worries as well as anxiety that one was not behaving in the proper gender-prescribed fashion (i.e., men being competitive and women being "good" wives and mothers).

Concerns about being seen as properly feminine and masculine may exacerbate psychological denial, which is always a part of addiction, and keep both women and men resistant to admitting they have an addiction problem. In other words, a woman would stubbornly refuse to acknowledge her alcoholism, as drunkenness is considered to be unladylike. Similarly, a male would deny being alcoholic as it suggests being out of control. That admission would be contrary to being a "real man."

Feelings of inadequacy, of not "fitting in," because the person does not conform to traditional gender roles can be antecedent to the development of addictive behavior. Individuals may feel some sense of shame if they don't self-identify as conventionally masculine or feminine, and drinking, drug use, gambling, and so on may be used as a way to relieve the anxiety of feeling one doesn't "fit in."

Addiction as Stigma

Society tends to view those who are alcoholics, drug-dependent, eating disordered, gamblers or sexually addicted as morally weak and without "willpower." Hence, regardless of the addictive behavior, a similar outcome is for the addict to feel stigmatized. The most deleterious outcome of stigmatization is failure to get treatment; either because of one's denial and/or the lack of facilities for procuring treatment.

Although men with an addictive disorder experience censure, women are reproached to a greater extent. Stereotypically, those of the "fairer sex" are supposed to be society's moral guardians. Consequently, women are triply victimized when they develop an addiction by being seen as: unfeminine, morally weak and sexually promiscuous. Sexual promiscuity is associated, in a stigmatized way, with alcoholism and with female alcoholics in particular. Because of societal double standards regarding sexual behavior, greater sexual assertiveness when drinking would be accepted in men, while being censured in women (Sandmeir, 1980).

The most insidious impact of stigmatization is that the addiction goes "in the closet." That is to say, women try to hide it, treatment is delayed; and therefore, greater damage can occur (physically, emotionally, financially, etcetera). Lesieur and Blume note that female gamblers tend to pursue their compulsion alone. Women alcoholics are significantly more likely to isolate themselves than their male cohorts and this remains true even for those on "skid row." Hiding one's addiction is particularly problematic for older women, who by virtue of their age and life circumstances are already at risk for isolation and depression due to losses accruing from health and financial problems as well as the death of friends and partners.

Stigmatization of female alcoholics is not a contemporary phenomenon.

For example, the code of Hammurabi (for the Babylonian civilization) contains the edict that any woman who had previously been a priestess or holy sister and then opened a wine shop, should be burned. In Rome, a man was allowed to kill his wife if she drank since it was assumed that drinking and adultery were related (Youcha, 1978). Emmanuel Kant, the eighteenth century philosopher, noted that it was important for women to avoid getting drunk, as community status rested on them being seen as pious and chaste.

Although both women and men can be scorned for the addiction, the stigma tends to be worse for women since they are held to higher standards of "moral behavior" than men. The greatest problem associated with stigma is that individuals will be inclined to deny they have a problem; hence, the addiction worsens.

The above discussion has underscored that a variety of factors place women, in particular, at risk for developing an addiction. Genetic predisposition has an impact in predicting propensity for the ingestive disorders (i.e., alcoholism, eating disorders) and physiological factors related to metabolism cause women to be at significantly greater risk than men for alcohol-related health problems. Family and societal forces ranging from stereotyped, pejorative beliefs to discrimination and victimization are also risk factors since individuals can develop an addiction as a panacea for the pain of discrimination, abuse and neglect. Having examined those risk factors, it is now appropriate to utilize a feminist analysis in synthesizing how those risk factors can propel an individual into addiction.

FEMINIST PERSPECTIVES ON THE DEVELOPMENT OF ADDICTIONS

The social, political and economic forces associated with patriarchy create conditions conducive to the development of addictive behavior. This is because the primary process associated with patriarchy is one of control and domination, whereby a few have power over many. The intersection of capitalism with patriarchy adds additional social, political and economic realities that can create conditions that engender addictions. This is particularly true for women and ethnic minorities who historically have experienced discrimination and powerlessness in a capitalistic system where they have been occupationally segregated and economically disadvantaged. Capitalist patriarchal values of acquisition, competition and conquest can also predispose to the development of addictions. This is because they promote the view that an individual's value is derived by acquiring "commodities" external to the self, such as wealth, victories and so on. Rather than being based on a philosophy which promotes the inherent worthiness of an individual, capitalist patriarchy associates a person's value with what that person has amassed. This can create a dynamic whereby people begin to look for something outside of themselves as the solution to their sense of personal inadequacy and inferiority. Grabbing for that which is external to the self, in order to make the self complete and whole, can become another predisposing factor to addiction development. Additionally, the capitalistic patriarchal value placed on competition and conquest promotes a drive for perfection. This creates psychological stress that can lead to the seeking of analgesic relief in compulsive drinking, eating, gambling, etc. Persons precluded from the means of exercising capitalistic patriarchal control judge themselves inadequate and inferior. This also can establish a psychological foundation for addiction's development.

Power and Powerlessness

Patriarchy mandates conformity in order to effectuate the dynamics of power and control over others. Consequently, those who are different from the norm (primarily white, male and Anglo-Saxon) are looked at both with contempt and fear.

The pervasive need to control sets up a context that allows for the development of discrimination, victimization and oppression. If one believes that success is measured by having power over others, then schema are created which allow for the categorization of people into groups to be controlled. Consequently, racism, sexism, homophobia, etcetera, become functional belief systems that give individuals reason to behave pejoratively and oppressively toward others, in order to maintain their power.

One can argue that in a paradoxical way, the greater the need to control, the more intrinsically powerless an individual may feel. Patriarchy has devalued that which represents femaleness, such as dependency, since feminine traits are associated with weakness. Fear of one's own vulnerability and doubts about one's ability to succeed can generate a sense of powerlessness which an individual can attempt to compensate for by seeking to control others. For example, most rapists do not seek sexual gratification, rather, they seek to subdue and conquer a woman who serves as an "object." Incest perpetrators are motivated by the sense of power and control they have over a victim. Additionally, the theme of much pornography is bondage and submission. Power, then, takes on an addictive, aphrodisiac quality which allows for an obsessive and compulsive quest.

Addictions, then, emanate from a sense of powerlessness and one's ongoing addictive pursuits can be for the purpose of feeling, albeit temporarily, powerful. As previously noted, some research on male alcoholics has suggested that drinking gave a sense of power. While this motive has not been found when studying older female alcoholics, it may be a more salient theme for younger women drinkers. The desire for a sense of power has definitely been substantiated for compulsive gamblers, eating disordered clients, sex addicts and codependents. Anorexics and bulimics recount feelings of social impotence and experience a sense of power by their rigid weight control efforts. Female gamblers acquire a sense of power by competing in a "man's world." Codependents and relationship addicts acquire a sense of power through their efforts to control others. Unfortunately, all these addictive pursuits provide only a temporary sense of power and its aftermath tends to exacerbate an already low self-esteem.

Feelings of powerlessness are an obvious outcome of experiencing many realities of a patriarchal culture. The feminization of poverty, sexual victimization and objectification as well as institutionalized sexism and racism, (which preclude equal protection under the law or access to resources and opportunities) are all associated with limiting the control that women and other minorities can actually exercise over their own lives.

Dichotomous Thinking

A second factor associated with development of addiction is the societal strategy of dividing and conquering and the related individual tendency to dichotomous or compartmentalized thinking. These characteristics of separating, dividing and splitting are associated with the scientifc method and logical positivism. It is a typically Western view to seek truth and knowledge by looking at component parts, rather than the whole. Society encourages "specialists" rather than "generalists." Looking at the parts rather than their interrelationship as a whole tends to generate thinking in terms of dichotomies, polarities and opposites; either/or, win/lose, good/bad dynamics are established. On the individual level, thinking in terms of dichotomies can become a problem since it can lead to feelings of inadequacy. Traditional notions of masculine and feminine sex roles are constructed according to the dichotomy model. If one does not conform to the model of either conventional masculinity or feminity, then one is aberrant, abnormal, impaired, weird or mentally unhealthy.

The tendency to dichotomize and compartmentalize also sets up the conditions for feeling a sense of emptiness, void or vacuum. Believing that an important "component" is missing, an individual can seek to fill up that empty space with something extrinsic. For example, a woman who questions her own femaleness could develop an addiction to squelch the uncomfortable feelings associated with being "faulty." She might engage in compulsive sexual behavior, repetitively seek romantic interludes or drink and take drugs to escape her discomfort.

An additional problem associated with splitting relates to spirituality. Within Judeo-Christian as well as Muslim religious traditions there is a theme that one must look inside of oneself to develop a sense of spirituality. This causes people to think that they cannot develop a relationship with a higher power through their own pursuit. Remember, Eve and Adam were banished from Eden because of their independent pursuit of knowledge, rather than simply accepting what was placed in front of them. Carl Jung, when writing to the founder of Alcoholics Anonymous (AA), Bill Wilson, suggested that alcoholism seemed to be a perverse outcome of man's search for some sense of "spiritedness" within living, by seeking feelings of joy and happiness through drinking. Because patriarchy does not encourage people to believe in their own value and worth as individuals, people can feel separated from that which provides meaning and purpose to life. Hence, they look outside of themselves to find "it," so that "it" can fill the internal spiritual void.

Valuing Outcome at the Expense of Process

A third theme associated with patriarchy that can engender addiction is a focus on ends rather than means. Being driven to win, succeed and to be "best" sets up a demand for perfectionism that invariably leads to anxiety, frustration and despair. Pursuing certain addictions, initially, aggrandizes one's sense of perfection through mood-altering experiences giving a feeling of "winning," such as with gambling or sexual and romantic conquests, being in "control" (anorexia/bulimia and codependence) or being "high" (drugs and alcohol). A "grab for all the gusto" mentality is also related to a focus on outcomes rather than process. But, because humans are inherently fallible and imperfect, striving to be the best will create stress and despair that one may exacerbate by going for a "fix" in order to feel better.

The Invalidated Self

Finally, living within patriarchal cultures can cause individuals to question their own reality and experience a loss of self. If norms are based on realities specific to only one group, but generalized to everyone, then those who are "other" will feel discounted, misunderstood, invalid, wrong or invisible. The impact of being left out or subsumed within another's experience can result in feelings of inadequacy, impotence, and incompleteness. Those feelings create an uncomfortable affective context that addictive behavior seeks to soothe.

The conditions of patriarchy, then, create a cultural milieu in which individuals can feel powerless, split, inadequate and experience a loss of self-definition and meaning. Addictions then become a way to either temporarily experience a sense of omnipotence and control, or a way to escape from feelings of helplessness, despair and powerlessness. Having used a feminist perspective to analyze addictive causes, it is now appropriate to look at feminist visions for treatment.

FEMINIST PERSPECTIVES ON TREATING ADDICTIONS

Obstacles to Treatment

The most salient point to make in terms of feminist perspectives on treatment is that it must be provided. As noted previously, there is a significant imbalance between addiction prevalence and treatment rates for many addictive disorders that affect females. Although the male/female alcoholism rate is 2:1, women make up less than 20 percent of the clients in drug and alcohol programs (NCA, 1988). Despite women constituting 33 percent of compulsive gamblers, they are only 2 percent to 7 percent of those in Gamblers Anonymous and other treatment programs.

Why are women underrepresented in much addiction treatment? Many of the same conditions that put women at risk for the development of addictions also preclude women from getting treatment. These include stigma, sex role stereotypes and lack of financial resources. It is interesting to note that while family and friends frequently are motivators and proponents for men to get treatment, those same groups have actually been shown to deter women from getting help (Beckman & Amaro, 1984), One may assume that the reluctance of family members and friends to support a woman's treatment is highly attributable to stigma. That is, they may feel it will bring shame to the family or sex role stereotypes could deter them from seeing a female friend's or family member's problem.

The prevalence of female poverty was previously noted as a sociocultural reality that can become a dynamic underscoring addiction. Lack of financial resources has obvious implications for the receipt of treatment. Because women tend to be occupationally segregated in jobs that are low paying, they are also less likely to be recipients of health care insurance that could offset the costs of treatment.

Women's responsibilities as primary caretakers for children also serve to deter their access to treatment services. First, many women may fear losing their children through a family court action if they admit to an addiction problem. New York State averted this dilemma by providing immunity from custody proceedings for women who voluntarily entered treatment (Blume, 1985). Second, provisions for the care of one's dependent children must be arranged if a woman is to enter treatment. If she does not have family or other social network resources to assist her, and if a treatment center has no provisions for assisting women with child care needs, entry into a treatment program becomes precluded.

Characteristics of treatment programs in terms of staffing and types of services provided can also deter women's involvement. Because women's experiences differ from men's, in general as well as in being addicts or alcoholics, it is crucial that there are female staff and clients with whom recovering women can relate. Also, the confrontational model often associated with "old guard" Alcoholics Anonymous is opposite to how most women relate to others; being forced into that kind of process will be frightening and alienating. Additionally, sexual victimization and abuse are common among addicted women and having to share those experiences in a primarily male milieu could be felt as humiliating.

Treatment professionals' attitudes toward women in general, and female alcoholics in particular, will have a profound effect on treatment outcome. It has often been felt that female alcoholics are harder to treat and have a poorer prognosis than men. Yet Vanicelli (1984) in researching women's treatment outcomes found, through a study of thirty years of treatment research having sex-related outcome information, that 78 percent of the studies reviewed showed no significant difference between male and female alcoholics in treatment success. Hence, pejorative beliefs about women alcoholics, based on adherence to sex role stereotypes, may be at the root of the prevalent myth that women tend to be treatment failures.

Having looked at some obstacles to women receiving treatment, it is now important to consider how feminist principles can inform the treatment provision process.

Using Feminist Principles in Treatment

Reconceptualizing power.

The great paradox of recovery is that one must first admit powerlessness. Ostensibly, this may seem an antifeminist principle, if looked at as an admission of weakness and failure; in fact, it is a statement of freedom. As long as a woman's psychic energy is engaged in a perverse attachment to a substance, person or process, then she is not able to utilize her intrinsic abilities in her life. To admit powerlessness is to disengage from an obsessional compulsive pursuit and to have use of that previously diverted psychic energy for one's own growth and development.

Power also becomes reconceptualized as what one can do for oneself (empowerment) rather than how one can control another. This means encouraging addicts (particularly women) to take responsibility for making things happen in their life rather than being reactive. This is tantamount to helping the client build more of an internal locus of control.

As people move into recovery, it is common that they experience anger; this emotion can be used in a positive way, if framed as an energy available to the client for directing change to get what she or he needs. For example, anger at being abused can be channeled in assertively setting boundaries or seeking to get a need met.

Additionally, reconceptualizing power includes changing the client's attributional patterns so that she or he takes credit for successes achieved rather than dismissing them as due to luck or something other than personal effort.

Renaming.

Discovery of self is a fundamental goal of recovery; the operationalization of renaming means that clients are encouraged to define what is appropriate for themselves, rather than pursuing conventionally established norms. Steps four through nine of AA's Twelve Steps help facilitate this process. They encourage the individual to undergo an honest self-assessment, to be willing to alter ways of being that are dysfunctional and to acquire the willingness to acknowledge one's mistakes. A bottom line of recovery is self-acceptance, authenticity and humility. Although the term humility may seem disparaging, its root is the latin *humus*, meaning grounded. Therefore, to rename one's experience is to get back to the basics of being only who we are, rather than feigning to be something different.

Consequently, another paradox of recovery is that the admission of one's faults and fallibilities allows the obsessive drive for perfection to end; it allows one to be free to be one's authentic self.

Movement towards authenticity also allows for spiritual growth. Often individuals who do not accept themselves, or who believe they are "wrong" or "bad," have a sense of shame. They fear censure, rebuke and usually have equated spirituality with aspects of patriarchal religiosity. By increased acceptance of self, it becomes possible to redefine spirituality.

Treatment within all female groups or residential programs enhances the process of renaming. Women can serve as mirrors for each other, seeing their experiences as more common than unique. It is empowering to realize one is not alone and that others have similar views or realities. Seeing the common denominators facilitates self-acceptance and helps to solidify a sense of identity and purpose.

Eliminating false dichotomies.

Healthy recovery promotes choices; a feminist perspective includes the premise that there is no "right" way to proceed which everyone should follow. Some people may be able to cure their addictions by involvement in a Twelve Step program, others may need an in-patient facility, while some may use a combination of approaches including psychotherapy and self-help. The important principle to impart is that there is not a "perfect" way to proceed, applicable for all. Since so many addicts have succumbed to "split-thinking," seeing everything in dichotomies of good or bad and right or wrong, processes must be established that enable seeing the middle ground. It is often helpful to encourage their acceptance of being average, rather than seeking to be "perfect" as the obverse of their fear of being "imperfect" (example of a false dichotomy).

Clients must also be assisted in modulating the dichotomies that may have been a part of their identity. A woman may have defined herself as both bad and unfeminine because of not being chaste. A man who is not comfortable within a competing environment or who does not have athletic ability may feel he is not masculine. Clients need to be assisted in seeing the acceptability of gradations.

Valuing process equally to product.

This feminist principle applied to treatment means that clients must be assisted in seeing that recovery is not finite; there is no specific end point one can achieve. Rather, recovery is an ongoing process in which the individual continues to practice dealing with "life on life's terms." One of the benefits from recovering through a Twelve Step program is that the participants can hear how people with "time on the program" handle the frustrations, fears, anxieties and joys that one encounters as endemic to living. It is one thing to cease an addictive behavior; it is quite another to move through life, day by day, not succumbing to obsessions and compulsions.

Curbing the need to be perfect may be an addictive person's greatest challenge. It is fear of failure and fear of exposure as imperfect that drives much compulsive addictive behavior. Consequently, it is crucial for clients to accept that recovery is not easy; there will still be pain, fear and anger. However, one reason why recovering people describe themselves as "grateful" is because exposure to the Twelve Steps and other programs provides them with methods and options for dealing with the vagaries and vicissitudes of life. Therefore, if one has a "slip," and re-engages in an addictive behavior after some abstinence, it needs to be reframed as a learning experience and an opportunity to accept more help than one may have been willing to ask for previously.

Several AA adages underscore the process nature of recovery including: (a) "progress before perfection," (b) "easy does it, and (c) "one day at a time." The feminist principle of emphasizing the importance of process when applied to recovery means that it is not important when something is done; what is valuable are the steps taken in moving toward the goal.

The personal is political.

Applying this feminist principle to treatment means assisting clients to see that the sociocultural context in which they live promotes the development of addiction. Helping clients to see the relationship between patriarchy and addictive behavior does not absolve them of personal responsibility to undertake their own recovery. However, it does help attenuate client tendencies to self-disparage, to believe that she or he is "terminally unique" in what brought them down an addictive path. For example, in working with eating disordered clients, it is extremely helpful for them to begin to see that they have over subscribed to societal stereotypes about what women should look like. For both men and women, it can be psychically freeing for them to reflect on how their discomfort with sex role stereotypes may lay in the roles rather than in themselves. Additionally, it is helpful for both men and women to see that conventional definitions of success, which measure what one has acquired, accomplished and looks like, negate their own intrinsic value. This, in turn, has led them to seek meaning and purpose in life by looking for a ''fix'' outside of themselves.

It may be that one reason there has been a burgeoning self-help movement in the United States is that people feel a kind of solidarity and community through participation in Twelve Step programs. Patriarchy engenders isolation and anomie; recovery groups provide an antidote to the pain and angst of believing one is alone. Individuals come together to share their ''experience, strength and hope;'' through that process a feeling of personal empowerment as well as community affiliation is experienced.

CONCLUSION

A feminist perspective suggests that the development of addictions can be related to the isolating and oppressive conditions engendered by patriarchal cultures. Getting by within a milieu that requires one to exert power over others in order to be successful and where success is measured by extrinsics rather than one's innate qualities can generate feelings of inadequacy, powerlessness, hopelessness and loss. One can become involved in an addictive behavior both for its analgesic potential as well as because the addictive behavior provides an illusory sense of omnipotence and control. Ultimately, however, the addiction depletes one of psychic energy needed for both self-nurturance and growth; if unabated, it will bring an individual to her or his ''bottom.''

Using a feminist perspective to treat addictions starts with seeing the addicted person as someone split off from her or his authentic self. Recovery becomes a process of rediscovering oneself and reclarifying one's meaning and purpose in living. In that process differences become accepted, as do deviations from conventional norms, and an emphasis is placed on being rather than doing, living rather than competing.

The context for recovery is to see oneself as part of the human condition rather than as being ''terminally unique'' and apart from one's fellows. In a way, addiction becomes a blessing as the individual is afforded an opportunity to reclaim the self and to participate in a collaborative venture—recovery—where one can share a sense of ''experience, strength and hope.''

This chapter's purpose has been to provide a feminist framework for view-

ing addiction causes and cures. In the next chapter, Nol articulates how
the conditions of patriarchy can negatively affect psychological development by impairing development of a strong sense of self as well as connectedness to significant others. These first two chapters, comprising Part
I, provide a sociopolitical, economic, and clinical analysis of the impact
of a capitalistic patriarchal culture on the development of addictive behavior.

In Part II, a feminist perspective is provided on selected substance dependencies, including alcoholism, drug addiction and eating disorders.
These are the "ingestive addictions." Part III focuses on process dependencies; these are addictive behaviors in a particular activity such as gambling, sex and work.

The unifying theme of this volume, as noted within all chapters, is that
the patriarchal culture in which we live engenders conditions that cause
people to feel inferior, powerless and alienated. Addictions develop as a
way to anesthetize the pain of being "less than" and "left out." Hence
it is unlikely that the solution for addictive behavior can be achieved by
a patriarchal process such as a "war on drugs;" the cure is much more
likely to be achieved by a sociocultural milieu that encourages individual
growth and the development of efforts undertaken to ensure collective well-
being and welfare.

REFERENCES

Babcock, M., & Connor, B. (1981). Sexism and treatment of the female alco-
    holic: A review. *Social Work, 5*, 223-238.
Bass, E., & Davis, L. (1988). *The courage to heal: A guide for women survivors of
    child sexual abuse.* New York: Harper & Row.
Beckman, L., (1978). Sex role conflict in alcoholic women: Myth or reality?
    Journal of Abnormal Psychology, 84, 408-417.
Beckman, L., & Amaro, H. (1984). "Patterns of women's use of alcohol treat-
    ment agencies." In. S. Wilsnack & L. Beckman (Eds.), *Alcohol Problems in
    Women.* New York: The Guilford Press.
Belle, D. (1982). *Lives in stress.* Beverly Hills: Sage Publications.
Blume, S. (1985). Women and alcohol. In T. Bratter & G. Forrest (Eds.), *Alco-
    holism and substance abuse* (pp. 623-638). New York: Free Press.
Braiker, H. (1984). Therapeutic issues in the treatment of alcoholic women. In
    S. Wilsnack & L. Beckman (Eds.), *Alcohol problems in women* (pp.
    349-368). New York: The Guilford Press.
Braverman, L. (1986). Reframing the female client's profile. *Affilia: Journal of
    Women and Social Work, 1*(2), 30-40.
Celentano, D., & McQueen, D. (1984). Multiple substance abuse among wom-
    en with alcohol related problems. In S. Wilsnack & L. Beckman (Eds.), *Al-
    cohol problems in women* (pp. 97-116). New York: The Guilford Press.

Corrigan, E. (1980). *Alcoholic women in treatment.* New York: Oxford University Press.

Courtois, C. (1988). *Healing the incest wound.* New York: W. W. Norton.

De Lange, J. (1982). Depression in women: Explanations and prevention. In A. Weick & S. Vandiver (Eds.), *Women, power and change* (pp. 17–26). Washington, D.C.: National Association of Social Workers.

Gomberg, E. (1980). *Risk factors related to alcohol problems among women: Research issues* (NIAAA Research Monograph, no. 1, DHEW publ. no. [ABM] 80–835). Washington, D.C.: U.S. Government Printing Office.

Gomberg, E., & Lisansky, J. (1984). Antecedents of alcohol problems in women. In S. Wilsnack & L. Beckman (Eds.), *Alcohol problems in women* (pp. 233–259). New York: The Guilford Press.

Goodwin, D., Schulsinger, F., Knop, J., Mednick, S., & Guze, S. (1977). Psychopathology in adopted and nonadopted daughters of alcoholics. *Archives of General Psychiatry, 34,* 1005–1009.

Kellogg, T. (1989). When choosing isn't choice: Addictions, compulsion and self-destructive behavior. *Quarterly News from the National Council on Compulsive Gambling. 4*(2), 11–12.

Johnson, N. (1989). Women drinkers die young in U.S. *Journal of Drug and Alcohol Dependence.* August. 9–12.

Leland, J. (1984). Alcohol use and abuse in ethnic minority women. In S. Wilsnack & L. Beckman (Eds.), *Alcohol problems in women* (pp. 66–96). New York: The Guilford Press.

Mendelson, J., & Mello, N. (1986). Clinical investigations of drug effects in women. In National Institute on Drug Abuse research monograph, series 65, *Women and drugs: A new era for research* (NIDA). Washington, D.C.: U.S. Government Printing Office.

National Council on Alcoholism (1985). *Alcoholism and alcohol-related problems among women.* New York: NCA.

National Council on Alcoholism (1988). *Women, alcohol and other drugs.* New York: NCA.

National Council on Alcoholism (1990) *NCADD Factsheet: Alcoholism, other drug addictions and related problems among women.* New York: NCA.

NIAAA (1985). *Alcohol and health.* Special Report to the U.S. Congress. Washington, D.C.: U.S. Government Printing Office.

Pape, P. (1986). Women and alcohol: The disgraceful discrepancy. *EAP Digest,* Sept./Oct., 50–53.

Peluso, E. & Peluso, L. (1988). *Women and drugs: Getting hooked, getting clean.* Minneapolis, MN: Compucare.

Sandmeir, M. (1980). *The invisible alcoholic.* New York: McGraw-Hill.

Schaef, A. (1981), *Women's reality.* San Francisco: Harper & Row.

Schaef, A. (1987). *When society becomes an addict.* San Francisco: Harper & Row.

Steinbrook, R. (1990, February 15). Research links enzymes to alcohol's effect on women. *Los Angeles Times,* pp. 27–28.

Van Den Bergh, N., & Cooper, L. (1986). *Feminist visions for social work.* Silver Springs MD: NASW.

Vanicelli, M (1984). Treatment outcome of alcoholic women: State of the art in relation to sex bias and expectancy effects. In S. Wilsnack & L. Beckman (Eds.), *Alcohol problems in women,* (pp. 369–412). New York: The Guilford Press.

Warren, M. (1980). *The nature of women.* Inverness, CA: Edgepress

Wetzel, J. (1982). Redefining concepts of mental health. In A. Weick & S. Vandiver (Eds.), *Women, power and change.* Washington, D.C.: NASW.

Wilsnack, S. (1973). Sex role identity in female alcoholism. *Journal of Abnormal Psychology, 82,* 253–261.

Wilsnack, S. (1976). The impact of sex roles on women's use and abuse. In M. Greenblatt & M. Schuckit (Eds.), *Alcoholism problems in women and children.* New York: Grune and Stratten.

Wilsnack, S. (1978). Sex roles and drinking among adolescent girls. *Journal of Studies on Alcohol, 39,* 1855–1874.

Wilsnack, S. (1984). Drinking, sexuality and sexual dysfunction in women. In S. Wilsnack & L. Beckman (Eds.), *Alcohol problems in women.* New York: The Guilford Press.

Women's Bureau. (1985). *The United Nations decade for women, 1976-1985: Employment in the United States* (USDL). Washington, D.C.: U.S. Government Printing Office.

Youcha, G. (1978). *Women and alcohol: A dangerous pleasure.* New York: Crown Publishers.

2

Selfobject Search: The Role of Addictions in a Patriarchal Culture

Jo Nol

INTRODUCTION

The condition of chemical dependency is a complicated one with a variety of possible contributing factors. In treating addicted people, the clinician must develop a broad knowledge base drawn from the biological and social sciences. I believe that our understanding of addictions cannot be complete without consideration of the social, psychological and cultural role of gender since this characteristic is an important component of human experience. Gender, in our culture, is a yardstick by which we are measured and addictions occur within the larger context of sexual inequality and gender role stereotypes.

There is a growing body of literature to draw on related to the origin of sexual inequality and its influence on the psychological development of females and males (Barwick 1971; Eichenbaum & Orbach 1983). Authors such as Dinnerstein (1976), Chodorow (1978), Baker Miller (1976) and Lerner (1988) have offered important works on the psychological cost of present gender role arrangements as well as powerful arguments on the origins of a ubiquitous devaluation of what is associated with femaleness.

This chapter will offer a feminist analysis of the link between the diverging experiences of the two genders within a patriarchal culture and the development of addictions. Using feminist and other contemporary psychoanalytic thought, the impact of stereotyped gender role expectations on early psychological development will be explored and how this may contribute to addictions. Specifically the contributions made by Kohut (1977, 1984) in his theory of self-psychology are considered by this author to be a useful framework for both conceptualizing the intrapsychic process of addiction, as well as providing a treatment method (Levin, 1987).

GENDER AND ADDICTION

Addiction occurs within the context of our patriarchal culture and clues to the explanation for this painful problem can be found there. Central to a patriarchy is the need to dichotomize the sexes, while also devaluing femaleness and controlling that which represents female power, or conversely, male vulnerability. This need to control the "female element" is reflected in the addiction process. Several preliminary studies suggest that in this culture, addictions for men have to do at least partially with repressed dependency needs, while women's experiences of addiction may have to do with unconscious gender role conflict (Wilsnack, 1973; Child, Bacon & Barry, 1965; and Blane, 1968). The reciprocal relationship between cultural influence and individual development is integral to understanding the addiction experience.

In our culture maleness and femaleness are considered to be on opposite ends of a positive/negative polarity. Those characteristics that are positive and valued more highly are those connected to self-reliant, autonomous and separate strivings and are defined as the essence of healthy masculinity. Dependency feelings, urges for connectedness with others and normal regressive wishes are associated with femaleness. Although the latter traits are sometimes acceptable in women and children, they are often rejected as evidence of weakness and inferiority in men.

More men than women seem to have difficulty accepting their affiliative needs and will engage in activity designed to defend against their longings for connectedness as well as the sense of loss and the expression of pain that accompanies inevitable failures. More women than men seem capable of acknowledging in themselves experiences of helplessness and powerlessness. Many men, through projection of these unacceptable aspects of themselves onto others, appear compelled to erect barriers engendering a host of positive/negative dichotomies, (i.e., racism, classism, ageism, sexism, speciesism, nationalism and other related biases). It seems that the individual psychological struggle to ward off the helpless and powerless segment of one's self has been woven into a social system that rewards individualism, power, control and cognition unaffected by emotion.

Marilyn French (1985) discusses the way in which this patriarchal need to control manifests itself in all "human" institutions from politics and religion to the history of our own helping professions. She delineates between the urge to dominate, as one form of power, versus the ability to express oneself, as a "power to" do something. In our culture, although both are valued and overlap in manifestation, the power over, or domination of someone or thing that is "other," is the much more prevalent and dangerous mode of operation. "Other" takes the form of women, children, people of color, nonhuman animals and the earth itself. This other is unconsciously perceived to contain that which is feared in the self (i.e., vulnerability), and is experienced as a threat to male independent separateness, which must be controlled. For many men, the struggle to "split" off their "female" selves results in a constant need to stay psychologically separate from "bad" others and to control those aspects of self that present a perceived threat to their independence, invulnerability and "maleness." Women, too, must labor under the falsehood that their value is determined by gender rather than their humanness. Patriarchal definitions of femininity reinforce denial of women's aggressive impulses and their need for experiencing self as a powerful, and actionable being. To sustain the dichotomy, both genders, in varying degrees, are culturally socialized to assume prescribed sex roles rather than accepted for their individuality.

The power of this socializing experience translates into a sometimes overwhelming fear of normal affective experiences and as a result, a correspondingly complex system of denial can develop. Both women and men can become afraid of how they feel or think if it doesn't correspond to gender expectations. Instead of learning acceptance of socially nontraditional aspects of the self, that which is unacceptable is repressed. Repression can often result in delayed or stultified psychological development. Instead of building an increasingly mature system of self-regulation, the person remains at an archaic level of reactivity and fear. This inability to develop an internalized self-soothing mechanism and to tolerate uncomfortable intrapsychic sensations leads many people to seek external methods of relief.

The initial reason for substance use often has to do with one's discomfort with her or his affective state. Drugs and alcohol are used as a way to fit in, to be accepted, to be attractive, to lessen inhibition, to relieve unpleasant feelings such as sadness or helplessness, to overcome intimacy fears and to regress in a socially acceptable manner. For men it is commonly included in social rituals to give permission for closeness or as a measure of their masculinity. Alcohol is often used to control unmasculine affect or to make legitimate the expression of this same affect. The masculine need to control extends to the drug as addiction develops. One reason that denial of addiction is so resilient in men is because in acknowledging addiction, one admits to being out of control, which is to acknowledge unmasculine "weakness." Thus, the same substance that initially was used to control affect can become that which must be controlled because being out of control by and of alcohol and drugs does not fall into acceptable male gender role expectations. To be controlled is to be female.

The key to the psychological aspects of addiction in women is in understanding the impact of being female in a society that not only limits their gender role but also devalues it. Thus a woman who attempts to adhere to a feminine sex role can never reap the reward of complete acceptance because her very gender is not acceptable. This dilemma is often unconscious and can lead to depression, which women may seek to attenuate through substances.

In our patriarchal efforts to deny the vulnerable aspects of ourselves, we can embrace a blinding array of substances designed to mask any evidence of the ordinary aches and pains inherent in being human. In addition, there are behaviors that do not readily fall into the category of addictions, but can be seen as symptoms of the constant battle to counter one's sense of vulnerability through dangerous pursuits and conquests. These behaviors include rape, molesting children, driving fast, pursuing more money than can be spent, gambling and hunting. While the above noted activities tend to be male antidotes to vulnerability, women tend to turn the struggle back onto themselves in forms such as eating disorders, depression and submission within relationships.

Having looked at some of the gender-linked underpinnings of addiction, we can turn to psychoanalytic and developmental theory as ways to explain the intrapsychic experience of addiction in a patriarchal society.

PSYCHOANALYTIC CONTRIBUTIONS

Many feminist therapists and chemical dependency treatment providers have indicated a distrust of psychoanalytic theory and held that it had little to offer them in their work. Often they responded to the sometimes sexist and antidisease position of the theory by rejecting the entire body of knowledge. Although one must be selective about which aspects to apply, psychoanalytic theory can be extremely useful in helping to understand the development of addictions as one symptom of a patriarchal culture. In fact, Mitchell (1974) argues that "psychoanalysis is not a recommendation for patriarchal society, but an analysis of one. If we are interested in understanding and challenging the oppression of women, we cannot afford to neglect it" (p. xiii). It can also help to understand the oppression men experience in this society. Two useful aspects of Freud's work and subsequent Freudian thinkers are the positing of the unconscious and the impact of historical family experiences on one's present functioning.

Both the Object Relations and Self-Psychology schools of psychoanalytic theory emphasize the relational context of psychological development. This seems congruent with our work in the field of addictions where the family experience is considered to be crucial in the history of addiction. Listening to our female clients we hear them talk about the use of substances in response to problematic recurring patterns in their relationships with others; these patterns often reflect early life struggles that have never been resolved. This is akin to Freud's repetition compulsion.

What many of these theories have in common is the impact of one's early bonding experiences on the development of personality and defense mechanisms. Central is the relationship between the infant and caretaker, which in this culture will be almost universally a woman. Not only is a newborn greeted by preexisting assumptions and expectations corresponding to the gender of the child, she or he is to be in the care of a person who received those same messages and to varying degrees internalized them. It is within the first three years of life that this relationship is most important in setting the groundwork for the person's sense of self both in relationships to other human beings and as a separate person. During these early years the baby learns about herself and the world through her relationship with the mother. Her personality develops as a result of the interplay between the endowment potential of the child to communicate with her caretaker and the mother's capacity to respond to that child. Initially, the child's world is completely comprised of this relationship and in fact, she experiences the mother subjectively as part of the self. Kohut's term (1977), selfobject, is useful to understand that the child and mother are experienced as parts of the child's self and that mother is not experienced as a distinct person. According to Kohut, the child has certain innate relational needs that she or he tries to get met through this selfobject context. The need for being accurately seen and admired (the mirroring selfobject), the need for merging with a sense of reassuring calmness (the idealized selfobject) and the need to feel a sense of belonging to the human species (the twinship selfobject) are selfobject needs that must be met to a minimal degree in order for the child to have a chance to develop a secure sense of self as separate from others (Mahler, Pine & Bergman, 1975).

There is an inevitable movement toward psychological as well as physical differentiation from the mother. This is motivated by an innate "lifeforce," that Freud (1961) termed the sexual drive, and Althea Horner (1984) named as aggression separate from anger. More contemporary thinkers refer to this as the need to experience oneself as actionable. For all infants, this process is frustrating, exhilarating and individually determined by the interplay between the developed personality of the mother and the emerging pliable one of the child. The child learns about the world and her or his own place in it from both painful and pleasurable experiences alike. At the core of this process is the infant's gradual realization that the caretaker is not a part of the self but is indeed a separate being with its own set of bodily and psychological needs (Kohut, 1977; Mahler, 1975). Within this intricate psychological dialogue the child must be allowed to integrate (called transmuting internalization by Kohut) the selfobject tasks into itself that had formerly been provided, more or less adaquately, by the caretaker. The child then is not only physically dependent on the caretaker for survival but is also psychologically dependent for her or his personality development.

This entire process takes place within the cultural reality of female inferiority. Gender is an important distinction made in human culture and gender identity formation is considered to be a crucial aspect of personality development. It can be argued that gender identity touches, consciously and unconsciously, most aspects of one's life (Eichenbaum & Orbach, 1983; Gilligan, 1982; Baker Miller, 1976). Thus, the differing values assigned to the two genders are important not only for the child's sense of oneself but also in understanding the impact of the caretakers' gender. Some authors, (Dinnerstein, 1976; Chodorow, 1978, 1989) contend that the root of female devaluation can be found in the process of separation from the mother. This is not because separation occurs, but because it is primarily from the mother, from women, that the child separates. Both genders must, through innate urges, move toward gradual differentiation from the primary parent and take on increasingly more complex psychological and physical self-care. This includes taking over the function of providing the self with those selfobject needs that were formerly met by the caretaker.

To develop a sense of identity within this increasingly separate experience, the boy can use the mother as a distinctly different person from which to move away. He can look to her as an example of who he is not and thereby define who he is as a human male. Combined with his experience of her as both a frustrating and pleasing selfobject, who is a different "other," the male child sees his mother as embodying all that is "unmale." In order to sustain his separateness of self, he must defend against ever getting too close to her again. Through projective identification he must deny all that appears to be "female" in himself. What seems most female is the role of emotional caretaker and the nurturer; consequently, experiences most uncomfortable for males seem to be those related to dependency needs. This is because those needs most closely associated with infantile urges to be taken care of by the mother engender feelings of helplessness. Ironically, the male need to maintain a separateness from others must be done within the context of a relationship. One cannot be separate without someone from which to be separate.

For girls the road toward separateness is different because the person with whom she is expected to identify is also the person from whom she must separate. She must somehow incorporate social feminine roles and also be a distinct person from her mother. The child's mother is also attempting to behave in a sex role syntonic way, as is expected by society and her family structure.

Lerner (1988) and Bernardez-Bonesatti (1978) both discuss one major issue that may hamper this process: the prohibition of anger in women. They contend that there is a fear of female anger that appears culture-wide and this fear is attributed to the early infantile experiences of the mother's anger as potentially anathema to the child's survival. "Because of the child's heavy reliance on primitive projection, one aspect of the early maternal image that persists in the unconscious of even the most 'rational adults' is that of a vengeful, angry, possessive, all powerful 'bad mother' who restricts her child's autonomy, freedom and growth'' (Lerner, 1988, p. 139). Males and females contend with this archaic fear differently, although they both will unconsciously accept it as truth. It is quite possible that the anger that infants perceive is only partially explained by the infants' use of projection. Often maternal anger is real because for many women the pain of inferior status is heightened by the presence of a dependent infant. In addition, a male infant could trigger resentment and anger for some women, because of his higher status and opportunities denied her. Fear of female dominance becomes evident in cultural warnings to women that they should "let the man win" or "pretend he's smarter, more capable, etcetera." These admonitions are designed to limit the capabilities of women and paint a picture of the "weaker" sex whose destructive potential must be continually guarded against.

The task of separating from one's caretaker is even more complicated for the girl, as she must differentiate from a person who is culturally inferior. This is because a mother's own sense of self can be affected by women's second class status and as a result, she may convey to her child a sense of fragility. This fragile structure may appear to be endangered by the child's movement toward separateness. The limits imposed on females by the cultural definition of femininity will have had some impact on the mother. The mother's longings and experiences of missed opportunities may be heightened by the daughter's strivings toward psychological independence, to which the child will respond. A daughter, more than a son, will represent for the mother an opportunity to redo something missed in her own life. Any movement on the part of the daughter to act in her own separate interest may trigger such uncomfortable reactions in the mother that she cannot provide the needed selfobject tasks. The daughter may then fear for the integrity of their relationship; consequently, she may sacrifice her needs for self-actualization so as to save the mother-daughter bond.

Bernardez-Bonesatti (1978) has written that the experience of anger separates one from others, and establishes the angry person as temporarily separate, different and unconnected. Therefore, while men may use anger defensively to deny their feelings of vulnerability, women expressing anger are perceived as violating their well-being. Bernardez writes, "In anger, the person establishes automatic aloneness and makes herself temporarily separate from the object of the anger'' (1978, p. 216). Lerner adds that for a girl ''the feeling of separateness stirs separation anxiety and an unconscious fear of object loss'' (1988, p. 141). It is suggested by Lerner that the fear has as its source the girl's difficulty with attaining an adequate separation from her mother:

> When mother and daughter cannot negotiate an adequate degree of separation between them, the daughter may sacrifice her own growth and avoid autonomous functioning in order to preserve an unconscious tie with her mother, who is experienced as too possessive or fragile to tolerate the girl's developing autonomy. When it is not safe to express one's separateness and difference from mother, the experience of separateness and difference inherent in the expression of anger may also be taboo. Healthy expressions of anger and protest may be replaced by masochistic solutions; by daughter's becoming the hurt or dependent child, an unconscious bond with mother is maintained (Lerner, 1978, pp. 141–142).

Although the experience of separation is much broader than the girl's ability to sustain her own anger, it is a major factor in working with adult women who are addicted. This will be addressed further in the discussion on treatment.

The role of the father is of crucial importance in this process since he is most likely absent or emotionally unavailable; therefore a murky model for maleness is provided. Experience suggests that a significant number of addicted people come from families who functioned along traditional gender role lines. Chodorow (1978) contends that because of the father's inaccessibility, a boy must often use cultural stereotypes of masculinity as a model for male behavior. A father often functions as a peripheral figure until his child is older; his absence can convey a mysterious excitement to both boys and girls. He can represent the adventure of the outside world and separateness (an idealizable selfobject). For the most part, he is not available for early identification for the girl and reinforces the idea that there are distinctly male and female realms when it comes to nurturance and socialization of children.

In either early male or female experience the movement toward autonomy and identity development is colored by the matriarchal world of the child, within a family system and a larger culture espousing certain gender role requirements. With present gender role arrangements both men and women are likely to have unmet selfobject needs that impair the development of a core sense of self. In the place of the self is a profound psychological emptiness. It is the pain of this emptiness that the adult person attempts to soothe through the use of drugs, alcohol or other external means. Reaching for a substance becomes a way to recreate an idealized mother-child dyad. For both men and women the substance or behavior can become a selfobject to provide a false sense of power, and to soothe from the outside what is not possible to do internally. A mood-altering drug can create the illusion of well-being, potency, and a sense of belonging that was not adequately provided for during the original infant experience.

TREATMENT CONSIDERATIONS

Implications of feminist psychoanalytic treatment for both chemically dependent women and men are extensive; however the two most important emphases are to (1) support sobriety, and (2) encourage adaptive authenticity.

Clinical Example

Ann, a 26-year-old single woman with a 4-year-old daugher, entered treatment right after her live-in man friend had proposed marriage. She had stopped drinking several years previously but had recently begun to drink again. After a rapid deterioration to previous drinking patterns and a course of treatment in an inpatient unit, she had entered outpatient therapy. Therapeutic exploration revealed that Ann's mildly negative description of the relationship masked a strong fear of resisting pressure to marry from members of her family system. Her description of her traditional parents further illuminated the origins of her reticence. Both her guilt over having a child out of wedlock, and her fears of further resisting familial and cultural expectations led her to passively accept the proposal. She turned to alcohol to soothe the psychological dissonance rather than do what she genuinely wanted to do, which was to reject the offer.

The ideological position of the therapist could serve to direct the focus toward or away from the underlying issue, which in this case was the client's struggle with a need to express herself differently than expected by family and culture. The therapist became a mirroring selfobject in acknowledging Ann's real wishes not to marry this man. As the therapy progressed, the therapist weathered a storm of increasing anger that had been held in check by a paralyzing depression. Eventually the therapist provided the vehicle though which Ann could explore her fear of asserting herself in a manner that differed from familial expectations. The therapist identified the ways in which Ann, although not consciously acknowledged, had all along been asserting her needs, however dysfunctional they had appeared (i.e., getting pregnant and drinking). Rather than risk a more direct challenge, she sacrificed her own growth and her selfobject needs to be seen accurately.

In another case, Jane, a divorced woman in her early twenties, sought treatment for a conflictual relationship with her 6-year-old daughter, Ellen. Through the course of the therapy, it became apparent to Jane that at times she was using alcohol to medicate her anger at her daughter. On further exploration of this anger Jane began to talk about her frustration and impatience with what seemed to the therapist to be normal 6-year-old behaviors on Ellen's part. This led the therapist to wonder about Jane's experience as a little girl herself. As the therapist encouraged Jane to explore her own background, Jane began to remember her father's impatience with her.

Jane—"He was always hurrying me and yelling when I couldn't do it faster. I felt as if I was in the way, an irritant, and somehow it was connected with being a girl."

Therapist—"You mean that it felt as if there was a different value placed on being a girl?"

Jane—"It didn't just *feel* like it, it was that way! He never missed an opportunity to say so. They were so happy when my brother was born! Three girls and finally a boy! And the thing that really bothers me about it, is that I have a hard time with my brother, and I really wish we could be closer."

As clinicians and therapists, it is not enough to acknowledge the possible effects of cultural dichotomizing on our clients' attempts to free themselves from addictions. We must also examine in ourselves the unconscious ways that we contribute to maintenance of the gender role expectations— and we all do. In fact, I believe that therapist stance plays perhaps a larger role than therapist theoretical orientation. One way that therapists' attitudes are revealed is in the organization of our treatment programs. An obvious manifestation is who sits where in the organizational hierarchy. Another more subtle indication is reflected in what we encourage or discourage clients to express in groups and in our individual work with them.

While in the earlier stages of recovery it is important to provide the addict with an external programmatic structure: selfobjects to replace the drug and the lack of internal sturcture. It is also important not to reinforce sex stereotypes. For example, helping a woman to feel better about herself by encouraging her to "put on her makeup and find her best color" does not address the profound need that she has to be seen and accepted as she is, the need for a mirroring selfobject. Instead it again speaks to our cultural need to have women be attractive for the other and to deny her differentness, her autonomous self. This may appear to be a trivial point, but treatment programs for women that focus on "Color Me Beautiful" may reinforce attention to extrinsics, rather than encouraging acceptance of oneself.

We must encourage women to talk about their experiences, and we must have the courage to provide alternative models for how women and men can be in the world. For example, our inpatient facilities must provide childcare options, and the caretakers shouldn't only be women. In fact, it may be therapeutic for male clients to spend time with children, in order to promote the development of nurturance. We must encourage our female clients to experience their anger by not discouraging its expression. For example, Dawn, an early recovery alcoholic, had used alcohol to medicate painful obsessive thinking. She and her therapist discovered that her obsessions were used to defend against anger. The therapist acknowledged and encouraged any sign of anger, providing a calm accepting presence as Dawn tenuously began to express her anger more directly. Gradually Dawn's anger became more intense both in the real relationship as well as in the transference. The therapist continued to weather the storm and as Dawn was able to experience the therapist as an idealized selfobject in addition to having greater understanding of her anger, the obsessive symptoms receded. Dawn's sobriety was strengthened.

Often, when the drug of choice is no longer an option, clients will initally step up their attempts to attain acceptable masculinity or femininity as a defense against further narcissistic injury. Both male and female clients may resort to stereotypic gender behavior; males by devaluing women and women by being flirtatious. Both these activities are often heavily tinged with hostility, which can be understood to be anger in response to helplessness. Because client populations in many treatment programs are predominently male, the cultural power inequality between the genders is heightened. An environment of safety for both must be provided. This safe structure should include rules against sexual intimacy. Another very useful tool is the establishment of same gender groups. It's important to provide this for both women and men, in order to minimize the message that women's needs are an addendum.

While in outpatient treatment, women should be encouraged to develop support structures from community resources while strengthening individual boundaries and limits. For many of my female clients the struggle to pursue an understanding of themselves as differentiated beings and the counter pressures of narrow sex role expectations manifests in distorted use of support networks. One woman I saw had difficulty resisting requests for rides to AA meetings and wound up constantly driving all over the city. For a time the focus of our work was on helping her to say no and to attain a balance between always and never saying yes. This was an important opportunity to explore with her fears of resisting the expectation to be of service to others and to stand firmly on the side of her own self-interest.

This can also be true for male clients. A 25-year-old man entered outpatient treatment after completing a thirty-day inpatient alcohol treatment program. A struggle with his male identity consolidation emerged when he stopped drinking. He had drunk addictively since he was thirteen years old. David's metaphor for this was an ongoing theme around hunting, which is not uncommon for male addicts. Over the course of a year, he spoke of guns, hunting trips with his father and friends, even dressing the animals. As the therapist stayed attuned to David's view of himself and the subtleties of his affective experience, David grew more able to express his experience more directly. He had gradually less need for the metaphor as he found safety and acceptance from the therapist for the more non-traditional aspects of himself, such as his fears and sadnesses. Close to the end of treatment, David went hunting and upon his return he described one experience with a deer.

> I had him in the sight of my rifle, my finger on the trigger. He was a big beautiful buck; the biggest I'd seen. I just kept watching him and I discovered that I couldn't shoot. I looked for a long time, both of us together there and I decided that I wasn't going to do it. How could I kill something that was so magnificent in life! I don't think I'll go hunting anymore, I don't need to.

In the cases of Dawn and David, the therapist stance was an important ingredient. In Dawn's case the therapist could have supported her helping stance as a step toward recovery, which might have reinforced Dawn's acceptance of the ''correct'' role for women. With David, this therapist had strong feelings about hunting as a negative activity and, if expressed, might have prevented him from exploring the meaning for himself. The first example illustrates a possible clinical mistake in overlooking the client's acceptance of traditional roles. The therapist in the second case, who saw herself as a feminist clinician, could have made an opposite error. She could have let her feminist view of hunting as unacceptable prevent the client from doing the therapeutic work in his own metaphor. This is an example of supporting authenticity in all its configurations; which is the goal of feminist therapy.

The road to recovery from addictions for women parallels their movement toward autonomy. When we recognize and aid our client's attainment of authentic expression of the self, we are helping to insure that she will have little use for a substance as a poor substitute. We must be willing to examine our own attitudes about gender expectations and to provide a ''holding environment'' (Winnicott, 1965) for our female clients to explore whatever possibilities there are, including activities that have been traditionally masculine. We must allow ourselves to be the selfobjects for our clients and acknowledge the strivings of the female self toward autonomy and self-dignity. At the same time, we must allow men the same room to not always be the boss. We must support their humanness, which includes their sadness and fears.

> As long as men are the makers and shapers of culture in the world outside the home, as long as women are not free to define the terms of their own lives,

as long as society continues to convey the message that mother *is* the child's environment, then the basic dysfunctional triad of distant father, emotionally intense, overinvolved mother, and child with little room to grow up is a natural outgrowth and microcosm of the culture (Lerner, 1988, p. 251).

I add that as long as this culture continues to deny expression of normal human strivings, both for connection and separateness, people will continue to seek relief in a variety of avenues, including mood-altering substances.

REFERENCES

Barwick, J. (1971). *Psychology of women: A study of bio-cultural conflicts.* New York: Harper & Row.

Bernardez-Bonesatti, T. (1978). Women and anger: Conflicts with aggression in contemporary women. *Journal of American Medical Women's Association, 33,* 215–219.

Blane, H.T. (1968). *The personality of the alcoholic: Guises of dependency.* New York: Harper & Row.

Child, I., Bacon, M. & Barry, H. (1965). A cross cultural study of drinking. *Quarterly Journal of Studies on Alcohol,* Supplements 3.

Chodorow, N. (1978). *The reproduction of mothering: Psychoanalysis and the sociology of gender.* Berkeley, CA: University of California Press.

Chodorow, N. (1989). *Feminism and psychoanalytic theory.* New Haven, CT: Yale University Press.

Dinnerstein, D. (1976). *The mermaid and the minotaur: Sexual arrangements and human malaise.* New York: Harper & Row.

Eichenbaum, L., & Orbach, S. (1983). *Understanding women: A feminist psychoanalytic approach.* New York: Basic Books.

French, M. (1985). *Beyond power: On women, men, and morals.* New York: Summit Books.

Freud, S. (1961). *The standard edition of the complete psychological works of Sigmund Freud.* (J. Strachey, Trans.). London: Hogarth Press.

Gilligan, C. (1982). *In a different voice.* Cambridge, MA: Harvard University Press.

Horner, A. (1984). *Object relations and the developing ego in therapy.* Northvale, N.J.: Jason Aronson Inc.

Kohut, H. (1977). *The restoration of the self.* Madison, CT: International Universities Press, Inc.

Kohut, H. (1984). *How does analysis cure?* Chicago: The University of Chicago Press.

Lerner, H. (1988). *Women in therapy.* Northvale, NJ: Jason Aronson, Inc.

Levin, J. D. (1987). *Treatment of alcoholism and other addictions: A self-psychology approach.* Northvale, NJ: Jason Aronson, Inc.

Mahler, M. S., Pine, F., & Bergman, A. (1975). *The psycological birth of the human infant: Symbiosis and individualism.* New York: Basic Books.

Miller, J.B. (1976). *Toward a new psychology of women.* Boston: Beacon Press.

Mitchell, J. (1974). *Psychoanalysis and feminism.* New York: Basic Books.

Wilsnack, S. C. (1973). Sex role identity in female alcoholism. *Journal of Abnormal Psychology, 82,* 253–261.

Winnicott, D. W. (1965). *The family and individual development.* Harmondsworth, England: Penguin.

PART II

Substance Dependencies

3

Sex Role Setups and Alcoholism
Cynthia Downing

INTRODUCTION

Sex roles socialization practices have a profound effect on the development, diagnosis and treatment of alcoholism in women. The differential sex role socialization system in America has the following effects on women alcoholics: (1) the damage done by active alcoholism is increased and prolonged; (2) the diagnosis of alcoholism is more difficult; and (3) treatment for and recovery from alcoholism is more difficult for women alcoholics than it is for male alcoholics.

Both alcoholism and sex role socialization involve the process of being controlled by a power stronger than one individual can withstand. Women in our culture have been taught that they have less power than men. When alcoholic women use chemicals to cope with problems, they are rendered even more powerless than they were before they used chemicals. This article will examine ways in which sex role socialization contributes to and exacerbates alcoholism in women.

SEX ROLE STEREOTYPING

Males and females are viewed and treated differently on the basis of their sex in our society. Sex role stereotypes are deeply embedded in American culture (Unger, 1989; Sandmaier, 1980) and women are assigned traits of being dependent and unaggressive with accompanying low social status. Literature in the mental health field has empirically documented characteristics associated with femaleness to be seen as less healthy than those considered masculine (Broverman, Broverman, Clarkson, Rosenkrantz, & Vogel, 1970). Consequently, women can be considered as a kind of deviant group in that they possess characteristics that are negatively valued and stigmatized. Goffman (1963) defines social deviance as a property that is assigned to a person by those who are threatened by that person's behavior and/or attributes.

Although alcoholic women are seen as more deviant than their nonalcoholic sisters, female alcoholics and drug addicts tend to abuse substances in ways that do not conflict with their traditional roles. As a result, women's patterns of chemical use are different that those of men's since females remain motivated to act in ways that will be accepted be others.

CHEMICAL USE PATTERNS IN WOMEN

Alcoholic women often discover that drinking or drug taking initially reduces the pain and conflict produced by sex role stereotypes related to deference, dependence, and acquiescent behavior. However, when her drinking inevitably gets out of control, the female alcoholic's pain and conflict increase because being out of control is not consistent with the stereotype of being unassertive and "in the background." Therefore, alcoholic women hide their drinking more often than men. Additionally, they often become more traditional in their roles so as to draw attention away from their secret deviance. Thus, behavior in a stereotyped feminine role can be accentuated and perpetuated by alcoholism in women.

Women hide their drinking both because of the inevitable denial that accompanies the disease as well as the considerable stigma associated with being a woman alcoholic. Blume (1985) elaborates:

> The woman who drinks to excess is triply stigmatized. First, she is included in society's negative attitude toward all alcoholics. Secondly, she is subject to a special disgust focused on the intoxicated woman. Lastly, the idea that drunkenness and sexual promiscuity are linked add to the burden of disapproval (p.625).

Because women hide their drinking or drug use more than men, women are less likely to drink in public places, to drive while intoxicated, or to be exposed to cohorts who urge them to drink. Women are more likely to be exposed to alcohol in supermarkets and drug stores, and thus be tempted to buy alcohol to take home (Ferrence & Whitehead, 1980).

Because of the surreptitious way in which many women drink, their alcoholism may have progressed to a later stage than men's by the time the illness is discovered (Fillmore, 1984). Mental health practitioners may actually collude in the female "hidden drinking" syndrome by mistaking the effects of alcoholism for mental illness. When alcoholism is misdiagnosed (for example as depression) the symptoms are treated, but the drinking or drug taking is never addressed. Because submissive behavior is socially sanctioned for women, most females are probably more comfortable with a psychiatric diagnosis of depression than alcoholism. Hence, the primary disease can progress and actually be exacerbated by dependence on psychotropic drugs if they are prescribed as part of the "solution" in a misdiagnosed case.

In addition to alcohol, women often turn to the use of prescription drugs as a socially sanctioned way to alter their moods. Prescription drug use is the perfect way to hide chemical dependency for women. Drugs don't smell like alcohol; therefore, drug use is harder to detect. In addition, if a physician has prescribed a drug, the traditional female role would indicate that a woman "should" obey her doctor, and take the medicine. Mulford (1977) found that 24 percent of women who were newly admitted to treatment facilities reported regular use of prescription drugs as opposed to 9 percent of newly admitted men. Ferrence & Whitehead (1980) found major sex differences in the use of psychoactive drugs. Men were found to be more likely to use or abuse illegal drugs, while women were found to be more likely to use or abuse prescribed drugs. Prescription drug use is one of the major differences between men and women in treatment for chemical dependency (Curlee, 1970).

In summary, the chemical use patterns of women make clear that a primary problem in female alcoholism and addiction can be its "invisibility." As a result, many women alcoholics and addicts are inaccurately treated or untreated for the primary disease.

Separation of the Disease from the Meaning of the Disease

Alcoholics drink and/or take drugs because they suffer from a primary, progressive and fatal biopsychosocial disease. Current research suggests that the predispostion for alcoholism is present in the brain at conception. Empirically based data have suggested that ethanol (alcohol) is metabolized differently by alcoholics and that they have an innate enzyme susceptibility for developing tolerance. Increased alcohol consumption leads to psychological or thinking problems that, in turn, cause social difficulties (Downing, 1989).

A person who is alcoholic is acting within the context of his or her own particular life. Thus, the meaning of the alcoholic's drinking and/or chemical taking will be different for each individual. Researchers in the past have confused the *cause of drinking* (a physical illness) with the *meaning of drinking* (to dull the pain, to feel better). Since one's idea of the etiology of any illness will determine how that illness is treated, it is important to keep in mind the difference between cause and meaning.

Two etiological theories of chemical dependency are directly related to sex role stereotypes. McCord & McCord (1960) pose the "dependency theory," which was based on interviews with 225 men. This study suggested that drinking satisfied hidden dependency needs: men drink to feel taken care of while maintaining the independent, masculine facade associated with drinking in our culture. The authors extended their conclusions to alcoholic women, although no women were studied.

McClelland, Davis, Kalin & Wanner (1972) posited that alcoholics drink to gain the illusion of power over others; men drink to feel powerful. McClelland's study was entitled *The Drinking Man;* it was based on the study of men only. McClelland himself did not claim that his results applied to women. As is true of much research done exclusively on males but generalized to the population at large, the pattern of data may not pertain for women.

Neither McCord and McCord's nor McClelland's theory has been confirmed in clinical practice with alcoholic women. Neither theory takes the biological nature of the disease of alcoholism into account, thus neither one can be properly espoused as a plausable explanation for the existence of the disease. The theories are a good example of mistaking a possible *meaning* of the disease for a possible *cause* of the disease. In the past it has been assumed by many in the addiction treatment field that the feminine role protected women from being alcoholic. State McCord and McCord:

> A woman who suffers from intensified dependent longings can find satisfactions simply by living the role most approved by her society. Her conflicts can be assuaged through marriage and homemaking; her need for alcohol as a vicarious outlet is consequently reduced (p. 162).

It is to be hoped that views such as this will cease to be included in the literature of alcoholism.

Dr. Sharon Wilsnack, a Harvard research psychologist, decided to address the theories of female "deviant sex role adjustment" and "defective femininity" prevalent in the scientific literature as explanations offered for female alcoholism. She hypothesized that women may drink to resolve sex role conflicts connected with their inability to attain the unattainable feminine ideal as prescribed by the culture. Contrary to McClelland's idea that people drink in order to feel *more* powerful, Wilsnack found that women with strong drives for power drank more *because the effects of alcohol diminished their need for power and made them feel more feminine!* Wilsnack's findings have been replicated in a number of other studies done on middle-class alcoholic women over 30 (Wilsnack, 1976).

Some ideas about women's sex roles have been changing in our culture, which may impact the development of alcoholism in women. Young women today have more options for "acceptable" behavior than did their mothers. Wilsnack & Wilsnack (1978) found that heavy drinking in younger women was linked to rejection of traditional femininity and in older women, drinking was linked to conscious feminine role reference. Thus women may view their drinking as a way to attempt to resolve their sex role conflicts. While older women strive to feel most in conformity with feminine norms, younger women may desire to acquire more masculine traits as they are societally valued. Hence, alcohol can serve as the illusive "magic potion" to resolve sex role conflicts related to desires for more or less femininity.

SEX ROLES AND THE ALCOHOLIC FAMILY

Sex roles are acquired by children through the process of parental as well as societal socialization, and knowledge of one's sex role is integral to the formation of identity (Block, 1984). If a child is raised by an alcoholic parent, then the impact of that parent's disease on the child, coupled with sex role socialization, can have a very negative outcome on personality development.

The alcoholic family is a dysfunctional family system whereby members deny their problems, bury feelings, develop strong and rigid personal defense mechanisms, exhibit low self-worth, communicate indirectly and encourage the formation of rigid roles for each family member. Family system rigidity is necessary for the unit to maintain homeostasis. Rigid survival roles are also influenced by gender and status within the family. Some of the common roles identified by Wegscheider (1981) include the Enabler, the Hero, the Scapegoat, the Lost Child and the Mascot.

It has also been found that birth order, IQ and physical attractiveness influence the assignment of survival roles in an alcoholic home. For example, the first child is generally assigned the role of Hero. If female, she will assume many of the primary caretaking duties in the household. And, if the Hero is physically attractive, she may be cast as a Heroine who is usually self-sacrificing, rather than heroically assertive. A Heroine with a high IQ will often be taught to hide her intelligence in order to be more completely, heroically female. Alternatively, she will be taught that she can use her intelligence only after her traditional role has been satisfactorily filled (See Wegscheider-Cruse, 1985; Black, 1985; Woititz, 1984).

In an alcoholic home, everyone is powerless over the alcoholism. Therefore a female child who grows up in an alcoholic home is powerless over both alcoholism and the demands of her traditional female role. When that child grows up to become alcoholic, her own alcoholism renders her even more powerless over her choices and actions. It is because she needs to reduce the risk of alienating those upon whom she is dependent that an alcoholic female will often accentuate her traditional feminine role. The difficulties of acting outside society's norms (Unger, 1979) are thus compounded by the rigidity of the alcoholic family's own norms

(Sandmaier, 1980).

How does reaction against sex roles apply to lesbians, who clearly are not "traditionally feminine?" Although age and life experience need to be considered, it may be that many women choose to be lesbian as a reaction against societal female stereotypes. This is probably particularly true for those who have "come out" since the rebirth of feminism in the 1970s. However, making that choice is not without conflicts. It has been estimated that the rate of alcoholism and drug addiction in the lesbian/gay community may be two to three times greater than in the population at large. One could argue that both lesbians and gay men challenge traditional stereotypes and seek a "crossover" identity. Although this is not true for all lesbians and gay men, many lesbians seek the opportunity to manifest more "masculine" traits while the reverse is true for gay men. However, both familial and societal censure of a lesbian/gay lifestyle can lead to internalized homophobia. If the person is genetically predisposed to develop alcoholism, he or she may inevitably turn to alcohol and/or drugs to assuage the pain of homophobia and censure.

Violence and alcoholism are frequently related (Sandmaier, 1980; Frieze & Knoble, 1980; Frieze & Schafer, 1984). Disproportionately, women have been victimized in alcohol related battering (Rada, 1975), and sexual abuse cases including rape (Groth, 1978). Child abuse by alcoholic parents is frequent and usually takes the form of neglect rather than physical violence (Frieze & Schafer, 1984). Neglect is a form of emotional violence. When a child's basic needs are not met, profound psychological damage can result, impairing both identity and the ability to form relationships. Unfortunately, such impairments can contribute to the development of the child's own alcoholism or drug addiction. This is because family victims of alcoholic neglect and abuse must form defenses such as cognitive distortion and self-blame in order to survive the abuse. Such defenses allow bizarre behavior such as alcoholic drinking and drug taking to flourish unchallenged for a long time. Many children of alcoholics must suffer enormous consequences before they notice they are alcoholic.

It is not surprising that women from alcoholic families become disproportionately depressed, and perceive themselves as being helpless more often than do women from non-alcoholic families. As was previously mentioned, there is often confusion between the diagnoses of depression and alcoholism (Cermak, 1986). If one has been trained within a family context as part of a prescribed role, then a "setup" for depression exists (Radloff, 1978). So, the depressed Heroine or Enabler may inadvertently turn to substances for analgesic relief. If she is alcoholic or has an eating disorder, the Heroine or Enabler's disease may be initially hidden, particularly if she tries to be "Superwoman." Both career wives/mothers and housewives might initially hide their disease by appearing productive on the outside and never letting anyone close enough to see how out of control their behavior is. But control inevitably fails as the disease progresses. The meaning of loss of control is hopelessness and helplessness, which worsen and prolong depression.

Sex role stereotypes prescribe that women are most valued for their nurturance functions and their roles as wives and mothers. Consequently, an alcoholic female will tenaciously try to hide her alcoholism to retain her status based on those roles. Discovery or acknowledgment of her disease often means being deserted. Over 90 percent of women stay with alcoholic husbands, but over 90 percent of husbands leave alcoholic wives (personal communication, St. Mary's hospital, 1982). Youcha (1986) points out that alcoholic women are generally left alone by their husbands both during their drinking and during treatment. This may suggest that a man's sex role is affronted by having an alcoholic wife. How can a man maintain his image of masculine dominance if his wife is "out of control" by virtue of alcoholism? The high desertion rate by husbands may be attributable to men attempting to salvage a faltering sense of "machismo."

Because females are deemed acceptable as long as they *look* good, hiding chemical use will be particularly important to them. If a woman looks good by continuing to nurture the other people in the family, then the chances of others discovering (or challenging) her chemical use are lessened. Many alcoholic women are married to alcoholic men. This state of affairs decreases the woman's chances of her alcoholism being diagnosed, especially if she does not complain about his drinking (Forrest, 1983).

Changing roles is difficult if not impossible when alcoholism is active. Dating and marriage reinforce sex role stereotypes previously learned in the home. The powerlessness, learned helplessness and rigidity of roles in an alcoholic family further complicate recovery for alcoholic women. It is only after a woman's alcoholism has been diagnosed and treated that she is free to examine the other issues that can keep her dysfunctional. However, even if a woman has been correctly diagnosed as having alcoholism, there is no guarantee that treatment will be available to her.

CLINICAL AND TREATMENT ISSUES

More than half the alcoholics seen by physicians are not recognized as alcoholics, in part because many physicians view alcoholics as the stereotypical "drunk under the bridge."

> To overcome their own myopia and the alcoholic's denial, both relative and clinician must learn to conceive of alcoholism as a disease that *causes* depression, marital breakup, and unemployment, not as a sympton that *results from* such distressing events (Vaillant, 1983, p. 295).

As with sexism, alcoholism is often subtle, hard to detect and based on stereotypes; therefore, its denial is perpetuated.

Therapists frequently deny that clients are alcoholic or drug dependent because of their own denial and lack of information. Because of sex role stereotyping, male clinicians may diagnose women as depressed rather than alcoholic. Seeing depression rather than addiction would more likely conform to male clinicians' own traditional conceptions about women. Apathy, listlessness and repressed anger exhibited by a female alcoholic in a therapist's office could be symptomatic of depression. A conventional therapist could misdiagnose alcoholism based on what he wanted to see.

Once over the hurdle of diagnosis, getting to treatment is a problem for women. The Junior League found in its 1988 nationwide survey that women are underrepresented in treatment facilities and that there are three major barriers to women for receiving treatment: (1) personal denial by the women themselves; (2) lack of child care for dependent children; (3) family denial and opposition to treatment. The survey noted that family support for the alcoholic woman may be a most important resource in ensuring that she receives treatment (*Woman to Woman*, 1988).

Even after she has been properly diagnosed and has entered treatment, other problems exist for the alcoholic woman. Alcoholism counselors working in treatment facilities tend to be either recovering alcoholics or codependents (Brown, 1985; Lawson, Ellis, & Rivers, 1984; Wegscheider, 1981). Although sensitivity to the disease through personal experience is a plus, personal recovery does not guarantee that a treatment professional will be free from biased or sexist assumptions. This is true for both male and female counselors. Because there is much to be gained by gender sensitivity, it is now considered prudent to offer same-sex group therapy within treatment programs.

Most existing treatment centers in the United States are based on the Minnesota Model of treatment, which evolved from Alcoholics Anonymous. The typical alcoholic who joined AA was, until recently, a late-stage, male alcoholic. Consequently, the literature of Alcoholics Anonymous is not ''gender sensitive,'' which could be alienating for women with a proactive feminist philosophy. Additionally, most AA literature refers to the abuse of only alcohol; hence, a woman who abused psychotropic or illicit drugs may not initially relate to what she reads. There is some evidence that the membership and literature of AA. is changing to include more women and more people who exhibit polydrug use; however, the basic philosophy remains the same as it was in 1935 and will change very slowly (Downing, 1989).

Feminist Treatment for Alcoholism

Some of the strategies for treating the unique problems of alcoholic women are social solutions that address the problems of women in general. Social programs that address women's issues can be a valuable adjunct to treatment of alcoholic women, such as job skills training and child care facilities.

In general, we must encourage physicians and therapists to get more training in the diagnosis and treatment of alcoholism, with special attention to the features of the illness particular to women. An alcoholism curriculum should be required in professional schools. Physicians need to be aware of the dynamics of addiction when treating women for pain and anxiety. A woman who repeatedly requests pain and anxiety medication over a long period of time should be routinely assessed for alcoholism or drug addiction.

We must encourage law enforcement agencies to go beyond their own stereotypes and refer women to weekend DWI programs so they can get help. A program that perpetuates hiding women's alcoholism by "overlooking" drunk driving is a program that perpetuates the illness and prolongs the suffering of the woman who has it.

Other treatment strategies will specifically address the problems created by the interaction of sex role socialization practices and alcoholism. Many treatment facilities have therapy groups for women only. These groups explore the issues, such as shame about being an alcoholic woman, having been a victim of sexual abuse or having been cast in a stereotyped role, in an atmosphere that encourages honesty about the consequences of the illness. Alcoholism is an ugly illness that creates shame in its victims. The act of saying out loud what one is ashamed of dissipates some of the power of the shame. When one woman shares her deepest secrets, another is invariably inspired to speak up about her own secrets. Each woman can learn that she is not alone, that her illness is like the illness of every other woman. Thus women end up learning to support one another in their recovery. Women should be encouraged to seek out all-female aftercare groups and AA meetings for the same reasons.

Family therapy should be used at a number of different points in the recovery process. Family therapy is used in primary treatment to educate family members about the disease, to begin to stop secret keeping, to identify problems caused by the alcoholism and to get each individual member started on his or her own recovery program.

With few exceptions, family therapy has incorporated feminist literature only within the last five years (Avis, 1988). As feminist theory has been added to family therapy, the interaction between the cultural and societal environment and the family has been properly acknowledged. This is an especially important principle in the case of alcoholism, since people have traditionally blamed the alcoholic for his or her disease. The tendency to blame the victim is harmful to the alcoholic and to his or her family. Special care must be taken to model a "no-fault" attitude toward the disease. The therapist may have to teach the disease concept to the family; special attention should be paid to the overwhelming evidence for genetic transmission of the illness. The therapist needs to help the family see that alcoholism is genetically programmed in a similar fashion to genetic programming of eye color or the shape of one's nose.

After the initial treatment goals have been met, individual family members need to pursue their own recovery programs for 6 months or so before more family aftercare therapy is undertaken. By the end of 6 months of sobriety, the alcoholic has been sober long enough to get the habit of sobriety and has sobriety firmly incorporated into her life. The ability to withstand the stress of examining beliefs and behavior patterns held for a lifetime depends on solid sobriety. A good guideline to gauge readiness for family therapy might be to wait at least 6 months after the start of sobriety.

A second reason for postponing family therapy is that women tend to try to overcompensate for having been dysfunctional by becoming over-responsible. In an attempt to "make up" for her inability to nurture properly, the recovering alcoholic mother in early sobriety may silently allow her family to put blame on her for her illness, thus buying into the "don't talk, don't trust, don't feel" rule. By pretending that the problem is over (because it was the woman's problem in the first place and she is now "cured"), the family colludes to hide the illness from the world. A recovering alcoholic woman needs time to fully forgive herself for the behavior resulting from the disease before dealing with family role and power dynamics. Because of an alcoholic woman's tendency to feel shamed and over-responsible for family problems, other family members may conveniently resist any change in their own behavior and fail to accept their own roles in the family dysfunction.

In a discussion about possible causes of this "silent conspiracy" to hide a woman's alcoholism or drug addiction, Peluso and Peluso (1988) state:

Women are cast as the bearers of virtue in our society... (there is a great) emotional stake that parts of our society have in maintaining the image of a virtuous, self-disciplined womanhood.... 'For every woman drug addict hiding in a closet, there are usually several family members leaning against the door' (p. 7).

Individual aftercare for the alcoholic woman needs to help her pull away from codependency, and to focus attention, in a healthy way, on her own growth and development. If a woman lets go of the need to get approval from others, she will learn to resist the demand of others that she be blamed and shamed. Learning to forgive oneself for being alcoholic is a complex task, but a crucial one for maintaining lifelong sobriety.

Women can benefit from reading such books as *Women and Drugs: Getting Hooked, Getting Clean* (Peluso & Peluso, 1988); *The Responsibility Trap* (Bepko & Krestan, 1985); *A Different Voice* (Gilligan, 1982); and *The Dance of Anger* (Lerner, 1985). All are books that are consistent with feminist principles and that can help the woman question her assumptions.

Long-term cognitive therapy is extremely valuable for long-term alcoholism recovery. Cognitive disputation of mistaken beliefs is a necessary strategy in the treatment of alcoholism (Downing, 1989); it is particularly important for women with mistaken beliefs about sex roles. For example, a woman might say to herself: "If my children need something done for them, I should never be too tired or too busy to do it, and I shouldn't have to ask anyone else to do it. Everyone in this family has been inconvenienced enough." One strategy for disputing this mistaken belief would be for the woman to write notes to herself such as: "I have the right to my own time," and "I can't always do what others want me to do." One particularly successful disputing statement is: "If I can't pretend that everything about running the house is my responsibility, then I will have to know how much of myself I have given away."

It takes about 5 to 7 years to address all the issues created by alcoholism, and to get the person's life into a Maintenance Stage of recovery (Gorski, 1988). Group aftercare therapy in an all-female setting has the potential for dealing with women's issues on a long-term, ongoing basis. Group therapy should be directive in its subject matter if it is to teach the woman new life skills. Subjects such as "What are sex role stereotypes?"; "Dependency in relationships"; "Value clarification"; and "Assertiveness training" can be brought to the group as topics. Each group member can then work on her own issues around the subject.

It has also been suggested that feminism is a good treatment approach for alcoholic women (Schultz, 1977). For example, a feminist therapist would model new behavioral standards for the alcoholic woman that were assertive and proactive. This would be a valuable therapeutic course as many alcoholic women have never had a healthy, functional female role model. Schultz helped set up a program that modeled feminist principles; women in her program made exceptional progress, with a recovery rate far above the norm. Schultz' program included group work on acceptance of and practice in using anger, group discussion disputing stereotyped standards for female behavior and work assignments within the program based on abilities rather than on sex.

Feminist therapy has empowering women as a focus. Oftentimes empowerment can mean acceptance of one's experience. This feminist principle is very apropos for working with alcoholic women who feel remorse about their role as mothers while drinking. Feminist therapy will encourage women to forgive themselves for not knowing how to parent, and will help parents to have the courage to learn new ways to relate to their children. Children need to learn that sex role stereotypes about mothers and fathers are incorrect and damaging to both parent and child. Parenting skills that encourage parents and children to become real people to each other can be learned in sobriety (Porterfield, 1984).

CONCLUSION

Sex role stereotypes are labels that limit the lives of all those they touch. Alcoholism increases and prolongs the damage done by the limitation of sex role stereotyping by creating more limitations than already existed. Many alcoholic women feel powerless because of sex role assumptions; this powerlessness is compounded by the existence of alcoholism. Additionally, the diagnosis and treatment of alcoholism in women is more difficult than it is with men. This is because of the female alcoholic's invisibility by virtue of drinking at home, and because of assumptions about women's mental health that can create misdiagnoses such as depression and/or anxiety. Feminist therapy for alcoholism encourages women to challenge sex role assumptions and to be involved in behaviors that are more proactive and assertive. Most basically, a feminist approach encourages a woman to accept herself, and self-acceptance is the cornerstone of recovery.

REFERENCES

Avis, J. M. (1988). Deepening awareness: A private study guide to feminism and family therapy. In L. Braverman (Ed.), *A guide to feminist family therapy.* (pp. 15–46). New York: Harrington Park Press.

Bepko, C., & Krestan, J. (1985). *The responsibility trap: A blueprint for treating the alcoholic family.* New York: Free Press.

Black, C. (1985). *Repeat after me.* Denver: MAC.

Block, J. H. (1984). *Sex role identity and ego development.* San Francisco: Jossey-Bass Publishers.

Blume, S. B. (1985). Women and alcohol. In T. G. Bratter & G. G. Forrest (Eds.), *Alcoholism and substance abuse: Strategies for intervention.* (pp. 623–638) New York: Free Press.

Broverman, I. K., Broverman, D. M., Clarkson, F. E., Rosenkrantz, P. S., & Vogel, S. R. (1970). Sex role stereotypes and clinical judgements of mental health. *Journal of Consulting and Clinical Psychology, 34,* 1–7.

Brown, S. (1985). *Treating the alcoholic: A developmental model of recovery.* New York: John Wiley & Sons.

Cermak, T. L. (1986). Diagnostic criteria for codependency. *Journal of Psychoactive Drugs, 18,* 15–20.

Curlee, J. (1970). A comparison of male and female patients at an alcoholism treatment center. *Journal of Psychology, 74,* 239–247.

Downing, C. (1989). *Triad: The evolution of treatment for chemical dependency.* Independence, MO: Herald House.

Ferrence, R. G., & Whitehead, P. C. (1980). Sex differences in psychoactive drug use: Recent epidemiology. In O. J. Kalant (Ed.), *Research advances in alcohol and drug problems* (Vol. 5: *Alcohol and drug problems in women)* (pp. 125–201). New York: Plenum Press.

Fillmore, K. M. (1984). When angels fall: Women's drinking as cultural preoccupation and as reality. In Sharon C. Wilsnack & Linda J. Beckman, (Eds.), *Alcohol problems in women* (pp. 7–26). New York: The Guilford Press.

Forrest, G. G. (1983). *Alcoholism and human sexuality.* Springfield, IL: Charles C. Thomas.

Frieze, I. H., & Knoble, J. (1980). *The effects of alcohol on marital violence.* Paper presented at the Annual Convention of the American Psychological Association Montreal, Canada.

Frieze, I. H., & Schafer, P. C. (1984). Alcohol use and marital violence: Female and male differences in reaction to alcohol. In S. C. Wilsnack & L. J. Beckman (Eds.), *Alcohol problems in women* (pp. 260–279). New York: The Guilford Press.

Gilligan, C. (1982). *In a different voice: Psychological theory and women's development.* Cambridge, MA: Harvard University Press.

Goffman, E. (1963). *Stigma.* Englewood Cliffs, NJ: Prentice-Hall.

Gorski, T. (1988). *The staying sober workbook.* Independence, MO: Herald House.

Groth, A. N. (1978) The older rape victim and her assailant. *Journal of Geriatric Psychiatry, 11,* 203–215.

Lerner, H. G. (1985). *The dance of anger.* New York: Harper & Row.

Lawson, G. W., Ellis, P. C., & Rivers, P. C. (1984). *Essentials of chemical dependency counseling.* Rockville, MD: Aspen.

McClelland, D., Davis, W. N., Kalin, R., & Wanner, E. (1972). *The drinking man: Alcohol & human motivation.* New York: The Free Press.

McCord, J., & McCord, W. (1960). *Origins of alcoholism.* Stanford, CA: Stanford University Press.

Mulford, H. A. (1977). Women and men problem drinkers. *Journal of Studies on Alcohol, 38,* 1624–1639.

Peluso, E., & Peluso, L. S. (1988). *Women and drugs: Getting hooked and getting clean.* Minneapolis, MN: CompCare.

Porterfield, K. M. (1984). *Keeping promises: The challenge of a sober parent.* Center City, MN: Hazleden.

Rada, R. T. (1975). Alcoholism and forcible rape. *American Journal of Psychiatry, 132,* 444–446.

Radloff, L. S. (1978). Sex differences in helplessness, with implications for depression. In L. S. Hansen & R. S. Rapoza (Eds.), *Career development and counseling of women* (pp. 137–152). New York: Charles Thomas.

Sandmaier, M. (1980). *The invisible alcoholics: Women and alcohol abuse in America.* New York: McGraw-Hill.

Schultz, A. P. (1977). Radical feminism: A treatment modality for addicted women. In E. I. Rawlings & D. K. Carter (Eds.), *Psychotherapy for women: Treatment for equality* (pp. 350–369). Springfield, IL: Charles J. Thomas.

Unger, R. K. (1979). *Female and male: Psychological perspectives.* New York: Harper & Row.

Vaillant, G. E. (1983). *The natural history of alcoholism: Causes, patterns, and paths to recovery.* Cambridge, MA: Harvard Universitiy Press.

Wegscheider, S. (1981). *Another chance: Hope and help for the alcoholic family.* Palo Alto, CA: Science & Behavior Books, Inc.

Wegscheider-Cruse, S. (1985). *Choicemaking.* Pompano Beach, FL: Health Communications, Inc.

Wilsnack, S. C. (1976). The impact of sex roles on women's use and abuse. In M. Greenblatt & M. A. Schuckit (Eds.), *Alcoholism problems in women and children* (pp. 37–63). New York: Grune & Stratton.

Wilsnack, R. W. & Wilsnack, S. C. (1978). Sex roles and drinking among adolescent girls. *Journal of Studies on Alcohol, 39,* 1855–1874.

Woititz, J. (1984). Adult children of alcoholics. *Alcoholism Treatment Quarterly, 1,* 71–99.

Woman to Woman: Community Services Survey. (1988). The Association of Junior Leagues, 660 First Avenue, New York, NY 10016.

Youcha, G. (1986). *Women and alcohol: A dangerous pleasure.* New York: Crown Publishers, Inc.

4

Psychosocial Factors in Women's Alcoholism

Eileen M. Corrigan

Just as there has been an increase in our understanding of the differences between women and men with drinking problems, so there has been a sharpening of the implications of those differences for treating women. Both physiological and psychosocial factors have been identified in recent years as the basis for addressing women's treatment issues. Some of the physiological factors concern lower rates of consumption (Plant & Plant, 1979) but accelerated consequences (Ashley et al. 1977; Hill, 1984), especially alcoholic hepatitis and ethanol-induced cirrhosis, (Gavaler, 1982). An explanation of the latter has more recently been suggested by the differences in ethanol's metabolism by women, increasing the bioavailability of alcohol (Frezza et al. 1990) and the likelihood of hepatic consequences.

Psychosocial aspects that are distinctive for women concern their rejection by others, the greater stigma experienced, identity issues and a persistent belief that women do less well in treatment (Corrigan, 1980; Beckman, 1978; Vanicelli, 1984; Gomberg, 1988). The totality of women's different experiences is a major reason for identifying and examining their unique treatment needs.

Within a feminist framework, this chapter will focus on distinctive psychosocial aspects of women's development with such issues as self-esteem and depression highlighted; the relationship to drinking and treatment will also be described. Both the theoretical and empirical underpinnings for understanding treatment outcome for women will be examined as well as the practice knowledge required to treat alcoholic women.

WOMEN'S SELF ESTEEM AND DEPRESSION

Self-esteem

Whatever particular constellation of problems is a consequence of drinking, the one area that requires the closest attention is women's self-identity. Feminist theoreticians perceive women as psychologically defined through their relationships (Miller, 1976; Gilligan, 1982; Berzoff, 1989). It is women's connection with others that promotes psychological growth. Gilligan (1982), in her development of women's distinctive psychology, notes women's greater orientation toward relationships and interdependence. The achieving of autonomy then is seen as accomplished through a connection with others. Miller (1976) describes women's sense of self as "... organized around being able to make and then maintain affiliations and relationships" (p. 83). The need for connection may be of critical importance in understanding the alcoholic women's relationships, many of which may be destructive. Gilligan (p. 156), notes that this process of women's attachment "... creates and sustains the human community" but at the same time promotes feelings of helplessness, powerlessness and constant compromise. The implications of this view for treatment will be returned to later.

Beckman (1978) and Turner (1987) examined one aspect of women's identity by following changes in their self-esteem over the course of treatment. Beckman (1978) originally pointed to the lower self-esteem of alcoholic women as compared to nonalcoholic women and alcoholic men. Both researchers report finding an improvement in self-esteem following treatment. Turner (1987) specifically examined self-esteem as it relates to drinking patterns after one year of treatment. She reported that while 67 percent of the women showed low self-esteem on entering treatment, this decreased significantly after one year of treatment to 30 percent. When this change in self-esteem was related to the women's drinking pattern after one year of treatment, it was found that those who decreased their consumption were most likely to have an improvement in self-esteem. The time frame for the Turner finding is quite similar to that of Beckman's study since it is based on an earlier research study (Corrigan, 1980).

It can be hypothesized that those whose drinking decreased were then able to realistically assess their self-worth; those who did not alter their drinking continued to be at risk of poor self-esteem. As noted above a considerable number of women continued to have low self-esteem. To further elaborate and test feminist theory, an important direction for future research would be to explore the alcoholic women's relationships to elicit their role in the women's identity as measured by their self-esteem.

Depression

The diagnosis of depression has plagued the alcoholic woman and confused treatment strategies. The frequent placement of women in this diagnostic category and their higher psychiatric admissions for depression (Weissman & Klerman, 1979; Braverman, 1986) are thought to mask alcohol related problems in some women (Merikangas, Weissman, Prusoff, Pauls, & Leckman, 1985).

Since alcohol is classified pharmacologically as a depressant, it obviously will have that effect if its intake is sufficiently high. How to sort out the diagnosis of alcoholism versus depression has intrigued clinicians and researchers alike. It is evident that the withdrawal of alcohol may well provide the answer; if the depression persists, then the separate diagnosis of depression can more easily be made.

Yet the question remains whether the depression preceded the onset of alcoholism, and if so whether drinking reinforced it or indeed exacerbated depressive features. This is more commonly seen as an underlying depression. Certainly when women have been known to practitioners prior to the onset of their drinking problem, such a differential diagnosis can be made. But long-term familiarity with a patient will no doubt apply to a relatively small fraction of the treated population.

Schuckit and Winokur's early work focusing on women (1971) and the Turner findings (1987) also concerning women, reflect a persisting need to examine the intertwined diagnostic categories of alcoholism and depression in women. Turner reports that at the beginning of treatment 59 percent of the women in her study were depressed but fewer, 32 percent, remained depressed at the follow up.

Depression was examined in relation to drinking behavior and both abstinence and a reduction in consumption of alcohol were found to have a significant relationship to the course of depression. Depression persisted for 19 percent of the abstainers and for 17 percent of those who reduced alcohol consumption. Thus a minority of women will find their depressive symptoms persisting even after altering their drinking pattern. At follow up, Turner (1987) found that the only demographic variable related to depression was socioeconomic status: women of lower socioeconomic status were more likely to find their depression persisting. It can safely be stated that the depression of poor women is very much related to their status in society, even after they enter treatment. Women continue to be clustered in lower-level jobs and occupational segregation also persists. The context of depression is oftentimes society's denigration of women. Many women also experience helplessness when faced with power and domination by others. When women use such relationships as their definition of self, then depression will persist for many.

Studies of men enlighten our understanding of depression in women. The work of Schuckit (1983) and more recently Brown and Schuckit, (1988) has added to the literature for men and depression. Using a different methodology and depression scale, Brown and Schuckit (1988) found fewer of the male alcoholics to be depressed at intake, (42 percent), and only 6 percent having depressive symptoms persisting after four weeks of treatment. Although the data set used by Turner (Corrigan, 1980) did not allow for a 4-week analysis of the depressive symptoms, it is likely that this same rapid decrease in symptoms would occur for women, since withdrawal of the depressant (alcohol) seems to account for this finding in men.

What is noteworthy, however, in these two research studies is the higher proportion of women with depressive symptoms both at the beginning and conclusion of treatment. While this is not surprising, the possibility exists that it is an artifact of using different scales to measure depression in the two studies cited. This would need to be tested by studying women and men as they begin treatment, and evaluating depression with the same standardized scale.

PERSPECTIVES ON TREATMENT

Clinical Experiences

Staff who work in programs for women alcoholics make a clear distinction between clinical depression and the depressive symptoms associated with alcoholism, (NIAAA, 1982). A report on a conference attended by the directors and staff of a number of programs for women noted there was less concern about depression than some other issues since "clinical experiences indicate that as the women become sober, depression diminishes" (NIAAA, 1982, p. 44). Yet we have evidence that for some women the depression will persist, although for the majority it will remit. This is no longer solely based on clinical experience since these views are now buttressed by research.

The staff singled out issues of stigma, trust and role identity as requiring primary attention during treatment. Further, they believe that women's treatment facilities should be staffed by women, both in clinical and management positions; there should also be women on the board of directors and/or advisory boards (NIAAA, 1982, p. 10).

Separate women's programming is also thought to be necessary for the treatment of women alcoholics; some believe that women do better in a total female facility:

Role modeling, an "insiders" sensitivity to women's problems and willingness on the part of staff to face their own sex role attitudes and biases form the philosophical base for the advocacy of separate women's treatment programs (NIAAA, 1982, p. 9).

Their experience also points to greater reluctance by women to reveal previous sexual abuse, such as incest and rape, in mixed groups as opposed to women's groups. Two programs for women reported sexual abuse among patients ranging from 70 to 90 percent (NIAAA, 1982, p. 17). These data are much higher than previously reported and merit further research. This issue has recently surfaced in almost every arena where women in treatment are discussed. Until studied, we will not know if such experiences are idiosyncratic to these women's treatment programs, or if it is a more universal experience.

It is not surprising to learn that almost all the programs represented at the conference just described favored single sex therapy groups and a predominance of female staff to treat women. Despite the popularity of this view among many clinicians, it is almost devoid of empirical groundings. One research study (Bournazian, 1987, p. 99) reports no relationship between the gender of the primary care provider and abstinence:

> Rather the one attribute of the treatment provider which tended to be significant in forecasting success was the number of alcoholic patients with whom the practitioner had worked. Therefore, experience rather than congruity in gender may be the more essential treatment ingredient.

There is clearly a lack of sufficient rigorous research on this issue. The view that women would fare better if treated by women can best be characterized as a hypothesis requiring testing under differing conditions. Yet this is a most important treatment and research issue and the lack of scrutiny of this assumption is symptomatic of the lack of consistent attention to issues affecting women. The views concerning women have too often been reflective of research based on men and this has clearly been challenged by women clinicians and researchers. What must be avoided now is the promulgation of additional notions about women without empirical grounding. The assumptions of the conference participants can be formulated as research questions and, if pursued systematically, could add immeasurably to our understanding of the most effective approaches to treatment of alcoholic and drug dependent women. Lacking more specific data in the areas just discussed, the research on treatment outcome, in general, will be scrutinized as it relates to women.

TREATMENT OUTCOME

Treatment evaluation studies form the connecting link with the clinicians' views. There are now two excellent reviews of treatment outcome that focus exclusively on women: Annis & Liban (1980) and Vanicelli (1984). Both reviews incorporated studies from outside the United States and Canada. The most recent review (Vanicelli, 1984) covers a 30-year period, 1950–1980 and 51 studies on treatment outcome for women were examined. Despite strong and compelling evidence to the contrary, the view that women alcoholics do less well than men alcoholics in treatment seems to persist in the folklore of alcohol studies and among some treatment personnel. The objective reality is that women alcoholics do as well as men in treatment. A number of researchers have alluded to this continuing erroneous perception of the alcoholic woman's response to treatment. Consistent with the earlier assessment by Annis and Liban (1980), no differences were found in treatment outcome between women and men in 43 studies; seven studies report women doing better and five showed men having a better outcome. Vanicelli (1984) quite rightly concludes there is no evidence to support that women have a poorer response to treatment, (p. 386).

There also appears to be an adherence to citing outdated research concerning alcoholic women, ignoring recent research (Corrigan, 1986). This could well be a function of journal authors and then reviewers being unaware of recent research. Yet, the older literature consistently presented alcoholic women most negatively, for example, "sicker," more difficult to treat and having a poorer treatment outcome (Braiker, 1984, p. 353). There is no basis for such a view, other than possibly an historically differing perception of what constitutes good mental health for women and men. The current research supporting "no difference" in treatment outcome must be called to the attention of journals when articles containing such errors are published. No doubt sexism also prevails among reviewers and journals and this institutional sexism, which is so insidious, affects the social sciences as it does all the sciences.

CLINICAL VIEWS AND RESEARCH

There is little scientific data on treating women separately from men or the merits of female as compared to male therapists (Vanicelli, 1984). Annis and Liban (1980) concluded that the major determinants of treatment outcome are linked to the characteristics of patients rather than to the treatment modality. Note, however, that the research they examined did not include any that compared the results of treatment of women by women to treatment by men. When describing the patient characteristics found to be of some importance, a "... trend toward greater improvement among married female alcoholics" (pp. 405–406) was observed. In addition, high social and economic status of the patient also results in a more positive treatment outcome (Ogborne, 1978; Corrigan, 1980). These particular variables may well be masking other variables such as the connections available to married women and those of higher social class. The many dimensions of a supportive social environment that reinforces a positive outcome in treatment may be a powerful variable influencing treatment outcome. This is a hypothesis that lends itself to testing in future research. This theoretical perspective is reinforced by a recent report of a longitudinal study of male alcoholics (Vallant, Milofsky, Richards, and Vallant, 1987) which reports that "... occupational and marital stability, not the complexity of treatment, predicted short term outcome" (p. 173).

An additional hypothesis needing to be examined concerns the beliefs of treatment staff about the likely outcome of treatment for women. There is evidence that the mind set of staff contributes to a positive or negative outcome. This has been variously referred to as the expectancy effect or the self-fulfilling prophecy (Bournazian, 1987). Only two studies that have concentrated on the relationship of treatment provider's predictions to actual outcome have included alcoholic women in their sample (Vanicelli & Becker, 1981; Bournazian, 1987). In Vanicelli and Becker's study (1981) predictions made by the patient about future drinking behavior tended to be more accurate than that of staff. In contrast, Bournazian (1987, p. 131) reports:

> Positive predictions by treatment staff were found to be significantly related to positive outcome as were negative predictions to negative outcome at the time of discharge. The close association did not persist when initial predictions were compared to drinking status reported by the women a year after treatment began, except for the women about whom negative predictions had been made. Active drinking was the result for women whose prognosis was poor upon entry into treatment.

In this study 60 percent of the staff responsible for treatment were women. Bournazian identifies a number of variables that contribute to the predictions and believes more attention to the treatment needs of women with poor prognoses would increase the likelihood of success. Since unemployed and single women were more likely to rate a poor prognosis, this "fits" with nontraditional women being perceived less positively by staff. The finding in Bournazian's study concerning the continuing relationship between negative predictions and a poor treatment outcome points to a possible troublesome area of staff attitudes. The power of such negative predictions is quite strong. It may well be that a staff member's belief system about a poor treatment outcome contributes to that result. Thus, where staff members negatively assess a woman, based on sexist, racist, class or other mythical notions, there is a good likelihood of that attitude permeating the treatment planning, relationship and outcome. The reality is that a heterogeneous population requires a fine-tuned treatment plan.

Thus, the connections available to a middle-class woman may not be there at all for a lower-class woman. This would imply that more connections need to be built where they are lacking. In addition, the staff may view the process of recovery as following a specified course. Is it conceivable that where the woman does not follow a preconceived response to the treatment regimen, the staff accelerates the outcome in a negative direction? Thus, the area of expectancy effects has been too little studied to date and is a promising one for future research efforts.

A SUGGESTION FOR CLINICAL TRAINING

There may well be a need for clinicians to first examine their own assumptions about women to determine if indeed they are harboring sexist views. Secondly, the attitude of the clinician toward the alcohol-dependent women is of primary importance. As just noted, this may be one of the most powerful features of treatment since it has been demonstrated to have a remarkable effect on outcome. For the clinicians who are seriously interested in examining their attitudes toward this dependency, a visit to AA is highly recommended. Participation over a period of months is seen as a helpful first step in coming to terms with attitudinal issues.

To be able to examine quite clearly the use of alcohol and its consequences for women, it is essential that there be a lack of ambivalence. This cannot be done if the clinician's views are still flawed with confusion around dependency. It is necessary to convey the essential elements of treatment—hope and the need to withdraw from alcohol and all other drugs. For some women it may be necessary to do this within a controlled environment where there are psychosocial and medical supports for detoxification (should withdrawal symptons such as convulsions occur) and treatment.

Extensive support for change must be built in for the individual—this includes support from family and friends as well as an affiliation with one or more AA groups. It has been noted repeatedly that the alcohol dependent woman needs to transfer this need to drink to other activities. Support groups within the patient's clinical setting are highly recommended and may be needed for an extensive period of time by some women.

Seasoned clinicians have learned to expect that some patients may experience "slips." They are to be viewed as exactly that. They are transient and sometimes of very brief duration, such as a day or two. Such backsliding may occur after some social activity where alcohol is prominently served. It may be the only discouraging incident in the woman's effort to achieve sobriety, an effort that needs to be supported in every manner possible. Here the optimism of the clinician must not flag since it is this positive view of the woman as someone whose illness can be treated which is so crucial to change.

CONCLUSIONS

The pervasive social acceptance of alcohol and more recently other mind and mood altering drugs such as marijuana, coupled with women's higher use of psychoactive prescription and over-the-counter drugs, indicates this will be a continuing major health issue for women. Progress has been made in calling attention to the very rapid pace at which women experience the consequences of alcohol.

Once the woman enters treatment, a positive outcome is now best understood in relation to the characteristics of the patient. Married women and those of higher socioeconomic status have a greater rate of successful treatment. Do perceptions of status influence the expectancies for a positive treatment outcome? If so, what about the other women who constitute the majority: poor women, single women and lesbian women.

A number of hypotheses have been suggested that need further study. These include the effects of women's social support, expectancies of staff and same-gender therapists. Finally the women's sense of her own identity and connection to others must be evaluated and become a central focus of treatment along with her alcohol dependency. If there is an impoverished self-concept and a destructive relationship that hinders development, then treating the alcohol dependence without attending to these connections is likely to result in a poor treatment outcome. Miller's caution (1976, p. 83) is most relevant here.

> Eventually, for many women the threat of disruption of connections is perceived not as just a loss of a relationship but as something closer to a total loss of self.

She adds that this can possibly lead to other problems singling out depression that is "... related to one's sense of the loss of connection with another(s)."

It probably needs to be underlined here that dependence on mind- and mood-altering drugs is not necessarily a symptom of an underlying emotional problem but must be treated for its health and psychosocial consequences. Gaining a better understanding of women's connection with others may be central to treatment and especially for those women whose treatment efforts have not been successful. Applying feminist theoretical perspectives to this group of women should greatly increase the likelihood of improving treatment and our grasp of deeply held resistance to change.

REFERENCES

Annis, H. M., & Liban, C. B. (1980). Alcoholism in women: Treatment modalities and outcomes. In O. J. Kalant (Ed.), *Alcohol and drug problems in women* (pp. 385–422). New York: Plenum Press.

Ashley, M. J., Olin, J. S., Le-Riche, W. H., Kornaczewski, A., Schmidt, W., & Rankin, J. G. (1977). Morbidity in alcoholics: Evidence for accelerated development of physical disease in women. *Archives of Internal Medicine, 137,* 833–887.

Beckman, L. J. (1978). Self-esteem of women alcoholics. *Journal of Studies on Alcohol, 19,* 491–498.

Berzoff, J. (1989). From separation to connections. Shifts in understanding women's development. *Affilia, 4,* 45–58.

Bournazian, R. (1987). *Treatment expectancies for women.* Unpublished doctoral dissertation, Rutgers—The State University of New Jersey.

Braiker, H. (1984). Therapeutic issues in the treatment of alcoholic women. In S. C. Wilsnack & L. J. Beckman (Eds.), *Alcohol problems in women* (pp. 349–369). New York: The Guilford Press.

Braverman, L. (1986). Reforming the female client's profile. *Affilia, 1,* 30–40.

Brown, S. A., & Schuckit, M. A. (1988). Changes in depression among abstinent alcoholics. *Journal of Studies on Alcohol. 49,* 412–417.

Corrigan, E. M. (1980). *Alcoholic women in treatment.* New York: Oxford University Press.

Corrigan, E. M. (1985). Gender differences in alcohol and other drug use. Brief Report. *Addictive Behaviors,* 313–317.

Corrigan, E. M. (1986). Professional roles—collaboration between clinicians and researchers. *Women and alcohol: Health related issues.* (Research Monograph 16, pp. 272–286) Rockville, MD: DHHS Publication No. (ADM) 86–1139.

Corrigan, E. M. (1987). Women's combined use of alcohol and other mind-altering drugs. In D. Burden & N. Gottlieb (Eds.). *Social work curriculum for practice with women.* (pp. 162–176). London: Tavistock.

Drug Abuse Warning Network. (1989). *Project DAWN annual report 1982.* Rockville, MD: National Institute on Drug Abuse.

Frezza, M., DiPadova, C., Pozzato, G., Terpin, M., Borgona, E., Lieber, C. (1990). High blood alcohol levels in women: The role of decreased gastric alcohol dehydrogenase activity and first-pass metabolism. *New England Journal of Medicine, 322*(2): 95–99.

Gavaler, J. S. (1982). Sex related differences in ethanol induced liver disease: Artificial or real? *Alcoholism: Clinical and Experimental, 6,* 186–196.

Gilligan, C. (1982). *In a different voice.* Cambridge and London: Harvard University Press.

Gomberg, E. L. (1988). Alcoholic women in treatment: The question of stigma and age. *Alcohol & Alcoholism, 23*(6) 507–514.

Hill, S. Y. (1984). Vulnerability to the biomedical consequences of alcoholism and alcohol-related problems among women. In S. C. Wilsnack & L. J. Beckman (Eds.), *Alcohol problems in women* (pp. 121–154). New York: The Guilford Press.

Merikangas, K. R., Weissman, M. M., Prusoff, B. A., Pauls, D. L., & Leckman, J. F. (1985). Depressives with secondary alcoholism: Psychiatric disorders in offspring. *Journal of Studies on Alcohol, 46,* 199–204.

Miller, J. B. (1976). *Toward a new psychology of women.* Boston: Beacon Press.

National Institute on Alcohol Abuse and Alcoholism. (1982). *Advances in alcoholism treatment services for women.* Rockville, MD: DHHS Publication No. (ADM), 83–1217.

Ogborne, A. C. (1978). Patient characteristics as predictors of treatment outcomes for alcohol and drug abusers. In Y. Israel, F. B. Glaser, H. Kalant, R. E. Popham, W. Schmidt, & R. G. Smart (Eds.), *Research advances in alcohol and drug problems, 4,* (pp. 177–223). New York: Plenum.

Plant, M. L., & Plant, M. A. (1979). Self-reported alcohol consumption for one hundred patients attending a Scottish alcoholism treatment unit. *British Journal of Alcohol and Alcoholism, 14,* 197–207.

Schuckit, M., & Winokur, G. (1971). A short-term follow-up of a group of women alcoholics. *Diseases of the Nervous System, 33,* 672–678.

Schuckit, M. (1983). Alcoholism and other psychiatric disorders. *Hospital and Community Psychiatry, 34,* 1022–1026.

Turner, J. M. (1987). *Alcoholism and depression in women.* Unpublished doctoral dissertation, Rutgers—The State University of New Jersey.

Vallant, C., Milofsky, E., Richards, R., & Vallant, G. (1987). A social casework contribution to understanding alcoholism. *Health and Social Work, 12,* 169–176.

Vanicelli, M., & Becker, B. (1981). Prediction of outcome in treatment of alcoholism. *Journal of Studies on Alcohol, 42,* 938–950.

Vanicelli, M. (1984). Treatment outcome of alcoholic women: The state of the art in relation to sex bias and expectancy effects. In S. Wilsnack & L. Beckman (Eds.), *Alcohol problems in women.* (pp. 369–412) New York: The Guilford Press.

Weisman, M. M., & Klerman, G. L. (1979). Sex differences and the epidemiology of depression. In E. S. Gomberg & V. Franks (Eds.), *Gender and gender disordered behavior* (pp. 381–425). New York: Brunner/Mazel.

5

Recovery Needs of Lesbian Alcoholics in Treatment

Brenda L. Underhill

There has tended to be a lack of information available in the field of alcoholism in regard to lesbian and gay alcoholics and the few studies dealing with that subject have tended to focus on gay men. Although both groups are subject to all of the prejudices and discrimination against homosexuals in general, lesbians differ from gay men in many aspects of their lives, just as men differ from women. From health care issues to the dynamics of intimacy in a couple, lesbian issues are by and large women's issues. Unlike gay men, lesbians also face socioeconomic discrimination based on gender. Lesbians of color are subjected to triple stigma based on race, gender and sexual orientation.

This chapter will present an overview of the specific needs of lesbian alcoholics in treatment and recovery. The underlying premise presented here is that the barriers to effective treatment for the lesbian woman with alcohol problems are cultural and external as well as intrapsychic and internal. The problems seen in treatment are, in fact, exacerbations of the problems any lesbian faces in her struggle to maintain a healthy, integrated emotional life in a heterosexually defined, homophobic and sexist culture. Thus it is homophobia, heterosexual bias and sexism that create the systems barriers that result in lesbians being an underserved population.

A feminist perspective places individual problems in a social context. A nonfeminist model personalizes social problems. Using a feminist model for lesbian alcoholics involves understanding the interplay between the nature of the disease of alcoholism and the realities of lesbians' lives.

A cause and effect relationship is not being proposed between sexism and alcoholism or feminism and recovery. However, it is necessary to acknowledge that there is a complex and intricate relationship between these issues. Lesbians, as women, must recover from the physical effects of alcoholism and the social diseases of sexism and homophobia. A feminist perspective on alcoholism is based on the understanding that an individual lesbian alcoholic must surrender to her powerlessness over alcohol and other mood-altering drugs while at the same time reclaiming her power as a woman and a lesbian. The design and delivery of services to this segment of the alcoholic population must address all of these factors if services are to be effective. These services are best provided within the framework of a feminist health model.

Although specifically focusing on the needs of lesbian alcoholics, most of what is presented here relates to women in general, gay men and other groups who are often referred to as "minority groups." These traditionally underserved groups all share the common factor of less power in society, discrimination and lack of services specific to their needs.

SCOPE OF THE PROBLEM AND CONTRIBUTING FACTORS

The available statistics indicate that 25 percent to 35 percent of the lesbian and gay community have serious problems with alcohol (Fifield, 1975; Lohrenz, Connelly, Coyne & Spare, 1978; Saghir and Robins, 1973; Morales and Graves, 1983). Although there are some concerns about the methodological limitations of these studies (Nardi, 1982), these rates are considerably higher than the 10 percent rate that is cited for the general population. It is generally estimated that for each person who has a drinking problem, four to six other individuals are affected. If these individuals are added to the statistics on lesbians with alcohol problems, the problems caused by alcohol abuse in the lesbian community can deservedly be considered pandemic.

Various sociological and psychological factors have been hypothesized in relationship to the high rate of alcohol abuse problems in the lesbian and gay community. In terms of cultural factors, the effects of minority group status, stigma and discrimination have been explored by various authors (Smith, 1979; Weathers, 1976; Ziebold, 1978). Weathers (1975) states:

> As is true of all minority groups that have been victims of ongoing and systematic discrimination, the dynamics of oppression manifest themselves in that community as low self-esteem, alienation, despair and higher rates of alcoholism and drug addiction. Many of these same characteristics, e.g., low self-esteem, a sense of inadequacy and loneliness are felt by informed alcoholism professionals to constitute an "Alcoholic Personality." When these feelings and behaviors are intensified by widespread and systematic societal oppression, alcoholism rates of the community involved take on a new and

more understandable perspective...the stages of addiction and progression of alcoholism are identical for the lesbian woman as for any other alcoholic, with alcohol in time becoming the problem rather than the solution. The critical point is that the adverse conditions which act on the lesbian community encourage a greater use of alcohol as a coping mechanism and produce a greater rate than in the heterosexual community (pp. 3–4).

The bars, as the traditional social setting for the lesbian and gay community, have also been proposed as a major factor in the high rate of alcoholism within the lesbian and gay community (Fifield, 1975; McGirr, 1975; Weathers, 1976). It may, in fact, be the only place a lesbian feels she can socialize and be open about her sexuality. This means that many lesbians spend much of their social time in alcohol saturated environments.

Ziebold (1978) on the other hand, feels that the above average incidence of alcoholism among gays is not related to the role of the bars in the gay community. He proposes a third factor, the interrelationship of the denial system of the disease of alcoholism and the strong rigid denial techniques that are required to survive in a hostile environment. He states:

Gays who build their ego defenses to protect their sexual orientation in a hostile society may unknowingly let the same psychic reflexes block awareness of a growing dependency on alcohol. This is not to say that all gays become alcoholic or that alcoholism is caused by one's being gay, but homosexuals are vulnerable to addiction because they may have learned how to cope with internal conflicts arising from sexual behavior or desires at the expense of self-acceptance and self-worth (p. 4).

A fourth factor that may also be involved in these rates is the lack of responsiveness to lesbians and gays by traditional alcoholism service providers. One study (Fifield, 1975) reported that out of a total of 54,000 clients treated for alcoholism in randomly selected alcoholism and rehabilitation agencies in Los Angeles County over a six-month period, known gay people numbered only five hundred to six hundred or about 1 percent. Only four of 46 agencies made attempts to do outreach to gay alcoholics. Only two agencies had meetings or group therapy designed for gay people. This finding was corroborated by Judd (1978) in a survey of 57 nongay alcohol treatment agencies. Only two of the agencies made any specific outreach to gay alcoholics and had workshops on gay lifestyles for their staff. In addition, Judd also found that, based on attitude test scores, the nongay alcohol abuse agency staff ''...hold more traditional attitudes towards women's sex roles, are more authoritarian and hold more negative attitudes towards lesbians and gay men than gay service organization staff'' (p. 545).

A recent study by Hellman, Stanton, Lee, Tytun, & Bachon (1989) confirmed these findings in a study of 36 government-funded agencies in New York City. The agencies were surveyed about their training for attitudes toward the treatment of gay and lesbian patients. The authors state:

> The results essentially support the conclusions of surveys of mainstream agencies in Los Angeles and San Francisco which found a significant lack of formal training in the treatment of homosexual alcoholics, limited knowledge of community resources, inability to identify gay clientele, little or no gay staffing, failure to actively address the unique treatment issues of this population, judgemental attitudes about homosexuality, and little or no priority for creating more supportive treatment environments for homosexual alcoholics. The conclusions may reflect a situation that is common and widespread in the health care field (p. 1168).

Most likely, all these factors are involved and interact in the high rates of alcohol abuse in the lesbian and gay community. Further empirical research is needed to more clearly define how these factors are interrelated. If all researchers investigating alcohol and other drug problems would identify the sexual orientation of subjects, the information base on lesbians and gays would greatly increase and the need for separate studies on lesbian and gays would decrease. However, regardless of the exact prevalence of alcoholism among lesbians and the reasons for this rate, considerable work has been done, since the women's movement of the 1970s, to develop effective treatment services to specifically address the needs of lesbian alcoholics.

TREATMENT

The need for a supportive, nonmoralistic, nonjudgemental treatment environment plays a critical role in the recovery process of every alcoholic seeking treatment. An environment that fosters trust and honesty is crucial if clients are to examine their lives and take the risks involved in initiating the changes needed to live a drug-free life. Much of what any alcoholism treatment program provides is an environment that offers the optimal conditions in which recovery can occur. For lesbians, this involves providing a *lesbian affirming* environment. Providers would gain from an examination of what creates a healing environment in which a positive lesbian identity can be nurtured. The importance of the environment in the healing process cannot be overemphasized, for as Ram Dass (1989) states:

> Whether our methods involve words or touch, meditations or medicines, our techniques and interventions are vehicles of transmission. What they transmit

is an environment in which healing can occur. Just as in a garden, we do not "grow" flowers; rather, we create the conditions in which flowers can grow (p. 171).

Lesbians as alcoholics face at least a triple stigma. Homophobia, "the dread of being in close quarters with homosexuals—and in the case of homosexuals themselves, self-loathing," (Weinberg, 1973, p. 4) is pervasive in our culture. Stereotypes continue to characterize lesbians as "man-hating, frigid, unfulfilled" women. The lesbian alcoholic faces the triple stigma of being a woman, a lesbian and an alcoholic.

Homophobia and the heterosexual bias of treatment staff are major issues to be addressed in recovery programs that serve lesbian alcoholics. This bias may take overt or subtle forms. Riddle and Sang (1978) state: "Therapists deal with their own negative attitudes toward homosexuality—or biases in favor of opposite-sex relating heterosexism—in several different ways: avowedly trying to "cure" lesbians, believing their biases to be irrelevant, or believing their biases to be non-existent" (p. 92). Morin (1977) has also discussed the adverse role of heterosexual bias in psychological research with lesbians and gay men.

If lesbian alcoholics are to confront their alcoholism and begin a journey of rigorous honesty, essential to recovery and advocated in Alcoholics Anonymous (AA), then alcoholism service providers, along with all mental health professionals, need training in dealing with homophobia and heterosexual bias. Programs that desire to meet the needs of recovering lesbian alcoholics must be staffed with service providers who are comfortable with their own sexuality, who have examined their homophobic feelings and who have owned any of their own homosexual feelings. This exploration, on the part of service providers, is crucial if the treatment barrier of homophobia is to be overcome (Clark, 1977; Finnegan & McNally, 1987).

Staff also need training in the realities of lesbian subculture. The lesbian community is invisible to most heterosexuals. Alcoholism professionals would never think to ask their alcoholic clients to take the responsibility to teach them about the disease of alcoholism. Service providers therefore must take responsibility to become knowledgeable about lesbian lifestyles and the resources available in the lesbian community. Since many clients will be returning to that community, after-care planning needs to be done with adequate information on the services available to a lesbian client. Lesbian alcoholics may also need special guidance in building a positive non-drinking support system in a community where alcohol abuse is pandemic. This includes knowing what resources are available in the lesbian community and what resources in the mainstream community offer quality services to lesbians.

Social isolation is a problem common to alcoholics. This problem for the lesbian alcoholic is doubled since social isolation is also one of the most devastating aspects of lesbian life. Many lesbians are well into their adult lives before they meet other lesbian women or even recognize their own homosexuality.

Lesbian reality is mystified. Little positive information is available regarding lesbian lifestyles in the media. These negative values about lesbianism are certainly internalized by lesbians as well as by nonlesbians. Individual counseling can continue to reinforce the problem of isolation through the process of one-to-one counseling and a concentration on an intrapsychic orientation. Lesbians need to feel the support of other lesbians that group therapy can provide. Group interaction can assist in breaking down the stigma experienced by lesbians through the same means that AA groups successfully help in breaking down the stigma of being an alcoholic. It takes positive social interaction with peers, whom you value, to help counteract years of conditioning related to feeling different and "queer." In group, lesbian alcoholics can see their lives as women, as alcoholics and as lesbians in a social context. This assists the women in sorting out which problems are individual and which are the result of minority group status. The entire process is an example of the feminist principle, articulated since the 1970s, that "the personal is political." In other words, by hearing the commonality between women's experiences, lesbians can come to see that the "problem" has a systemic root rather than being the exclusive outcome of individual psychopathology.

Sexual abuse is a common issue in working with recovering women (Evans & Schaefer, 1980; Covington, 1982). It will therefore be an issue in working with many lesbian alcoholics. While the subject of how to work with survivors in recovery is beyond the scope of this work, a note of caution to providers is indicated here. A woman's choice of sexual orientation is *not* related to the fact that she may have been abused as a child. Any provider bias or misconceptions in this area could be very damaging to a lesbian. As Bass and Davis (1988) suggest:

> People prefer sexual partners of the same or of a different gender for a multitude of reasons. Sometimes past abuse is one of a complex of reasons, but reducing sexual preference to a consequence of abuse is simplistic and disrespectful to lesbian clients. This belief is usually based on homophobia and on the false assumption that one would not be lesbian unless there has been trauma (p. 349).

Group therapy is also the preferred treatment modality for women and minorities (Christmas, 1978). Only when clients begin to see *all* the factors affecting their lives can they make informed decisions as to what they want to change, what can be changed and how to make those desired changes. The use of group also helps to underscore feminist premises related to the validity of renaming one's experience. The concept of redefining one's reality through one's own experience in living is an empowering process articulated by Mary Daly in *Gyn/Ecology: The Metaethics of Radical Feminism*, (1978). Feminist therapists encourage clients to name their own experience, their own realities, as opposed to accepting what others have said about them. Consequently a lesbian alcoholic can rename her sexual preference as a positive choice in affirming her love of women and her femaleness.

The principle of empowerment means becoming powerful by acquiring the resources and opportunities one needs to maximize one's individuality. As a member of a treatment group, a lesbian can hear how her peers have encountered problems and handled them. She then becomes privy to a kind of "collective wisdom" which she can call upon to assist her with the struggles she confronts. There is much love to be experienced within a group and the healing power of that unconditional positive regard should never be underestimated.

These treatment groups are preferably facilitated by lesbian staff. Not only does a lesbian staff member share many of the life experiences of the group members, but she is also a very positive and needed role model. How many alcoholism treatment centers would ever consider staffing their programs without recovering alcoholics? Alcoholism service providers know from experience the effects of the invaluable statement "I know how you feel." Recovering lesbian staff members are positive proof that recovery is possible.

Recovery groups play a role similar to that which consciousness raising groups provide for women in general. The group format is an excellent place for assisting lesbians in making the connection between the sociopolitical environment and the personal. It is in such a group that lesbians can explore their experiences as alcoholics and as women in order to find common denominators in their life experiences. This can also be the beginning of the development of a healthy support network which is essential to breaking through the barriers of isolation. It is here that lesbians can dispel their own internalized stereotypes and myths about lesbians as they are exposed to a variety of lesbians of many classes, races, cultures, vocations, etcetera.

GROUP FOCUS ON SPECIAL TOPICS

Topical groups for lesbian alcoholics are worth noting here. One example is a group that focuses on assertion techniques and anger. As alcoholic lesbians are exposed to supportive, knowledgeable staff, and peers who validate their feelings, anger usually begins to surface. This anger is often related to the pain of all those years of misunderstanding, guilt, self-doubt and self-blame. Lesbians are particularly vulnerable at this state in treatment to uneducated and homophobic counselors who harbor stereotypes of "boot stomping dykes."

Anger in general is an issue for all women in our culture as Miller (1973) so articulately points out:

> Anger is an especially important part of powerlessness. Remaining in a powerless position can be a refuge from one's fearsome anger. Recognizing and feeling anger is initially very frightening. If one has felt powerless for a long time, one has often reacted with anger. (People do not merely accept such things; they always react to them.) Even women who now want to be openly assertive can get caught in the fear of being angry, which they often don't want to do. It is frequently hard to separate the anger from the assertiveness. Sometimes, too, women are afraid that the degree of their anger is excessive or unjustified. Usually one can learn how to separate the two only if one allows oneself the right to test and explore the anger (pp. 122–123).

Providers involved in the recovery process of lesbian alcoholics need to view this anger as a positive step toward the development of a healthy self-concept and feelings of self-worth as women, as alcoholics and as lesbians. Groups specifically designed to deal with this anger in a safe and supportive environment can be a great asset in recovery. Here lesbians can have the opportunity to learn tools which will help them express their anger in constructive ways rather than reverting to the self destruction of drinking and using.

Some lesbian alcoholics may initially reject Twelve Step programs such as AA, confusing patriarchal religion that has historically rejected homosexuals as "sinners" with spirituality which is integral to AA and recovery. A spirituality group run by a trained alcoholism counselor can be very useful in helping lesbians find individual meaning in the concepts and principles of the Twelve Steps. Ratner (1988) in discussing the role of spirituality issues in groups that explore homophobia states: "Spirituality issues are also examined so that patients can authenticate their experiences as lesbians or gay individuals and overcome some of the shame instilled in them by society, family or religious traditions" (p. 40).

Another specialized group that many lesbians can benefit from is a mother's support group. About one third of all lesbians have children. Clunis and Green (1988) point out that:

> There are three kinds of families headed by lesbian couples: *nuclear*, with children who are born to or adopted by the couple; *blended*, where children are included who came originally from their mother's prior relationship (usually with a man); and *extra-blended*, where children come from both sources (p. 112).

Lesbian mothers face some unique and different problems. An alcoholic lesbian mother, particularly if she is poor, may face a legal system which judges her to be unfit based on her alcoholism *and* her sexual orientation. As Lowenstein (1980) points out: "The two implicit reasons for removing a child from a lesbian mother are that the child might adopt a similar deviant sexual orientation or that the child would be growing up in an emotionally unhealthy atmosphere." Referring to a study by Green (1978), Lowenstein also points out that growing up in a homosexual home does not contribute to a child's homosexuality.

But regardless of the lack of evidence for these negative assumptions that lesbian mothers will produce homosexual children or that these children will not be as emotionally healthy as children from heterosexual homes, stereotypes abound. Lesbian mother support groups can be very effective in dealing with the pain from societal prejudices and discrimination. Again, the feminist principle of the "personal is political" can help lesbians understand that one's personal experience is rooted within the dynamics of how society deals with women, people of color, mothers and lesbians.

FAMILY SERVICES

Much work has been done in the field of alcoholism in the last ten years regarding the role of the family in the disease of alcoholism. There now exists a recognition and acceptance that alcoholism affects each member of the family, and as such, every member needs assistance to learn new behaviors to replace the unhealthy coping mechanisms developed in living with an alcoholic person. However, as Crawford (1987) points out:

> Most literature on the family makes the assumption that *family* refers to the heterosexual unit of mother, father and children, or to the heterosexual single parent family. This image of the family has hung on tenaciously despite the existence of many lesbian-parent families with special characteristics and needs. Family therapy virtually ignores the lesbian family with children, although there has been an increase in materials on lesbian couples (p. 195).

To effectively work with lesbian alcoholic women, recovery programs need to expand the definition of "family" beyond the traditional nuclear family concept. A more inclusive definition would be of family as an emotional field or circle of the significant others who strongly influence one's feelings and behavior. Lesbians need access to counseling that includes significant others be they lovers, children, heterosexual family members or friends. In addition, methods and materials need to be developed which are specific to codependency issues within lesbian relationships. Due to a number of factors, including gender socialization and female role expectations, some of the dynamics present in heterosexual codependent relationships differ in codependent lesbian relationships. One such issue which Finnegan and McNally (1989) raise is the significance of the merging of the denial of self, common to codependency and the homophobic teaching of society. Thus, current theory and practice of codependency treatment cannot simply be applied to lesbian relationships.

Another issue in working with lesbians and their families is the importance of understanding the problems faced by lesbians in "coming out" to their family and nonlesbian friends. "Coming out" is defined by de Monteflores and Schultz (1978) as the "...developmental process through which gay people recognize their sexual preference and choose to integrate this knowledge into their personal and social lives" (p. 59). Various others have offered a stage model of the coming out process (Coleman, 1982; Cass, 1979). Regardless of the theoretical model used, it is critical to understand that acceptance of being lesbian is a *process*. Alcoholic lesbians seeking services may be anywhere on this continuum of acceptance from the closet of self hate to the freedom of self acceptance and openness. In addition, providers should also be aware that there is often a dual process occurring with an individual in coming out. There is both the acknowledgement to self and the acknowledgement to others of her lesbianism. The two often do not occur simultaneously. Hence, to work effectively with lesbians, providers need specific knowledge of the coming out process. Confidentiality is crucial and the service provider must be prepared to work with each individual client on her own time table of acknowledging lesbianism.

McNally (1989) addresses the issue of how alcoholic lesbians integrate the two stigmatized identities of alcoholic and lesbian into their recovery. In her doctoral dissertation she utilizes Cross's five stage structure of identity transformation (Cross, 1971) and Cass's ideas of homosexual identity formation. Her research indicates that a lesbian who is "out" before getting sober "comes out" again in her sobriety. That is, in recovery a lesbian reexperiences the stages of coming out, only now it is as a sober lesbian. In addition McNally indicates that a powerful and dynamic circular interaction occurs between the acceptance of an alcoholic identity and a positive lesbian identity, so that as each identity increases, it strengthens the other identity. This work would indicate that "coming out" is a process universal for all lesbians in recovery and cannot be avoided by providers if services are to be effective. The importance of provider knowledge of this process is then crucial when working with lesbians.

It is important to understand, however, that one source of conflict for recovering lesbian alcoholics who are still in the closet consists of the dishonesty required in concealing their true identity while being encouraged to engage in rigorous honesty as a part of their recovery program. Therefore, "coming out" to family members and friends may be integral to recovery for an alcoholic lesbian. Yet in making this choice to disclose her sexual identity, a lesbian may be rejected outright by family and friends and some women may even jeopardize their legal rights to custody of their children. In addition to that pain, a lesbian alcoholic so treated by her family will not have that family as a source of support in her recovery. Parents who attempt to accept their daughter's lesbianism may need help in working through perceived losses related to heterosexual dreams they had for their daughter. Parents and Friends of Lesbians and Gays is a national self-help organization which can be used as a referral source for parents.

In addition, many lesbian couples, contrary to popular opinion, are in stable long-term relationships. Agencies need to provide same-sex couple counseling that is not replete with heterosexual biases such as asking questions like "Who plays the man and who plays the woman?" Providers need to be knowledgeable about the specific dynamics of lesbian relationships (Kreston & Bepko, 1980; Loulan, 1984; McCandlish, 1982/1983), as opposed to heterosexual relationships. A lack of knowledge on these issues becomes particularly dangerous to lesbian couples in codependency treatment programs (Finnegan & McNally; 1989). Also, as with all individuals, family issues must be placed in a cultural context. Lesbians of color often have stronger ties to their family of origin than do Anglo lesbians. In addition the terms used in the alcoholism field, such as "codependency", have different meanings in different cultures. Services to lesbians of color must integrate issues of gender, sexual orientation and culture to truly be effective.

In addressing the special needs of lesbian alcoholics, care must be taken to treat each lesbian as a unique individual with unique problems and needs. In addition to being a lesbian, a woman comes from a particular racial, cultural and class background. Women of color and working-class lesbians face the burden of racism and class bias in their lives. The problems of lesbians of color are compounded since they must confront both the racism of the lesbian community and gay oppression within their own communities. The additional needs of other subgroups of lesbians, such as teenagers, lesbians with physical disabilities and poor lesbians, are also factors which must be taken into account in treatment. The point is that lesbians are not a homogeneous group in any sense. The differences must not get lost in attempts to take the variable of sexual orientation into account. However, by framing alcoholism services within a feminist perspective lesbians are able to receive support in an environment that acknowledges the role of sexism and homophobia and which assists each woman to begin to make the choices necessary to recover from the disease of alcoholism.

Recovery is about internal and external change. It is about owning individual responsibility and understanding the need to transform society from one that discriminates against lesbians into one that accepts all expressions of sexuality. Mander (1977) states: "Feminism, then is about self-exploration and about action. It is about integrating the two" (p. 286).

Feminism, applied to addiction issues, emphasizes that recovery is a paradoxical process that does not take place in a vacuum. It involves surrendering to the uncontrollable (the addiction) and empowering the controllable (responsibility for self). The challenge for feminist alcoholism service providers is to design and deliver services that address the devastation of the addiction process in a way that empowers lesbians to make the internal and external changes necessary to recovery.

REFERENCES

Bass, E., & Davis, L. (1988). *Courage to heal.* New York: Harper & Row.

Cass, V. C. (1979). Homosexual identity formation: A theoretical model. *Journal of Homosexuality*, 4, 219–35.

Christmas, J. J. (1978). Alcoholism services for minorities: Training issues and concerns. *Alcohol Health and Research World*, 2, 20–27.

Clark, D. (1977). *Loving someone gay.* New York: Signet Books.

Clunis, D. M., & Green, G. D. (1988). *Lesbian couples.* Seattle: Seal Press.

Coleman, E. (1982). Developmental stages of the coming out process. *Journal of Homosexuality*, 7, 31–43.

Covington, S. (1982). Sex and violence—the unmentionables in alcoholism treatment. Paper presented at the National Alcoholism Forum, Washington, D.C.

Crawford, S. (1987). Lesbian families: Psychosocial stress and the family-building process. In Boston lesbian psychologies collective (Eds.), *Lesbian psychologies* (pp, 195–214). Chicago: University of Illinois Press.

Cross, W. E. (1971). Discovering the Black referant: The psychology of Black liberation. In V. J. Dixon & B. G. Foster (Eds.), *Beyond black or white: An alternative America* (pp. 95–110). Boston: Little Brown & Co.

Daly, M. (1978). *Gyn/Ecology: The metaethics of radical feminism.* Boston: Beacon Press.

Dass, R. (1989). The intuitive heart. In W. B. Joy (Ed.), *Healers on healing* (pp, 171–172). Los Angeles: Jeremy P. Tarcher, Inc.

de Montef1ores, C., & Schultz, S. J. (1978). Coming out: Similarities and differences for lesbians and gay men. *Journal of Social Issues*, 34, 59–73.

Evans, S. & Schaefer, S. (1980). Why women's sexuality is important to address in chemical dependency treatment programs. *Grassroots*, September, 37–40.

Fifield, L. (1975). *On my way to nowhere: Alienated, isolated, drunk.* Unpublished manuscript.

Finnegan, D. G. & McNally, E. (1987). *Dual identities: Counseling chemically dependent gay men and lesbians.* Center City, MN: Hazelden.

Finnegan, D. G., & McNally, E. B. (1989). The lonely journey: Lesbians and gay men who are co-dependent. *Alcoholism Treatment Quarterly, 6*(1), 121–134.

Green, R. (1978). Sexual identity of thirty-seven children raised by homosexual or transsexual parents. *American Journal of Psychiatry, 135*(6), 629–97.

Hellman, R., Stanton, M., Lee, J., Tytun, A., & Bachon, R. (1989). Treatment of homosexual alcoholics in government-funded agencies: Provider training and attitudes. *Hospital and Community Psychology, 40*(11), 1163–1168.

Krestan, J., & Bepko, C. (1980). The problem of fusion in the lesbian relationship. *Family Process, 19* (September), 277–289.

Judd, T. D. (1978). A survey of non-gay alcoholism treatment agencies and services offered by gay women and men. In D. Smith et al. (Eds.), *A multicultural view of drug abuse* (pp. 539–547). Cambridge, MA: G. K. Hall/Shenkman.

Lohrenz, L., Connelly, J., Coyne, L., & Spare, K. (1978). Alcohol problems in several mid-western homosexual communities. *Journal of Studies on Alcohol, 39*(11), 1959–1963.

Loulan, J. (1984). *Lesbian sex.* San Francisco: Spinster Ink.

Lowenstein, S. F. (1980). Understanding lesbian women. *The Journal of Contemporary Social Work,* January, 29–38.

Mander, A. V. (1977). Feminism as therapy. In E. I. Rawlings & D. Carter (Eds.), *Psychotherapy for women* (pp. 285–299). Springfield, IL: Charles C. Thomas.

McCandlish, B. M. (1982/1983). Therapeutic issues with lesbian couples. *Journal of Homosexuality, 7,* 71–78.

McGirr, K. (1975). Alcohol use and abuse in the gay community: A view toward alternatives. In K. Jay & A. Youth (Eds.), *After you're out* (pp. 277-278). New York: Pyramid Books.

McNally, E. (1989). Lesbian recovering alcoholic identity. Unpublished doctoral dissertation, New York City University, New York.

Miller, J. B. (1973). *Toward a new psychology of women.* Boston: Beacon Press.

Morales, E. S., & Graves, M. A. (1983). Substance abuse: Patterns and barriers to treatment of gay men and lesbians in San Francisco. San Francisco: Department of Health.

Morin, S. F. (1977). Heterosexual bias in psychological research on lesbianism and gay male homosexuality. *American Psychologist,* August, 629–637.

Nardi, P. M. (1981). *The double doors of homosexuality and alcoholism: A sociological perspective.* Unpublished manuscript.

Nardi, P. M. (1982). Alcoholism and homosexuality: A theoretical perspective. *Journal of Homosexuality, 7*(4), 9–26.

Ratner, E. (1988). A model for the treatment of lesbian and gay alcohol abusers. *Alcoholism Treatment Quarterly, 5,* (1/2), 25–46.

Riddle, D. I., & Sang, B. (1978). Psychotherapy with lesbians. *Journal of Social Issues, 34*(3), 84–101.

Saghir, M., & Robins, E. (1973). *Male and female homosexuality.* Baltimore: Williams & Wilkens, Co.

Smith, T. M. (1979). Specific approaches and techniques in the treatment of gay male alcohol abusers. (Available from NALGAP, 204 W. 20th St., New York, NY 10011).

Weathers, B. (1976). *Alcoholism and the lesbian community.* Unpublished manuscript.

Weinberg, M. (1973). *Society and the healthy homosexual.* New York: Anchor Books.

Ziebold, T. O. (1978). Alcoholism and the gay community. *The Blade*, March.

6

Prescription for Despair: Women and Psychotropic Drugs

Jane E. Prather,
Nancy V. Minkow

Throughout Western Europe, North America and Japan women receive almost two thirds of all prescriptions for psychotropic or mood-modifying drugs: minor and major tranquilizers, psychostimulants (amphetamines), antidepressants, sedatives, and hypnotics. Women receive 80 percent of the prescriptions for amphetamines or psychostimulants, 71 percent of those for antidepressants (Mendelsohn, 1981, p. 60) and 66 percent of the tranquilizer prescriptions (Balter, Manheimer, Millinger, & Uhlenhuth, 1984).

Although these drugs have been popularized for over two decades, the problems associated with continuous use have only emerged publicly during the past decade. Minor tranquilizers are still reported in the United States as a major cause of drug-evoked emergency hospitalizations. Tranquilizers continue to be a primary tool for accidental death and suicide for women in the United States (National Institute on Drug Abuse [NIDA] 1984, 1986). The American Medical Association (1977) in their widely recognized publication, DRUG EVALUATIONS, asserted that the benezodiazepines had a wide margin of safety that virtually precluded their successful use for suicide. This conclusion was reached during the same year these drugs were a leading cause of female suicide (NIDA, 1978). The following year, the Federal Drug Administration declared there was no evidence that minor tranquilizers were effective in the long-term control of emotional problems with long-term defined as only four months (Silverman, Lee, & Lydecker, 1981, p. 50). However, it was 1983 before the American Medical Association changed its view that minor tranquilizers could be ingested for suicide (American Medical Association, 1983).

Major tranquilizers, widely acclaimed since their inception in the 1950s as a safe solution to psychotic problems, have now been shown to cause such problems as temporary or permanent brain damage. Other side effects of major tranquilizers include severe depression and lack of muscular and motor control resulting in Parkinson-like symptoms (Silverman et al., 1981, p. 49).

Barbiturates and amphetamines, when first introduced, were claimed to be reliable and safe, yet now have been recognized as extremely dangerous and highly addictive. Even when these drugs were declared to be so dangerous that production was halted in the United States, pharmaceutical companies continued to distribute them in Third World countries (Melrose, 1982).

Significant warnings about side effects of anti-depressants only emerged after they had been marketed for over a decade. Use of these drugs in the Western countries has not decreased and they are overwhelmingly prescribed for women. Warnings state that patients should avoid activities that require alertness and good psychomotor coordination. Does this imply that women rarely engage in such activities and hence can safely use the drugs? Perhaps stereotypes of women as depressed and emotional add to the continued prescribing of these drugs for women. The problem is even more acute among older women who are much more likely than elderly men to be prescribed antidepressants (Whittington, Petersen, Dale, & Dressel, 1981).

This chapter presents a feminist perspective on the issues affecting treatment for women who suffer from psychotropic drug dependencies. The purpose of this analysis is *not* to argue that psychotropic drugs never have an appropriate use, but to question why women, in contrast to men, receive almost two thirds of the prescriptions for these drugs. The first section of this paper reviews the psychotropic drug literature. Analysis of these studies reveals that assumptions are made about women's psychological status and mental health which should be challenged from a feminist perspective. As long as pharmaceutical companies and medical professionals perpetuate the belief that women need psychotropic drugs, which is reinforced by sex role stereotypes of women as dependent, then any consequences women suffer from overuse or abuse will be ignored. The chapter concludes with macro level recommendations for changes in social policy and social institutions and micro level suggestions for clinicians treating psychotropic addictions.

PRESCRIBING PSYCHOTROPIC MEDICATIONS: A CRITICAL REVIEW

Speculations on why women take more psychotropics than men, or why they are more frequently prescribed for women than men, are central themes in several literature reviews (see Cooperstock, 1974; Prather, 1990; Gabe & Williams, 1986; Smith, 1985; Marsh, 1982; Ogur, 1986). Justification for the higher drug usage by females appears based upon findings that women, more frequently than men, report such symptoms as nervousness, insomnia, despair, irritability (Verbrugge, 1982, 1985) or depression (Radloff, 1975). Whether women actually experience more symptoms or are simply more willing to admit them than men remains speculative.

The literature suggests that physicians who prescribe psychotropics perceive and diagnose female patients as suffering from symptoms that can be relieved by these drugs (see Cooperstock, 1974, 1976). Traditional medical training perpetuates stereotypes about women's health (Bourne & Wikler, 1978; Scully, 1980; Corea, 1977) and often includes misinformation about female patients (Scully, 1980; Campbell, 1973). Research indicates that physicians are more likely to describe a complaining patient as being a woman than a man (Cooperstock, 1971) or to discount female patients' physical symptoms (Armitage, Schneiderman, & Bass, 1979; Ruzek, 1978) while overemphasizing their psychological symptoms (Mendelsohn, 1982). Physicians (male) more frequently prescribe antidepressants to women than men who present depression symptoms (Rosser, 1981).

Traditional Western medicine has emphasized the physician's image as authoritarian and omnipotent; the infallibility of medical techniques and the treatment of symptoms with medication or surgery (Maykovich, 1980, p. 200). Little instruction is given in the sociocultural or psychoemotional factors that may affect both symptomology and presentation of symptomology (Mumford, 1983). Physicians often ignore the possibilities of poor or improper nutrition, inactivity, poverty, hygiene or sanitation as prime causes of health problems.

Few physicians receive training in identifying psychological symptoms, in spite of evidence that 50 percent of all patients treated by general practitioners (in the U.S.) have emotional problems affecting their health status (Follmann, 1970).

Prescribing of drugs is correlated with office visits and with physician-patient communication. Typically, office visits or physician consultations are short and rarely allow sufficient time for physicians to explore emotional or psychological symptoms. The average time spent per patient in an office visit is 15.3 minutes with a male physician and 17.8 minutes with a female physician (National Center for Health Services Research cited in Mumford, 1983, p. 381). When consulting with the doctors, patients are usually interrupted if they elaborate on their problem and male physicians interrupt their patients far more frequently than female physicians (West, 1984). The patient-physician relationship has been described as asymmetrical in power (see Parsons, 1975; Friedson, 1979) and if the patient is female and the physician male, this power differential may intensify communication problems. Physician-patient interaction is also complicated when differences occur between class, ethnicity, race, education and age. Moreover, the physician may not communicate in a vocabulary the patient can understand or may not be willing to listen to the patient's point of view (see Fisher, 1986; Pendleton, 1983).

Research on prescribing behavior suggests several reasons why women receive more psychotropic drugs than men. Most visits to a physician result in the writing of a prescription (Mumford, 1983; p. 381) and women (between ages 15 and 44) make almost twice as many physician visits as men (Silverman, et al., 1981, p. 39). Physicians tend to write prescriptions when they do not know any other solution, or to end an office visit (Muller, 1972) or when the physician reports difficulty relating to the patient or perceives only vague symptoms (Cartwright, 1974). Repeat prescriptions for minor tranquilizers reflect physician's attitudes more than patients' conditions (Melville cited in Pendleton, 1983).

Writing of a prescription satisfies both patient and physician that something tangible has been accomplished. The prescribing of a psychotropic drug may in addition legitimize the complaint for the patient (Silverman et al., 1981, p. 48).

Physician attitudes often infer that prescribing a medication is like issuing an order that should be followed without question. Medical texts and journals abound with comments on "patient compliance" and complaints about noncompliance such as the following: "Noncompliance, it may be concluded, is widespread, it is dangerous, and it is expensive to the patients themselves, to third party programs and to taxpayers" (Silverman et al., 1981, p. 42).

The extent to which physicians expect compliance from their patients is exemplified by the following description offered by a doctor: "I think the main thing is that the patient understands what I say, listens to what I say, believes what I say" (Scully, 1980, p. 92).

Physicians report difficulty keeping abreast of drugs. Since psychotropic drugs are such a new category, being on the market no more than 20 years, many physicians report limited knowledge of them (Gottlieb, Nappi, & Strain, 1978). Pharmaceutical sales representatives (also known as detailmen or detailers), whose training lies in marketing, not medicine or pharmacy, provide physicians with advice and information about drugs. General practitioners, who write most psychotropic prescriptions, report that the pharmaceutical sales representatives are their primary sources of drug information (Reinstein, 1975). In Canada 47 percent of physicians surveyed stated that the detailmen are the most informative and/or the most acceptable means of drug promotion (Anser & Grebin cited in Mumford, 1983, p. 463).

Research in Switzerland reveals a correlation between drugs that are heavily promoted and those frequently prescribed (Bethoud cited in Melrose,

1982, p. 64). Advertisements in medical journals have been criticized for their stereotyped portrayal of women depending on psychotropic drugs in order to cope (Prather & Fidell, 1975; Seidenberg 1971; Mant & Darroch, 1975; King, 1980). Ads depict women in roles as housewifes or mothers experiencing emotional symptoms that are to be alleviated through drugs (Hill, 1977).

Pharmaceutical companies have incorporated some of the most extensive marketing techniques to promote drugs. For example, when *Librium*, (a minor tranquilizer) was introduced to the medical profession, Roche Pharmaceuticals purchased eight-page advertisements in American medical journals and sent physicians long-playing phonograph records describing patients' positive results using *Librium*. In addition, Roche sent physicians over 40 separate mailings including drug samples (Moskowitz cited in Smith, 1985, p. 197).

TRADITIONAL FEMALE SOCIALIZATION: DEPENDENCY TRAP

In addition to the stereotyped images of women presented in medical training and portrayed in pharmaceutical advertising that may impact physicians' prescribing behavior, traditional female socialization may also promote drug taking. At an early age women are taught to be dependent, passive, home-oriented, nurturing, or other-oriented (see Maccoby & Jacklin, 1974; Block, 1984; Lipman-Blumen, 1984). The late developmental psychologist Jeanne Block (1984) described gender socialization for girls as promoting "roots" while boys acquire "wings." Girls are still protected more than boys and not allowed to wander far from home (Maccoby and Jacklin, 1974) or school (Serbin, O'Leary, Kent, & Tonic, 1973). Exploration of the environment, according to Block, is important for developing self-confidence, mastering new situations and learning problem solving. Often unintentionally, parents and significant others teach girls to be dependent upon others, to be afraid of new situations, and to sacrifice themselves for others (Lipman-Blumen, 1984, p. 62). Women are encouraged to control their anger and hostility and to become the family peacemaker or martyr (Lipman-Blumen, 1984, p. 63). In summary, traditional socialization, with all its variant forms, promotes feelings of helplessness, dependence and powerlessness. The result is that women begin to believe in their own powerlessness.

This socialization, no doubt, has implications for the mental and physical health of women (see Nathanson, 1975). Being dependent upon others, hiding or masking anger, feeling powerless can all lead to depression. Not surprising, women throughout the world (where data is available) report experiencing more depression than men (Weissman, Myers & Thompson, 1981). Excluding pregnancy and childbirth, women state they suffer from more illness than men (Verbrugge, 1985). Women also report experiencing more anxiety, insomnia and pain (Christie, 1978) than men. What is not known is whether women actually do suffer from more socioemotional problems or whether they are more willing to admit these problems than men. If women do experience more sociopsychological problems, is this due to their socialization, their status in society vis-a-vis men, or some biogenetic origin? Answering these questions appears critical before physicians and health professionals assume the only viable solutions are prescribing psychotropic drugs for long-term usage.

SUGGESTIONS FOR TREATING WOMEN WITH PSYCHOTROPIC DRUG DEPENDENCIES

1. The first step in recovery is a recognition that drug dependency exists. Although admission of dependency and denial of a problem are common for most addictions, these problems are even more complicated for women with prescription drug dependencies because they do not initially perceive themselves as having a drug problem. Instead they perceive a reoccuring health complication requiring a change in prescriptions or physicians. Furthermore, since using the drug, at least initially, had the tacit approval of a physician, the woman may consider the prescription—the drug taking—as an order she must follow even if she is suffering effects of dependency.

Psychotropic dependencies often remain hidden because the women are experiencing numerous health problems that they feel justify their drug use. They may be unaware that the complications for which they seek help may be related to drug usage. Physicians and other health professionals may inadvertently enable this hidden victim syndrome in a variety of ways, such as approving a prescription without ascertaining other medications the patient may be taking. Fearing his medical judgement might be questioned, the physician may deny the possibility of a patient developing a drug dependency.

2. Soliciting the cooperation of families and significant others becomes a vital component of the treatment process. Since every significant person in her life may be supporting her use of drugs, the drug-dependent woman needs to include family members in her recovery. As drug treatment counselors state: "We find at times the family is part of the problem." "The husbands don't want them to change—they don't want them well!" (see Prather & Minkow, 1986). Obligatory participation in family therapy

is probably required since in most cases family problems are related to drug problems. Groups for significant others, modeled after Al-Anon, focus upon ways families can be supportive of the drug-dependent woman without reinforcing drug taking behavior. Group programs assist the families in dealing with the problems the drug abuse may have caused for the family as well as the victim. In addition, family members can acquire skills that will strengthen rather than weaken the victim's self-esteem and assertiveness. Moreover, some significant others may be very threatened with the changing self of the drug-dependent woman and need extensive individual therapy to learn new ways of interacting with their partners.

3. Programs treating drug dependencies need to emphasize and advertise there is help available for prescription drug dependencies. Many agencies are not effective in recruiting and rehabilitating these clients (Prather & Minkow, 1986). As with other forms of drug dependency, treatment is more successful if the patient has a short-term usage and is not involved in multiple drugs. Yet frequently help is sought only when the woman begins to suffer intensely from symptoms due to the drug usage or when she abuses many drugs including alcohol.

Another barrier hindering the women with prescription drug dependencies from seeking treatment is ascertaining where to go for help. Since popular images of people with drug problems are individuals addicted to illegal drugs or alcohol, the woman dependent upon prescription drugs might not initially perceive herself as having a drug problem. Treatment programs traditionally designed for a population of working-class, street wise clients are not conducive for attracting a middle-class woman with a prescription drug addiction. Unlike users of heroin or cocaine, the psychotropic drug user does not initially seek the drug to obtain a high. Instead, she believes that her health and emotional problems justify using the drugs prescribed by her physician. Even after extensive therapy, the prescription drug-dependent person often seeks another drug to take, one that will be safe. As one drug counselor stated: "It is extremely difficult to get this person committed to a drug-free state because she is still convinced she needs a drug for some problem. And a lot of our doctors have the same notion—just find another drug for her" (Prather & Minkow, 1986).

4. Women need "women-only" groups for effective treatment. Women with prescription drug dependencies may have family problems that are best discussed in a women-only group. Most drug-dependent women experience low self-esteem and receive reinforcement from their families for being passive and acquiescent. Emotional, physical and sexual abuse are not uncommon in the lives of drug-dependent women (See Peluso & Peluso, 1988). Dealing with topics of incest, abuse or battering can best

be discussed in women-only sessions.

Another issue that underscores the need for all-women's groups relates to the feelings about one's role as a mother. In treatment women may need to deal with remorse and guilt about possible neglect or abuse of children while they were using drugs. Concern about one's mothering can actually be confounded when in treatment as most programs do not provide facilities allowing women to care for their dependents while in residence (Marsh & Miller, 1985).

Women undergoing treatment need the support of other women. They may have used drugs in isolation and hence do not know other women with the same problems; or they have a host of female friends who also take prescription psychotropics and perceive their usage as normal. All-women groups are also necessary so women do not play pleasing and passive roles toward men that could keep them from focusing on their own problems. One counselor observed that ''in all-female groups the extremely passive woman cannot remain in the background'' (Prather & Minkow, 1986). Finally, a woman-only group can effectively offer assertion training opportunities for women.

5. Drug-free alternatives for alleviating health or psychological problems need to be explored in spite of initial resistance. Such alternatives for reducing physical pain or mental stress might include biofeedback, relaxation, acupuncture, meditation, physical exercise or spirituality.

RECOMMENDATIONS FOR CHANGES IN SOCIAL POLICY AND SOCIAL INSTITUTIONS

1. The ''hidden problem'' of women's psychotropic drug dependency requires more public attention. Health professionals at all levels of patient care should receive training about the symptoms and treatment of prescription drug addictions with an emphasis upon women's propensity for this dependency. Treatment programs should include literature addressing the possibility of problems and/or addictions with long-term usage of prescription psychotropics. Treatment programs that currently focus only upon the street drug addict or alcoholic add to the invisibility of the prescription drug abuser. Advertisements should clarify that prescription drug dependency can be treated and, in fact, is not uncommon.

2. More funding is needed for treatment programs that focus on women's psychotropic drug addictions. Even though the National Institute on Drug Abuse has recommended legislation giving priority to funding of women's treatment and prevention programs since the 1970s, the num-

ber of programs providing special services to women remains limited (Beschner & Thompson, 1981; Marsh, 1982). Finding money for treatment is exacerbated for women with psychotropic drug abuse. If a woman suffered innumerable health problems, she may not have been employed; hence, qualifications for health insurance may be precluded. When psychotropic drug addiction becomes linked with alcohol, extensive detoxification may be required involving both inpatient treatment and follow-up outpatient services. Inpatient programs tend to be expensive, (approximately $14,000) which necessitates the patient having either financial resources or health insurance, neither of which is as common for women as men.

3. Alcoholics Anonymous and Narcotics Anonymous should produce literature specifically concerned with self-help recovery from prescription drug dependencies. Although *Pills Anonymous*, was available in some urban areas a decade ago, few groups are in existence today. Even though all drug addictions manifest similarities, victims of prescription drug addiction are not likely to initially identify with treatment programs focused on alcohol, narcotics or street drugs. More literature solely addressing prescription drug dependency and warnings about side effects through the long-term usage of such drugs should be accessible in public health centers, medical waiting rooms and pharmacies.

4, Health and mental health professionals should recommend alternatives to drugs for alleviating the stresses and health problems that women experience. Professionals prescribing psychotropic drugs should alert patients to possible side effects if they are taken longer than 4 months. That time parameter is now the AMA's recommendation for minor tranquilizers.

5. Pharmaceutical advertising necessitates scrutiny for misleading information about women's mental and physical health. Governmental agencies should establish some guidelines to regulate the kind and amount of drug advertising. This is in recognition of how powerful those sources are in providing current drug information for practicing physicians. Additionally, advertising revenues for drug companies should not be allowed to exceed research expenditures. Independent evaluations of drugs and assessments of drug safety are vitally important if health professionals are to access quality information about drugs that is independent from manufacturers' commercial position.

Psychotropic drug dependence by women has occurred through a mutually reinforcing process. Physicians, drug researchers, pharmaceutical companies, female users and their families have all bought the notion that women inherently suffer from symptoms that can best be relieved through prescription psychotropics. As long as a feminization of psychotropic drug use remains unquestioned, the problems associated with that dependence will persist.

From a feminist perspective one notes that throughout the history of medicine women have been designated as the weak and the powerless. Frequently they have been the human guinea pigs for modern medical and pharmacological research. Many in the medical community and the pharmaceutical industry have trivialized women's complaints about the abuse potential of these drugs and hence minimized the need for treatment. As long as psychotropic drug abuse remains feminized, several generations are at risk. The newborn may be at risk if a mother has taken these drugs during pregnancy. Teenage girls are introduced to psychotropic drugs when mothers share prescriptions with their daughters. As women advance in age they may feel even more powerless and compliant; whereby obeying their physicians' prescriptive orders is especially likely if they are institutionalized.

In conclusion, the solution to women's psychotropic drug abuse includes reconceptualizing what it is to be female. Rather than perceiving women as sick, compliant and dependent, women need to be treated as healthy, competent and self-reliant. To that extent, socializing women to be proactive in caring for themselves rather than reactive to others is preventive medicine that could have a significant impact on women's well-being.

REFERENCES

American Medical Association (1977). *Drug evaluations*. Chicago, IL: Public Sciences Group.

American Medical Association (1983). *Drug evaluations*. Chicago, IL: Public Sciences Group.

Armitage, K. J., Schneiderman, L. J., & Bass, R. A. (1979). Response of physicians to medical complaints in men and women. *The Journal of the American Medical Association, 241*, 2186–2187.

Balter, M. B., Manheimer, D. I., Mellinger, G. D., & Uhlenhuth, E. H. (1984). Cross-national comparison of anti-anxiety sedative drug use. *Current Medical Research Opinion, 8*, supplement, 5–20.

Beschner, G., & Thompson, P. (1981). *Women and drug abuse treatment: Needs and services*. National Institute on Drug Abuse. (ADM) 81–1057. Services Monograph Series. Washington, D.C.: Supt. of Docs. U.S. Government Printing Office.

Block, J. (1984). *Sex role identity and ego development*. San Francisco: Jossey-Bass.

Bourne, P. G., & Wikler, N. J. (1978). Commitment and the cultural mandate: Women in medicine. *Social Problems, 25*, 430–440.

Campbell, M. (1973). *Why would a girl go into medicine?* Old Westbury: The Feminist Press.

Cartwright, A. (1974). Prescribing and the relationship between patients and doctors. In R. Cooperstock (Ed.), *Social aspects of the medical use of psychotropic drugs* (pp. 63–73). Toronto: Addiction Research Foundation.

Christie, D. (1978). The analgesic abuse syndrome. *Internal Journal of Epidemiology, 7,* 257.

Cooperstock, R. (1971). Sex differences in the use of mood-modifying drugs: An explanatory model. *Journal of Health and Social Behavior, 12,* 238–243.

Cooperstock, R. (1974). Some factors involved in the increased prescribing of psychotropic drugs. In R. Cooperstock (Ed.), *Social aspects of the medical use of psychotropic drugs* (pp. 21–34). Toronto: Addiction Research Foundation.

Cooperstock, R. (1976). Psychotropic drug use among women. *Canadian Medical Association Journal, 115,* 760–763.

Corea, G. (1977). *The hidden malpractice: How American medicine mistreats women.* New York: Jove

Fisher, S. (1986). *In the patient's best interest.* New Brunswick: Rutgers University Press.

Follmann, J. F. (1970). *Insurance coverage for mental illness.* New York: American Management Association.

Friedson, E. (1979). The organization of medical practice. In H. Freeman, S. Levine, & L. Reeder (Eds.), *Handbook of medical sociology* (pp. 297–307). New York: Prentice Hall.

Gabe, J., & Williams, P. (1986). Tranquilliser use: A historical perspective. In J. Gabe & P. Williams (Eds.), *Tranquillisers: Social, psychological and clinical perspectives* (pp. 3–21). London: Tavistock.

Gottlieb, R., Nappi, T., & Strain, J. (1978). The physician's knowledge of psychotropic drugs. *American Journal of Psychiatry, 135,* 29.

Hill, S. (1977). Drugs and medicalization of human problems. *Social Science and Medicine, 9,* 461–468.

King, E. (1980). Sex bias in psychoactive drug advertisements. *Psychiatry, 43,* 129–137.

Lipman-Blumen, J. (1984). *Gender roles and power.* Englewood Cliffs, NJ: Prentice-Hall.

Maccoby, E. E., & Jacklin, C. N. (1974). *The psychology of sex differences.* Stanford: Stanford University Press.

Mant, A., & Darroch, D. B. (1975). Media images and medical images. *Social Science and Medicine, 9,* 613–617.

Marsh, J. C. (1982). Private problems: Women and drug use. *Journal of Social Issues, 38,* 53–65.

Marsh, J. C., & Miller, H. A. (1985). Female clients in substance abuse treatment. *The International Journal of the Addictions, 20,* 995–1019.

Maykovich, M. K. (1980). *Medical sociology.* Sherman Oaks: Alfred Publishing.

Mellinger, G. D., Balter, M. B., & Uhlenhuth, E. H. (1984). Anti-anxiety agents: Duration of use and charateristics of users in the U.S.A. *Current Medical Research Opinion, 8,* (supplement), 1–36.

Melrose, D. (1982). *Bitter pills, medicines and the Third World poor.* Oxford: Oxfam Press.

Mendelsohn, R. S. (1981). *MALePractice.* Chicago: Contemporary Books.

Muller, C. (1972). The overmedicated society: Forces in the marketplace for medical care. *Science, 16,* 488.

Mumford, E. (1983). *Medical sociology.* New York: Random House.

Nathanson, C. (1975). Illness and the feminine role: A theoretical review. *Social Science and Medicine, 9,* 57–62.

National Institute on Drug Abuse. (1978, 1984, 1986). *Annual Data from the Drug Abuse Warning Network.* Rockville, Maryland.

Ogur, B. (1986). Long day's journey into night: Women and prescription drug abuse. *Women and Health, 11,* 99–115.

Parsons, T. (1975). The sick role and the role of the physician reconsidered. *Milbank Memorial Fund Quarterly, 53,* 257–277.

Peluso, E., & Peluso, L. S. (1988). *Women & drugs getting hooked, getting clean.* Minneapolis: CompCare.

Pendleton, D. (1983). Doctor-patient communication: A review. In D. Pendleton & J. Hasler (Eds.), *Doctor-patient communications* (pp. 5–53). London: Academic Press.

Prather, J. E., & Fidell, L. S. (1975). Sex differences in the content and style of medical advertisements. *Social Sciences and Medicine, 9,* 23–26.

Prather, J. E., & Minkow, N. V. (1986). The search for help: Issues affecting women seeking treatment for psychotropic dependencies. Paper presented at the meeting of the Pacific Sociological Associations, Denver, CO.

Prather, J. E. (1990). Why do women use tranquilizers? In B. Forster & J. Salloway (Eds.), *The socio-cultural matrix of alcohol and drug use: A sourcebook of patterns* (pp. 302–318). Lewiston, NY: Edwin Mellen Press.

Radloff, L. (1975). Sex differences in depression: the effects of occupation and marital status. *Sex Roles, 1,* 249–269.

Reinstein, P., (1976). A regulator's perception of drug advertising. *Journal of Drug Issues, 6,* 60.

Rosser, W. W. (1981). Influence of physicians gender in Amitriptyline prescribing. *Canadian Family Physicians, 27,* 1094–1097.

Ruzek, S. B. (1978). *The women's health movement: Feminist alternatives to medical control.* New York: Praeger.

Scully, D. (1980). *Men who control women's health.* Boston: Houghton Mifflin.

Seidenberg, R. (1971). Advertising and abuse of drugs. *New England Journal of Medicine, 284,* 789.

Serbin, L. A., O'Leary, K. D., Kent, R. N., & Tonic, I. J. (1973). A comparison of teacher response to the pre-academic and problem behavior of boys and girls. *Child Development, 44,* 796–804.

Silverman, M., Lee, P. T., & Lydecker, M. (1981). *Pills and the public purse.* Berkeley: University of California Press.

Smith, M. C. (1985). *Small comfort: A history of minor tranquilizers.* New York: Praeger.

Verbrugge, L. M. (1982). Sex differences in legal drug use. *Journal of Social Issues, 38,* 59–76.

Verbrugge, L. M. (1985). Gender and health: An update on hypotheses and evidence. *Journal of Health and Social Behavior, 26,* 156–182.

West, C. (1984). *Routine complications.* Bloomington, IN: Indiana University Press.

Weissman, M., Myers, J. K. & Thompson, W. D. (1981). Depression and its treatment in a U.S. community 1975-1976. *Archives of General Psychiatry, 38,* 417–421.

Whittington, F. M., Petersen, D. M., Dale, B., & Dressel, P. L. (1981). Sex differences in prescription drug use of older adults. *Journal of Psychoactive Drugs, 13,* 65–73.

7

Double Jeopardy: Chemical Dependence and Codependence in Older Women

Eloise Rathbone-McCuan
Larry Dyer
Judith Wartman

Substance abuse problems and differential treatment of special populations have received much attention. While access to substance abuse treatment is easy for groups who have good insurance coverage and are in frequent contact with sources of referral, members of special populations who are not as socially visible or who do not have financial resources to cover treatment often do not have equal access to substance abuse treatment services. As a member of two such groups, the older woman who suffers from chemical dependence or codependence is in double jeopardy for falling through the cracks in a complex, reimbursement oriented service system and, consequently may not get treatment for alcoholism, drug addiction, and codependence. This chapter reviews pertinent literature regarding women and older adults in relation to the development and treatment of substance abuse problems, looks at special risk factors for older women, points out the barriers to treatment for older women who are either substance abusers or codependent, explores the special strengths that older women possess to facilitate recovery once assistance is offered and draws some implications for practice within this special population.

REVIEW OF THE LITERATURE

The epidemiological research on alcohol problems among women (Clemmons, 1985) and elderly populations (Maddox, 1988) is very problematic.

It is of concern that we do not know, with sufficient reliability, the nature and scope of problems in either population. National surveys of drinking in the general adult population have not produced accurate rates of heavy drinking and problematic consumption among older cohorts. Surveys of drinking practices among the elderly tend to produce more reliable rates for men than women while surveys of women's alcohol consumption detect rates more accurately for younger rather than older women.

Williams (1984) summarized the methodological survey problems in regard to older people. The great variance in the estimated extent of the problem of alcohol abuse among the aged speaks to the need to better identify elderly persons who are problem drinkers. Identifying alcohol problems among the elderly is especially difficult because many of the indicators that apply to the general population are not equally applicable to the elderly client. Graham (1986) offered a discussion of limitations of alcohol abuse indicators to measure older adults' alcohol abuse in such problem areas as employment, driving, legal matters and financial situations. Consequently, the best assessments of the elderly's potential drinking problems are completed in the home. It is important to observe for repeated injuries, certain patterns of confusion, violent or argumentative behaviors and alcohol containers on table tops or in trash cans as clues in the home environment (Rathbone-McCuan, 1988).

Estimates frequently quoted in the literature indicate that 12 million to 15 million Americans are alcohol dependent or in some stage of alcoholism. Up to 35 million more people are estimated to be affected by alcohol abuse. The range of problem drinking among the elderly falls somewhere between 2 percent and 10 percent in most studies (Williams, 1984). The 2 percent remains the most frequently mentioned in older men (Lawson, 1989).

Myers, Hingson, Mucatal, Hereen, and Goldman (1985) commented about the growing concern among clinicians and policy makers that there is epidemic alcoholism and alcohol abuse among older adults. His research on alcohol abuse among aged people was based on a subsample of 920 people 60 years and older drawn from a longitudinal study of drinking practices, life problems, and life satisfaction among adults in metropolitan Boston. The subsample was drawn from a larger adult metropolitan sample. The authors conclude from their results that older females in the sample are significantly more likely to drink relatively large amounts. Twelve percent of male respondents reported that they had two or more drinks daily compared to 2 percent of females. Gavaler (1985) reviewed the several studies that examined drinking patterns in women of postmenopausal age. Even though the percentage of drinkers who may be classified as heavy drinkers or misusers is low among postmenopausal women, cross-sectional studies address neither the issues of crossover drinking such as late onset problem drinking or late abstinence by alcoholic women.

The prevalence data on women's alcohol use is also questioned for its accuracy, and improvement in drinking survey methodologies remains a challenge to researchers. Wilsnack, Wilsnack, and Klassen (1984) reported data on the findings gathered from their survey of women's drinking patterns and compared those results to other national surveys conducted between 1971 and 1979. The percentage of women between 50 and 64 years of age who were classified as heavy drinkers ranged between one percent and 5 percent across the various surveys. The percentage rates of heavy drinking among women age 65 and older was between one percent and 5 percent; however six of the surveys placed heavy drinking among aged women at 2 percent. Based on further comparative examinations of these various surveys, Wilsnack, Wilsnack and Klassen (1984) noted a possible trend of slightly increased consumption among women in middle age, but could not substantiate the frequently quoted trend of marked increase of heavy drinking among younger women. From their data these researchers concluded that there was no evidence for the pronouncement that there was an epidemic of heavy drinking or drinking problems among women, even though there is some suggestion of modest increase to heavy drinking among younger women.

For the purpose of discussion, the assumption of epidemic increases of dangerous alcohol consumption among adult women is not supported by national data and that at least the present cohorts of elderly people who have been surveyed do not reflect excessive alcohol consumption in large scale proportions. It is probable that older women who have been lifelong or long-term abstainers from alcohol use do not likely have a high risk of becoming problem drinkers. It is rather those who make shifts from light to moderate drinking and experience problems with that level of use, or those who move from moderate to heavy drinking that have greater levels of risk. But merely measuring intake by standard quantity and frequency measures of alcohol consumption does not serve as a sufficiently accurate predictor of psychological, social, economic and health risks. However, the psychosocial stresses that older women are likely to suffer from, such as reduced income as compared to older males, increased risk of chronic illness resulting in medication use, loss of status, and widowhood, place older women in special risk for chemical dependence. There are millions of women who are 65 years of age and older and if only 2 percent are currently heavy drinkers, the significance of their consumption should not be minimized (Straussner, 1985). Given that persons over the age of 65 are the fastest growing segment of the population, this reality warrants concern.

Some community workers with extensive personal contact with older women note that the harmful impact of substance abuse is far broader than is evident from alcohol consumption measures. For example, (a) alcoholism is a serious problem among residents of nursing homes and institutional care facilities where elderly women predominate in the patient population; (b) much of the criminal victimization of older women involves factors of alcoholism; (c) countless older women are caretakers to dependent spouses and may suffer from physical and psychological abuse; and (d) stresses and burdens of many middle-age care giving women provoke conditions for their misuse of alcohol and other drugs. Sex role stereotyping results in the predominance of women in filling caregiver roles in families. It also results in the feminization of poverty, which especially hits older women who also suffer the reduced income effects of retirement and pension policies deferential to males. These situations can magnify the psychosocial risk for chemical and codependence among older women. Alcohol abuse plays a central role in many situations of self- or other-neglect among younger and older women.

Professionals in the fields of alcoholism and aging do encounter alcohol related problems among older women. Often they are faced with having to respond to the complex psychosocial and physical care needs of these women without adequate service resources to provide the appropriate care and treatment. Communities usually lack formal programs for the specific treatment of older alcoholics; aging women may lack funds to pay for private treatment, and the nonprofessional community support programs that do not cost much money are poorly organized to reach older women. Additionally, older women are coping with the pervasive and predominant influences of sexism as well as specific life conditions that manifest the powerlessness, victimization, abandonment, isolation, loneliness and dependency associated with growing old. Ours is a culture that clings to ageism and is very ambivalent about a national healthcare priority. Added to this is the reality that women are victimized by the social stigma of alcoholism and by their inability and growing unwillingness to meet cultural expectations (Lacerte & Harris, 1986) such as being super women or corporate mommies. The social stigma associated with alcoholic women can impede chances of recovery and the problem is compounded if the woman is older (Lasker, 1986).

SPECIAL RISK FACTORS RELATED TO ADDICTION

Older women face unique and intertwining situations, due to the combined status of being older and being women in today's society, that magnify the risk factors for the development of problems with substance abuse. The first of these factors involves isolation. Increasing isolation has long been known to be a risk for older people who are no longer working, frequently widowed, and frequently homebound due to physical disability (Rathbone-McCuan & Hashimi, 1982). Depression, also a greater risk as people age, adds to the circumstances that make older adults more likely to become isolated. When this is combined with the social stigma that is attached to female aging, in particular in this society, the subsequent potential for isolation lending itself to the development of substance abuse problems is tremendous. To avoid isolation the older woman must overcome obstacles such as living alone for perhaps the first time, physical incapacities that occur, society's seclusion of its oldest members, and the poor self-esteem that accompanies the stereotypes and myths surrounding older women who drink. The older woman would need to force herself out into a society that neither encourages older adult participation nor views older women who drink in a manner that is conducive to recovery. Loss and depression, previously mentioned in regard to isolation, need to be considered in their own right in relation to older women and alcoholism. The aging process itself, with its associated losses brings with it many causes for depression. The most obvious, perhaps, is loss of one's spouse; however, age-related losses are numerous and compounding. For instance, loss related to disability can result in an inability to get to outside activities or social events. Loss of sensory perception, loss of income and loss of status are among the most frequently cited losses in old age. Older people feel the loss of age-peer friends due to disability and/or death. Many lack the opportunity and/or ability to replace old friendships, leaving them vulnerable to increased social isolation. These losses compound for the older person who frequently does not have time to grieve one loss before another is added. There is even greater impact if an older alcoholic or drug addict has lost relationships due to alcoholic behaviors. Additionally, loss is experienced through employment that is often prematurely terminated, or physical processes that lead to disabilities. Consequently, the potential for age-related and addiction-related loss escalates exponentially. This social predisposition to depression places older women at special risk for the development of problems with addiction.

The physical correlate of depression in the older person is the development of chronic pain from the various insidious ailments that are more prevalent in aging. The pain associated with diseases such as arthritis can cause a constant awareness of pain. The temptation to self-medicate or to overuse prescription medication is great when the older woman is experiencing pain that she knows will not get better. This is further exacerbated by loss of physical mobility that results in a reduced ability to divert one's attention from the pain, as well as an increased sensation of the pain due to immobility. Thus, chronic pain can act as a precipitating cause for misuse of chemical substances to relieve both physical and emotional pain.

Another risk factor for older women in developing chemical dependency problems has to do with role changes inherent in the aging process. As children mature, women move from the role of mother, which frequently leaves them home alone with a lot of time to fill. Soon after the loss of the motherhood role, women are often forced to assume spousal caregiving and then the role change to widowhood, requiring additional economic, social and emotional adjustments. As women are socialized in this country to assume roles involving the care of other people, this role loss is also associated with a loss of self-esteem. The socialization of women involves subscription to roles defined in relationship to others; that is, into nonautonomous roles. Consequently, the socialization of the current cohort of older women directly places them in unique risk for alcoholism and drug addiction when combined with the role losses such as widowhood. In addition, if the older women works, the additional role loss associated with retirement brings further loss problems. Role loss for older women poses a special threat to self-esteem, leaving them more vulnerable to the development of chemical dependencies.

CODEPENDENCY AS A RELATED RISK

Just as women suffer from risk of developing chemical dependencies, older women also suffer special risks to encounter codependency, which increases the possibility of experiencing behaviorally entrenched relationships that are more impervious to change. One such risk that has been mentioned for the development of chemical dependency, role socialization, also plays an important role in the development of codependency in older women. The fact that women are socialized into roles that revolve around caregiving can place them at special risk for codependence. Caregiving can be a rewarding experience if the role is associated with normal human helping and the dependency is natural. Examples of this kind of caregiving experience involve child rearing or taking care of frail elders (Hasselkus, 1988). Caregiving becomes more taxing and longer term when it involves a physical or mental disability such as caring for a child with cerebral palsy, or caring for a developmentally disabled family member. Likewise, it can be a fulfilling experience that is mutually healthy. However, when caregiving is the result of a chemical dependency, the resulting codependency maintains the addiction within the family system. The codependent behaviors that result from being in a relationship with a chemically dependent person can create tremendous damage and stress. The underfunctioning of the chemically dependent person is buoyed up by the overfunctioning of the codependent. For the older woman who has been socialized to take care of children and spouse, the move into codependent relationships might also serve the function of insuring that the relationship stays intact. However, this occurs only at great expense to the older woman. The bitterness and anger involved in bearing all the responsibility in the relationship keeps the codependent older woman in constant threat of depression, which is a frequent concommitant of codependence. The older woman's socialization into caregiving roles makes this risk for codependent behaviors especially great.

Older women, as a characteristic of their age, often have been in codependent relationships for many years. Many older codependents might have been raised in alcoholic homes, thus creating the behavioral patterns associated with codependence at an early age. These behaviors would then be further reinforced during marriages and in raising children who might have addiction problems. The sheer reinforcement of a codependent style of relating over a lifetime would increase the possibility of the older woman's adopting new codependent relationships during her later years.

A risk factor that is somewhat unique to older women is the possibility of increased physical dependence upon other people, that sometimes accompanies increasing age. Indeed, older women are susceptible to a unique kind of codependent relationship where the chemically dependent person is actually the caregiver for the physical requirements that the older woman feels as a function of age. This arrangement produces a kind of dynamic that will make it very difficult for the older woman to accept and believe in change.

An example of an elderly woman, codependent in relation to her adult son and caregiver, illustrates some key patterns. This particular individual was blind, diabetic and had an amputation above the right knee. She was unable to use a prosthesis, although she had been fitted for one, and physical therapy was attempted. The woman was cared for by her 62-year-old son who lived with her. They had lived together off and on most of their lives and had bought their home together. He managed to assist her with medication and meals fairly well in spite of his lifelong alcoholism. He drank during all waking hours. They fought constantly about the situation surrounding their living together. However, for this woman to leave this codependent relationship inevitably meant going to a nursing home. Thus, the alternative to continuing the codependent relationship may be seen, by an individual, as less desirable than remaining in the dysfuntional relationship.

The older woman may also face a special risk by virtue of comparatively few financial resources available to her. The feminization of poverty has not excluded older women. For the current cohort of older women who have worked primarily in the home, neither social security nor private pensions provide for their financial equity. Thus, today's older woman has often experienced reduced resources compared either to younger women or middle-aged or elderly men. This places her in an unenviable position in terms of leaving codependent relationships where pensions may be shared. This gender inequity may be shifting in some states that have only recently passed legislation to assure greater pension equity between men and women. These special risk factors create, for older women, a situation that can result in the development of chemical and codependencies that can seriously jeopoardize their physical and mental health. When these are accompanied by the barriers to treatment that exist in a sexist and ageist society, the possibility for assistance in recovery needs special attention.

BARRIERS TO TREATMENT

There are barriers to treatment affecting older people and all adult women that need to be considered in a discussion of addictions and older women. For both older people and women, the issue of stigma surrounding alcoholism or drug addiction may be the most significant barrier. The current cohort of older people was raised at a time when all problems were kept within the confines of the family, and this was especially true of addictions. Having been raised prior to the currently popular disease concept of alcoholism and drug addiction, the older person equates addiction with moral decay, weakness and sin. If one suffers from these maladies or had a family member who did, the strong tendency is to deny and to hide the addiction from public or health professional purview. This makes it unusually difficult for older people to engage in a discussion of addiction with health professionals and, thus, to access treatment.

The issue of stigma is a complex and moralistic nightmare for the alcoholic or drug addicted older woman that results in treatment inaccessibility. To expose this nightmare to the light of day for women, one must first examine its historical roots. Historical analysis of alcohol abuse in America, and women's efforts to work against its proliferation, indicate several important points: (a) women recognized long ago the public and private damage caused by alcoholism, and (b) women have suffered its consequences, but not necessarily with quiet reserve. Lender (1986) wrote an insightful critique of gender related issues as they emerged within different historical periods; each period being characterized by a particular cultural response to alcohol.

By mid-nineteenth century the institution of the family had taken a predominant hold on this society and with it came the solidification of gender role concepts as central to the family. As the century closed, ''victorian'' roles of women, defined almost exclusively within the family context, had become the accepted standard of women's worth. One of the few positive impacts of the mores of that era may have been to allow women's voices to be heard against the social costs of alcoholism. The Temperence Movement, in its various and protracted stages, was a public response around which women gathered to create change which gave impetus to their own access to political and educational institutions.

Lacerte and Harris (1986) noted that the status of women as moral guardians was tolerated by the male dominated culture, thus they were allowed to speak out and work against the evils of the "drunkened state." Obviously, women could not save America from the presence of alcohol related problems, but that movement produced a significant collective force among women that led to the beginnings of a political voice heard throughout the country. The long established interplay between gender stereotypes of male alcoholism and female sobriety continued to prevail, while at the same time mid-twentieth century drinking practices were shifting among American women.

These contradictions and counterpoints of the past have a direct influence on conditions of today. Lender (1986) states:

> If the stigma grew as it did because of factors beyond drinking behavior alone—and even beyond the social sanctions brought against male alcoholics—it stands to reason that efforts to deal with alcohol problems in women today cannot be solely concerned with drinking either. For it is not just the familiar stigma against the alcoholic which women have contended with for over a century, but a stigma with roots deeply entrenched in attitudes towards what it means (and has meant) to be a woman in America. Perhaps it would be well to keep this historical legacy in view as society plans to help women alcoholics today (p. 55).

Given the unique role of women in our society in regard to temperance and sobriety, the female alcoholic then becomes severely stigmatized with characteristics much greater than that of suffering from a disease. The "moral guardian" then becomes the "fallen angel," which results in the incorrect positing of other characteristics such as sexual looseness, that is in reality unconnected with the existence of an alcoholism problem. This stereotype increases for the older alcoholic woman who is then thought of as sexually promiscuous in a society that demands that older people not be thought of as sexual.

The combined effects of the stigma around alcoholism and drug addiction for the older person and for the woman in our society makes the plight of the older alcoholic woman ever more precarious. For her to acknowledge an addiction problem is to admit to a variety of unassociated, but emotionally potent, characteristics that are often directly juxtaposed to her value system. Likewise, the older codependent has failed at her socially assigned task of moral guardianship when she admits to a relationship with a chemically dependent person, which further reinforces her need to control the chemical use of the other individual and keep it a secret. Thus, the prescription for both is to suffer in silence.

Interfacing with the barrier for the older women suffering from addiction is the powerful barrier of denial by health professionals. Service providers join in a subtle collusion with the family members and the older woman not to discuss issues of chemical dependency. This perhaps occurs out of a desire to protect the elder from the moral stigma of addiction; however, the effect of this benign neglect is a particularly malignant form of treatment discrimination. This leads to systematic denial with a reinforced belief that older women do not suffer addiction problems because none are seen.

Additionally, older women who suffer addiction problems do not engage with the community in a manner that is likely to result in the addiction's discovery. The older adult is usually retired, living alone, and does not drive. Family members may live out of town. The answer to social isolation lies in the older woman's decision to attend outside functions and she must overcome the transportation barriers in order to do so. However, for the older female alcoholic or addict, asserting that initiative would be uncharacteristic, given the stigma mentioned before and the disabling nature of addiction itself.

Finally, the barrier of financing of the treatment needs to be addressed. As was mentioned before, the older woman is more likely to be economically disadvantaged than either her male age peers or younger women. Further, chemical dependency treatment does not universally embrace clients who are either Medicare or Medicaid recipients. Thus, the problems of reimbursement leave this population particularly susceptible to systematic treatment neglect.

OLDER WOMEN'S STRENGTHS THAT
CAN BE MOBILIZED FOR RECOVERY

Older women who suffer from addiction problems possess special strengths that need to be considered. For instance, the same socialization that encourages nonautonomous role development can produce an opportunity for sobriety. Recovery from alcoholism, drug addiction and codependence can be facilitated by participation in self-help groups such as Alcoholics Anonymous, Narcotics Anonymous, Al-Anon and Nar-Anon. Since women are socialized into networking behaviors, they more easily accept the process of getting help from other people to resolve problems. Also, socialization into fiercely independent roles, a characteristic of male socialization that can impede recovery, is a trait older women may not have to surmount. Likewise, women are socialized to seek understanding of others and to value empathy. These characteristics make recovery from codependence, which is often characterized by critical and blaming behaviors, easier by helping them more easily accept the disease concept as an explanation of addictive behavior. Consequently, differential and gender-specific socialization may actually help older women accept interdependence and willingly agree to participate in self-help treatment programs. Indeed, this characteristic probably helps women during the aging process, regardless of addiction, as the process of aging demands greater degrees of assistance from others.

Older women also have accrued life experiences that they can draw on in making the necessary development changes required in recovery. By the time one is older, many life transitions will have been experienced. The coping mechanisms previously used can be mobilized to help older women with addiction problems examine their current situations and evaluate the possibilities for change.

IMPLICATIONS FOR PRACTICE

This discussion of older women who suffer addiction problems lends itself to certain implications related to meeting the unique needs and characteristics of this group. The first progressive and necessary step would be to confront professional denial as it operates with older women. Educational forums that help professionals see the significance of chemical and codependency problems in older women need to be developed so these problems can be detected in spite of their hidden nature. In order to be able to detect these problems, any educational effort must include training that helps professionals look at the myths surrounding addiction problems among older women. A belief in the recovery potential of older women must be nurtured and this cannot occur if the attitude of the "fallen gray angel" continues, which devalues aging women who are chemically dependent or codependent.

Associated with the problem of professional denial is the problem of service fragmentation. Just as the family is more capable of impacting a chemical dependency problem if they discuss the problem openly and organize around the issue of recovery, so must the social service networks be developed to support recovery efforts. Professionals need to become more aware of the Twelve Step programs such as Alcoholics Anonymous and Women for Sobriety (Kirkpatrick, 1989) and refer clients to these programs. Chemically dependent clients may have much initial resistance to the use of Twelve Step programs based on their fear of admitting to a problem. Brown (1985) suggests that psychotherapy and Alcoholics Anonymous can act in partnership to best serve the alcoholic client. However, this cannot happen if the professional stays aloof and uninformed. Attending some open

AA meetings might be a way to better understand the process that occurs in self-help groups. Further, becoming familiar with the Twelve Steps and their developmental significance can help the professional assist the older client in personal growth during recovery.

Finally, programs that currently treat alcohol- and drug-addicted people need to become more sensitive to issues of gender and age. Older adults with extensive sensory deprivation may not do well with adolescent clients who tend to run around the halls in a way that might frighten elders. The developmental issues involved in recovery likewise might be quite different. In a male-dominated treatment community, where entrance into treatment is often based upon employment or legal problems, gender issues can easily remain unaddressed. Age and gender issues need to be highlighted if treatment that truly meets the needs of older women suffering from addiction or codependence problems is to be offered.

REFERENCES

Brown, S. (1985). *Treating the alcoholic: A developmental model of recoverry* (pp. 267–280). New York: John Wiley and Sons.

Clemmons, P. (1985). Reflections of social thought in research on women and alcoholism. *Journal of Drug Issues, 15,* 73–80.

Gavaler, J. S. (1985). Effect of alcohol on endocrine function in post-menopausal women: A review. *Journal of Studies on Alcohol, 46,* 495–516.

Graham, K. (1986). Identifying and measuring alcohol abuse among the elderly: Serious problems with existing instrumentation. *Journal of Studies on Alcohol, 47,* 322–326.

Hasselkus, B. R. (1988). Meaning in family caregiving: Perspectives on caregiving/professional relationships. *The Gerontologist, 28,* 686–691.

Kirkpatrick, J. (1989). Women for sobriety. *The Counselor.* January/February, 9–10.

Lacerte, J., & Harris, D. L. (1986). Alcoholism: A catalyst for women to organize. *Affilia: Journal of Women in Social Work, 1,* 41–52.

Lasker, M. N. (1986). Aging alcoholics need nursing help. *Journal of Gerontological Nursing, 12,* 16–19.

Lawson, A. W. (1989). Substance abuse problems of the elderly: Considerations for treatment and prevention. In G. W. Lawson & A. W. Lawson (Eds.), *Alcoholism and substance abuse in special populations.* (pp. 95–109). Rockville, MD: Aspen, Inc.

Lender, M. E.. (1986). A special stigma: Women and alcoholism in the late 19th and early 20th centuries. In D. L. Stug, S. Piryadarsini & M. M. Hyman (Eds.), *Alcohol interventions: Historical and sociocultural approaches* (pp. 41–58). New York: Haworth Press.

Maddox, G. (1988). Aging, drinking, and alcohol abuse. *Generations, 12,* 37–40.

Meyers, A. R., Hingson, R., Mucatel, M., Heeren, T., & Goldman, E. (1985). The social epidemiology of alcohol use by urban older adults. *International Journal of Aging and Human Development, 21,* 49–59.

Rathbone-McCuan, E. (1988). Promoting help-seeking behavior among elders with chemical dependencies. *Generations, 12,* 37–40.

Rathbone-McCuan, E., & Hashimi, J. (1982). *Isolated Elders,* Rockville, MD: Aspen, Inc.

Straussner, S. L. A. (1985). Alcoholism in women: Current knowledge and implications for treatment. In D. Cook, S. L. A. Straussner, & C. H. Fewell (Eds.), *Psychosocial issues in treatment of alcoholism* (pp. 61–78). New York: Haworth Press.

Williams, M. (1984). Alcoholism and the elderly: An overview. *Alcohol Health and Research World, 8,* 3–9.

Wilsnack, S. C., Wilsnack, R. W., & Klassen, A. D. (1984). Drinking and drinking problems among women in a U.S. national survey. *Alcohol Health and Research World, 9,* 3–13.

8

Healing the Feminine: A Feminist Residential Model for Treating Chemical Dependency

Chandra Smith

Chemically dependent women are not only addicted to mood altering substances but have, at the heart of their disease, confusion about their female sexual self. Abstinence from mood altering substances is not enough since treatment must include healing the feminine. Treatment goals should encourage women's self empowerment through a redefinition of their own experiences as females.

This is best done in a setting exclusively for women clients with female staff as role models. Residence XII is an example of the treatment center which has goals directed toward the empowerment of women through self-acceptance, improved relationships with others and the development of a personal spirituality. Addictions treatment for women is a spiraling and interwoven process that is felt and perceived as well as linearly understood.

Residential treatment is a waystation on the path to recovery. It is a point where a woman consciously makes decisions about her life, free from the anesthetizing influence of drugs and alcohol. Working through her addiction(s) is a rebirthing of self; a conscious change in her life direction, whereas remaining addicted is tantamount to being unconscious. Active participation in any addiction ultimately is a contract with death, for all addictions have an onset, a progression that is observable and a terminal ending if there is not intervention.

FEMINIST TREATMENT GOALS

The initial immediate goal in treatment for chemical dependency is abstinence from mood altering drugs. Without abstinence, therapeutic interventions remain in the unconscious and are not consciously understood and available.

The role of the treatment facility is to manage a client's abstinence until she can manage it herself. The longer term goal of treatment is to engage the woman in the healing process; the process of becoming consciously female. This longer term goal can be described as having three parts. Each needs to be addressed in a treatment program for women: (1) the development of self acceptance; (2) the creation of a model for healthy relating to others; and (3) the development of a spiritual sense of self.

1. Self Acceptance

Accepting being female. At the heart of recovery is a rediscovery of self; the return to a more internal locus of control. It is critical for a woman to understand what it means, for her, to be female. This can be best assisted by listening and sharing with other women about their experience. Helping a woman to understand that her body has been objectified and devalued, because of sexist assumptions about women, is the beginning of understanding why a client may have devalued herself.

Women can only learn about how to live in a female body from other women. The first other woman is her mother. Chemically dependent women share a common thread in their perception of not having had a mother who was able to instill within them a sense of pride in femininity. It is not uncommon to hear women in treatment say that they live "from the neck up," meaning that they experience great discomfort about their bodies. Oftentimes those women who have been sexually abused view their bodies as a source of betrayal that brought physical and emotional pain. Additionally, they may have experienced maligning statements about menstruation, being pregnant or menopause. Unfortunately, if a mother was not a positive role model, the client may have been a "daddy's girl," which can engender the cultivation of seductress behavior.

Most clients observed at Residence XII have been emotionally enraged, even though they may appear passive. They are furious about their sex role and have gender confusion, in the sense of not clearly knowing how to be female. Depression accompanies the anger as it can be both the internalization of uncatharted rage as well as a sense of loss in not having "femaleness." Addiction to alcohol, drugs, etcetera, is often one way to self medicate a pervasive sense of dysphoria.

Accepting being an addict. To accept one's addict self simply means being able to identify those character traits and behaviors which, when manifested, do not help to maintain emotional serenity or sobriety. Some women may even give this persona a name or identify a mythological archetype to symbolize that part of the self. While not underscoring what is negative, it remains important to accept that one does have both a "dark" and "light" side. To manage one's dark side requires accepting it, not being in denial, and being willing to change those traits and behaviors.

In working with a client's "dark side," the therapist generally encounters some significant difficulties because of the absence of cultural archetypes that include the dark side as part of one's female self. For example, cultures that tend toward dichotomous thinking offer women a choice of being either a virgin or a whore. There is little capacity for an archetype that integrates the two into a completed whole. Another way of viewing this is to see that a destroyer aspect can become part of one's rebirth and renewal process. The death of one way of being allows for the creation of something new. New life emerges only after the pain and grief of loss is felt over the rampant destruction that occurs in the process of addiction(s).

2. Relationships

Women are relationally based and often describe that "hitting bottom" in their addiction occurred when their relationships were seriously deteriorating or had ceased to exist. Men, on the other hand, tend to talk about "bottoming out" when they lose income or their job.

Relating to others. Women frequently have difficulty being in relationships where there is integrity and authenticity, which means honoring the boundaries of oneself and others. Addressing the need to have clear differentiation in relating to others directly hones in on codependence. Women are socialized to be codependent in the sense that normative sex role socialization prescribes that they should be focused on the care and nurturance of others. The most hallowed of female images, such as the Virgin Mary, bespeaks the need to be a martyr. Being external in locus of control will breed despair. To anesthesize the pain accompanying relationship failure, women often turn to alcohol and drugs.

The goal for helping alcoholic women break out of codependent relating patterns includes setting parameters of acceptable and unacceptable behavior including feeling comfortable in saying no.

3. Spirituality

Becoming centered. Women are taught to be externally focused, as was previously noted. To survive as a female in our culture means to be hypersensitive to external cues and consequently to be more internal in one's focus. This is not easy for women. What we know of the spiritual in this culture is from religious institutions, which are patriarchal and externally oriented, where scripture is seen as law, written by men, about their relationship to a male God. Consequently, many women can feel alienated from the development of a personal spirituality if they sense that their femaleness is alien to what is traditionally honored as spiritual.

Recovery mandates the development of spirituality and the Twelve Step programs, such as Alcoholics Anonymous, are considered to be spiritually-based. To be spiritual means to have a sense of purpose, meaningfulness and mission in one's life. It also means believing that there is a power greater than oneself which influences one's personal direction as well as others. This power can be genderless, yet, it could be female or male.

Paradoxically, to believe in this ''power greater than one's self,'' an individual can feel more internally strengthened, thereby having the wherewithall to be more internal in one's locus of control.

To develop spiritually also means acquiring a sense of duality; being yin and yang, honoring one's feminine as well as masculine aspects. Because femininity is derided in our culture, it is a challenge for many women to honor their femaleness. However, to disparage one's nurturing, intuitive, sensing aspects is to neglect an integral component of oneself that is crucial for self-actualization.

Our sexuality and our spirituality are intrinsically connected. In *Knowing Woman*, de Castillejo writes that to have been sexually abused is to be spiritually damaged because the core of the female herself has been wounded.

The addicted female needs to experience a continuum of female metaphors, which include the child, maiden, and crone, in order to have an integrated sense of self. The maiden contains both the divine child and the wise old woman; whereas, the crone contains the child and maiden. All three are components of one's female self.

Addictions serve to keep one unconscious. So, if a woman began her addiction(s) as a child, her conscious maiden and crone are unknown to her and her child self is impaired due to the anesthetizing effects of the addiction. Her conscious reality is limited.

The task of treatment is to begin the connective process that starts with identification and data gathering. The more she knows about her divine child, maiden and crone, the more she will know about herself. The movement out of the addictive process is movement from unconsciousness to consciousness. Taken together, claiming child, maiden and crone is not a linear process but could be more accurately described as multidimensional, circular and it happens on many levels over time.

WHO IS THE WOMAN WHO COMES TO TREATMENT?

Miriam was referred to Residence XII by her therapist when she repeatedly shared her inability to stay clean and sober despite two prior episodes at coeducation treatment facilities, where she was assessed as late middle stage chemically dependent on alcohol and other drugs.

Miriam is a white female, 41 years old, divorced, with a daughter and son, both now young adults living on their own. She was raised in a Roman Catholic family. Her father drank excessively but was never labeled alcoholic. Her description of their relationship sounds covertly incestuous and overtly codependent. Miriam's relationship with her mother is distant, and her mother is described as passive. Miriam's role with her three siblings was as a caretaker, due to a recurring illness on the part of her mother. She tearfully describes two of her siblings as chemically dependent and she seems to feel responsible for them.

Miriam is currently in an unstable relationship with a man who is allegedly angry at her because she cannot remain clean and sober. She has a sense of shame about her abstinence failures and is apprehensive about coming to a gender specific facility.

Miriam has had many jobs, the majority of which cause her to be underpaid and underemployed. She discounts her one year at community college and seems to have no clear vocational goals.

In the interview she appears to be agitated and upset when talking about her own children. She is not on speaking terms with her daughter and she maintains sporadic phone contact with her son. Miriam reports that what she is most afraid of is losing her current partner who is verbally abusive, and whom she described as being alcoholic as well.

She does not talk about her slightly overweight condition, or the fact that one of the items she is wearing has been shoplifted from a local department store. Nor does she talk about her genuine frustration at why ''bad things keep happening to her,'' like her divorce or her failure to be able to pay her bills on time. It was not until participating in treatment that Miriam was able to talk about being raped in her extra marital affairs or the abusive behavior she perpetrated on her siblings as well as her offspring.

Miriam is typical of many women who come to a residential treatment program like Residence XII.

A common set of themes has been found to exist among women seeking residential care (Klaitch, 1989):

1. Early religious influence with later alienation.
2. A dysfunctional family of origin.
3. Externally appearing to be someone she isn't.
4. Lacking significant social support systems.
5. Alcohol or other drugs were used to deal with a sense of unmanageability in her life.
6. Lacking basic skills in areas such as money management and parenting.

7. Feeling shame-based and impaired.
8. Behaving in a codependent manner toward others.
9 . Displaying other addictive behaviors such as an eating disorder, nicotine addiction, shoplifting.
10. Perceiving herself as being a victim, (i.e., "Things just happen to me."
11 . Displaying sexual naivete, although she may have been sexually active.
12. Valuing men more than women.
13. Exhibiting a poorly integrated sense of femaleness.

The list suggests that women who come to treatment can have confusion about their female sex role. In great part this may be because many female alcoholic/addicts experience emotional, physical and sexual abuse within their families. As a result, they have become distrustful of others, both women and men. Since many chemically dependent females may not have had previous supportive relationships with other women, many women initially resist attending a women's only program. Miriam was not an exception.

THE TREATMENT PROGRAM

Following her admission to treatment, Miriam was given a daily schedule and guidelines regarding expected behavior in treatment. The morning schedule included meditation, breakfast, chores, movement therapy as well as small and large groups. The afternoon schedule included lunch, recreational exercise or rest, didactic and experiential classes.

During the evening Miriam attended a Twelve Step meeting, had visitors or worked on written assignments.

As is true with all clients, she was assigned to a primary counselor as well as a treatment group, which would never exceed more than eight clients. The size of the group is limited so that clients cannot "hide," a defense mechanism that many chemically dependent women attempt. The first week in treatment found her "on focus," meaning no receipt of outside phone calls or visitors. The concept "on focus" refers to the need for clients to self examine and introspect, which most find difficult.

Because staff knows that isolation is part of any addiction, Miriam was assigned to a room with eight other residents, which promoted making contact with her peers. Clients are expected to do their share in keeping the facility orderly and are expected to eat three meals a day. These meals are served without caffeine or sugar.

In the first week she was given an indepth assessment by her primary care counselor, which included a comprehensive autobiography. Together with her counselor she developed a treatment plan that would be amended or changed during the course of treatment. Additionally, clients are asked to record how unmanageable their lives had become through the disease and this written reflection is shared within one's primary group as a First Step.

Oftentimes a client can be told by her primary group that they do not feel she has been rigorously honest and thorough; hence, the resident may be asked to write another autobiography. Her peers are able to give her this feedback because they have heard parts of her story in their informal exchanges during the simple interactions of living together in a discrete setting.

Work within the group, on the First Step, occurs during the second week of treatment. Clients listen as other women present their First Steps and contribute to the group when asked to give feedback to a presenter. Through observing others share, a client can be assisted in recognizing those parts of her life truly affected by alcoholism/addiction. As an example, clients can be aided in understanding that the part of her which is an addict can be a "shadow self" that operated unconsciously. It is one's addict self that wants to run away, be dishonest, lie and manipulate.

When presenting a comprehensive autobiography to one's group, other members list the attributes and behavior of a client's addict self, which the resident can keep. The client is then asked to paraphrase feedback she has heard which can evoke painful emotions and memories. Because of the intimacy created through this process, other group members can also be restimulated in their own pain and also cathart strong feelings. Although a client will be left feeling very vulnerable, perhaps angry and embarrassed, the outcome of this experience is positive. Group members will feel closer to the client and share that by hugging, smiling and engaging with each other in a loving and accepting way.

One outcome of the initial First Step may be that the client is given direction to write about her resentment and fears toward abusive people, places or situations. This is very therapeutic, as a psychodynamic process is engaged for the release of long-repressed feelings that is ultimately cathartic and healing.

In the third week of treatment the client begins to actively acquire living skills. She will be encouraged by staff to particularly focus on the appropriate use of assertion. She will practice how to think through and articulate what she wants and how to go about getting it. For example, the client may express anxiety about returning to an unstable environment. She will be encouraged to identify what in that environment evokes the instability and to identify what she will need to be safe. She will set up an appointment with her counselor, the family counselor and significant others for a session in which she will express her needs and state her plan and engage in any planned negotiation, if necessary.

Generally during the third week the client will receive a full body massage. It is not uncommon for cellular memory to be evoked. It can be a positive restimulation of physical nurturance or a negative restimulation of an abusive experience. For example, a repressed experience of physical pain as a result of corporal punishment may surface.

In the fourth week of treatment the client begins to actively anticipate societal reentry. She presents written plans for her self-care following residency. She will be directed to focus her energy and attention on what she will need to sustain her recovery in all areas of her life. For example, by the fourth week it is not unusual for a woman to have become aware of physical processes, such as menstruation, that are causing her concern. She will be encouraged to make a plan to see a physician. Or, she may identify her emotions as being unmanageable. She will be given a list of therapeutic resources in her area. It is not unusual for anxiety to escalate during this time and for "secrets" such as past abandonment or overt abuse to be disclosed. Miriam chose this time to disclose having been sexually assaulted by a family member.

If this happens, the client will need to carefully assess, with her primary counselor and group, whether an extension of stay would be beneficial.

The residential phase of treatment for most clients, like Miriam, will end at 30 days. At exit women report having a clearer sense of self. This clarity has been acquired by telling their own story and by listening to the stories of other women. By sharing her own experience, the client is able to name and reclaim her life, however painful that life may be. Living in close contact with other women, the client learns that her peers are often mirrors for aspects of self that are outside her awareness. Treatment can be regarded as successful if the client has now internalized that she has a chemical dependency addiction that is progressive and terminal as well as believing that she can create her life in a direction that is more healthful.

The client's program of continuing care will need to be designed to sustain and strengthen the gains made. It needs to include ongoing regular contact with a counselor-facilitated recovery group as well as attendance at other supportive group meetings such as those offered through Twelve Step programs. In advance of leaving, it is essential to discuss and write out a plan of action for keeping recovery the first priority in her life. She should also be able to describe a plan of action for appropriate interventions should her disease become activated.

In the case of Miriam, she planned to attend aftercare one time a week for four months, three anonymous meetings a week and to continue in therapy once a week. In a family session she told her partner that alcohol and drugs could not be part of her living environment nor would she continue to accept his verbal abuse. If either were present, she would move out.

CONCLUSION

In treating chemically dependent women Residence XII utilizes a feminist approach that includes: (a) use of female staff as role models; (b) a safe and discrete environment that allows women to interact with one another so that they can identify their femaleness; (c) empowerment through telling one's own story and listening to other women; (d) development of assertions skills; (e) reconnection with pride in one's body; and (f) seeing the personal as political.

Women alcoholics actively engaging with others who are recovering creates a power greater than themselves that works on their behalf.

In short, women healing women is empowering.

REFERENCES

de Castillejo, I. C. (1973). *Knowing woman: A feminine psychology*. C. G. Jung Foundation, San Francisco: Harper & Row.

Klaitch, K. (1989). Preliminary work. Unpublished doctoral dissertation, University of Washington. Work done in collaboration with C. Smith.

9

Reclaiming Women's Bodies: A Feminist Perspective on Eating Disorders

Sue A. Kuba
Susan Gale Hanchey

INTRODUCTION AND ETIOLOGY

Ninety-five percent of eating-disordered patients are women. There are three major types of eating disorders: anorexia nervosa, bulimia and compulsive eating.

Anorexia nervosa is characterized by severe weight loss or, in the case of prepubescent girls, by a failure to gain weight. Anorexics are overly preoccupied with food, perceiving themselves as too fat, while in reality, they are maintaining themselves in a state of chronic starvation. Weight is lost through a variety of methods, including severe caloric restriction, fasting, relentless exercising, use of over-the-counter diet aids, diuretics, laxatives, and in some cases, self-induced vomiting. Anorexia nervosa commonly begins in adolescence. Approximately six in one thousand young women are anorexic (Fairburn, 1988).

Bulimia consists of episodes of binge eating, which can be followed by some form of purging and/or severe dietary restraint. A "binge" is the secretive consumption of large quantities of food over a discrete period of time. Bulimia may be accompanied by other compulsive behaviors such as shoplifting, self-injury and chemical abuse. Bulimics can be obese or of average weight. Five to 10 percent of females between the ages of 12 to 24 display significant bulimic behavior (Fairburn, 1988). Even though bulimia tends to develop in late adolescence and early adulthood, it may occur at any age. Some women suffer simultaneously from anorexic and bulimic symptoms. Boskind-White and White (1983) estimated that 40 percent of eating-disordered patients are bulimarexic.

Compulsive eaters usually binge in secrecy and rapidly ingest huge quantities of high-calorie foods. It is the most prevalent eating disorder affecting approximately one in four women (Kano, 1985).

All three types of compulsive food-related behaviors develop before a young girl reaches maturity and seem to be related to a cluster of personality traits. The girl at risk is generally perfectionistic, demanding absolute conformity to external criteria for success. She is often emotionally isolated while appearing socially gregarious. Her own needs, anxieties and values are subjugated to the demands of others, leaving her with unexpressed resentment and loneliness.

Eating disorders are multicausal and causality differs for each woman. In adolescence, girls are expected to form their own identity by separating from their familes and by developing their values through experimentation. Eating disorders can be an expression of unresolved role conflict within the family. Often these families demonstrate sex roles that are stereotypical; the mother fulfills a traditional role and experiences her life as unfulfilled. The father may be emotionally detached yet professionally successful. Adolescents in these families can experience a profound conflict because they are expected to transform their gender identification from mother to father (Wooley, 1987). In addition, the daughter may develop a unique role as family caretaker and mother's confidante. These factors can make individuation difficult.

By the time the family presents for treatment, they often appear to fall into two groups: controlling and rigid or emotionally enmeshed and conflictual. Some families combine features of both types. Often a careful history will reveal parental chemical dependency, child abuse or incest.

This intrafamilial conflict is exacerbated by certain sociocultural pressures on women (Chernin, 1981; Woodman, 1980). The direction of women's identity development has been confused by two conflicting cultural ideologies: traditional right-wing conservatism and liberal left-wing feminism. Today's young woman grows up with the expectations of maternal and wifely fulfillment, subjugation to male needs, and a limited perception of competence. She also experiences a broadening of opportunity, demands to be self-sufficient, and a lack of faith in long-term marital commitment. Vascillating between these sets of expectations, she fails to develop a cohesive set of values upon which to build the sense of self and regresses into the relative safety of the family environment.

Another sociocultural pressure is the use of body weight as a measure of attractiveness and competence. This focus on thinness interferes with the normal health development of many teenage girls and directs them to develop their self-image in terms of their body size. Society tends to stereotype overweight adult women as lazy or out-of-control (Orbach,

1979). These overweight women diet in response to the sociocultural pressure to be thin, often developing an eating disorder in the process.

Even the medical establishment fails to challenge misinformation about weight. Fat women are fat due to genetic predisposition and physiological factors, not lack of self-control. Perhaps the best example of this misinformation is the misconception that dieting may cure obesity, when in fact diety may cause obesity (Orbach, 1979; Wooley & Wooley, 1981). Failures at weight loss condemn American women to a life of chronic dieting and continuous low self-esteem (Steiner-Adair, 1987). Becoming a woman and developing an eating disorder thus share in common the characteristics of powerlessness and loss of control.

INTEGRATION OF A FEMINIST APPROACH

The basis of a feminist approach to any addiction or psychological treatment is the primary understanding of the oppression of women. Eichenbaum and Orbach (1983) stated that "women discover . . . that they share . . . feelings of powerlessness and rage, of frustration and underdevelopment, a sense of themselves as being less than whole people." (p. 3). This oppression, resulting in a sense of victimization, is culturally most powerful in the form of fatism (Orbach, 1982; Surrey, 1984). Reduced to a sense of self as based primarily on external validation, women strive to become one dimensional, a portrait without depth or sense of self. Price (1988) validated the sense of women's inability to make a worthwhile contribution to a culture in which the woman's internal strength and basic herstory are denied.

Combating this oppression and resultant feelings of worthlessness is the primary task of therapists and health care professionals working with eating-disordered women. The first step is the expansion of women's options and sense of choice. Keeping choices and options open can be as basic as providing the opportunity for the least restrictive means of treatment. A continuum of treatment approaches—inpatient, day treatment and intensive outpatient which combines group, family and individual therapies—is the minimum standard for a feminist approach to treatment.

For too long, women have been diagnostically degraded, overmedicated and invalidated by the psychiatric establishment (Mitchell, 1974). Any feminist approach must take strenuous precautions to avoid further disempowerment by developing supportive-nurturing environments of women caring for women. Such an environment can create a healing community rather than a demoralizing male-dominated infliction of "treatment."

The creation of such a community requires a basic belief that women's development is different than that of men. Gilligan (1982) and Steiner-Adair and Surrey (1988) have documented these developmental differences and the need to nurture women's relational identity. This can be accomplished through the use of group treatment, which encourages relationships between women, expanding beyond the boundaries of therapy itself.

In order to encourage the development of these relationships, women must expand their knowledge and skills. Practically, women need more information about their unique history. They need to understand the suppression of women's culture and experience archetypal images as new role models for the development of their own identity. Skill development needs to be specific and should incorporate anger facilitation, assertiveness training and sexuality education. Basic texts include *The Dance of Anger* (Lerner, 1985) and *Our Bodies, Our Selves* (Boston Women's Health Collective, 1971). Fedele and Miller (1988) stated that "women's masochism" (p. 5) is an accurate perception of their reality. This reality needs to be confirmed through the use of herstory and skill development so that anger and pain cease to be internalized in a masochistic way.

One primary source of a woman's sense of failure is her relationship to her children. Mental health professionals often contribute to this by intervening to judge a woman's suitability for motherhood. In treating eating-disordered women, special attention must be paid to their relationships with their children and the unmet and unrealistic expectations of their own mothering. Practically, this means creating therapeutic time for mothers and children, developing prevention strategies and helping children to understand their own feelings about their mother's eating-disordered behavior.

Women's sense of themselves as caring mothers, spouses and friends creates a unique relationship with food. In eating-disordered patients, food assumes mythical proportions. It becomes "Nurturance" itself, deemed appropriate for others but denied for the self. For anorexic women, this denial of self-need for nurturance requires heroic strength. The bulimic woman alternates between heroic denial and extravagant indulgence followed by remorse, guilt and self-cleansing through purging. Compulsive eaters live in chronic shame for their willingness to replace their sense of self-starvation with perpetual indulgence (Orbach, 1979).

To break this cycle of shame, doubt and powerlessness, therapists working with eating-disordered patients must be aware of women's oppression. They must be willing to set aside some previous assumptions about treatment and engage their real selves in therapeutic alliances with the women they treat. Therapeutic relationships become real as well as transferential (Eichenbaum & Orbach, 1983), with appropriate limits which do not further victimize the women in treatment. Male therapists can be very effective in working with eating-disordered women, if they are capable of denouncing the cultural norm. This requires a sense of comfort with their own masculinity and femininity; a strong sense of self which can tolerate rage without suppressing or interpreting it. Similar demands are made upon female therapists. They must be clear about their own androgeny and be capable of supporting the development of other women. Both male and female therapists should exemplify the possibility of alternative roles and lifestyles.

Supportive-Nurturing Environment

The creation of a feminist environment for women's healing involves some practical and some elusive elements. Practically, one begins with the primacy of choice and the assertion of responsibility for one's own healing. Margaret is a bulimic woman who entered treatment on an emergency basis because of suicidal thoughts and ideas. Her life, controlled by an emotionally abusive husband and three male children, had created a desperate search for, and destructiveness against, the self. She entered an inpatient treatment program against the wishes of her husband who believed she did not have the right to enter into a financial contract without his approval and consent. Validation of Margaret's choice for self-healing meant first accepting her ability to make independent decisions. It required a strict sense of confidentiality about that decision and her progress in treatment, despite desperate manipulations by key people in her life.

For Margaret and other eating-disordered women, the issue of choice is based primarily on their relationship to food. It is here that a feminist eating-disorder therapist must defeat a sense of externally based control. Food programming must create a sense of options. This is best accomplished by providing healthy guidelines. Food prescriptions and plans can be established by a registered dietitian. Unlike diets, these plans must focus on the consumption of adequate amounts of healthy food without calorie counting. Social eating should be encouraged in a variety of settings.

The amount and variety of food should be contracted by the woman in group meetings with her peers. In the meeting, her goals may be presented so that she may receive feedback about her choices. Modifications or additions to goals should be determined by the woman herself. For example, an anorexic woman may initially contract to consume 25 percent of her food plan, gradually increasing until she consumes 100 percent.

The management of purging behavior requires the establishment of certain rules, whose impact can be experienced as supportive if they are not overly restrictive. A woman's choice to purge should be acknowledged. The rules focus on the abolishment of secrecy associated with this activity and the replacement of guilt and shame with support from staff and peers. Most women will discuss their purging and are first supported for acknowledging it, then challenged to understand the feelings that created it. Generally, the woman seeking to heal herself will respond to this

structure by eliminating purging within 6 to 10 weeks. Failure to stop purging behavior can be addressed by pairing the woman with another group
member who will accompany her while she purges. Another option is to
suggest the woman restrict purging to the bathroom at the therapist's office
or the home of a friend.

Monitoring the weight of patients presents another challenge. A patient's
weight is an objective criterion for monitoring the decrease in obsession
with food. Yet, women who have determined their daily lives by the scale
need to be encouraged to give up this tyranny. Group members should
be instructed to remove scales from their homes. Pamela, a bulimic woman in outpatient therapy, insisted that physicians and health care providers
weigh her backwards in their office. After a lengthy and self-disclosing explanation of her need for this, she was reassured by a nurse that "127
pounds isn't so bad." Clearly, combating weight obsessiveness requires
heroic measures in our fat-phobic culture.

The elusive elements of creating a supportive, nurturing environment
are most profound in the development of relationships between women
patients. An environment can be established that supports these relational ties. The depth of them is determined by the patients themselves. To
encourage this, activities may be done in groups. Patient cohesion seems
to build as thoughts, feelings, dreams and recreation are shared.

Women are encouraged to spend time together. Some choose to live
together for added support. In one case, a 24-year-old anorexic chose to
share an apartment with the daughter of a 47-year-old anorexic in her
group. These connections outside of group therapy can be encouraged by
therapists rather than discouraged as they might be in a traditional approach. Touch between patients might be considered normal and supportive. Many anorexic and bulimic women fear touch from others, so the
first abilities to reach out to supportive women friends are growthful and
a sign of health.

The continuation of these relationships outside the bounds of therapy
requires the establishment of a new support group. From the time a woman enters treatment for her eating disorder, she may be required to attend
appropriate Twelve Step support groups. The primary one is Overeaters
Anonymous, which has expanded in recent years to accommodate all wom-
en with food obsessions. Overeaters Anonymous (OA) has redefined abstinence as the removal of compulsive food behaviors. In OA the
eating-disordered woman establishes a group of peers who are combating
the cultural obsession with weight reduction and dieting. She begins to
understand that her struggle with food will be lifelong and that she will
never be "cured" of her disorder but faces a lifetime commitment to recovery as a process.

Women's relationships become more open through the process of mutual decision making. The feminist movement has advocated decision making by consensus since the early 1970s. Practical steps for implementing this involve helping women to provide peer feedback. This may be accomplished through structured peer feedback groups that meet without professional facilitation.

The overall needs of women must come before the needs of men with eating disorders. Very few men present for treatment; however, the decision to place those few on a unit predominantly female, or in a women's group, is always weighed against the possible adverse effects. Admitting one male patient to a group has potential positive benefits for the man as well as the women. The man who has succumbed to culturally based stereotypes for thinness suffers from oppression similar to that of his female counterparts. His identity is also confused and underdeveloped. Often, he attempts to overcompensate by rigidly adhering to traditional views of women. In order to relieve his own suffering, the man must confront his role in this oppression and his stereotypes of women's roles. Healing can occur for the women in such a group when their collective power impacts the male's attitudes and beliefs.

There are obvious dangers involved. The male's impact must be monitored to see that he does not become the group's pivotal point. Such distortion of his importance in the group can create a recapitulation of the women's lives as they existed before treatment began.

Group Treatment as Method of Choice

Group treatment of eating disorders is found to be the most helpful because women can develop a sense of self in relationship to others (Surrey, 1984). When a woman begins to build trust and empathy with others, she also develops these feelings for herself.

The primary group is best composed of up to eight eating-disordered patients regardless of diagnosis. Generally, it is best to separate adult and adolescent women in order to meet their differing needs. Each patient has a goal to develop healthy eating habits and a moderate exercise program. Other goals are developed, depending on the patient's particular needs. Helpful requirements include OA meeting attendance, suggested readings and daily food diaries. Written feedback from the group therapist is especially helpful.

Powerful therapeutic techniques are required to dismantle the facade that eating-disordered patients create. Reenactments of past events can uncover painful issues and bring the group closer together. Guided imagery of past experiences can create new insights. Sometimes an indirect paradoxical approach may be necessary to break through resistance to change. Cognitive distortions need to be labeled and understood in light of the sociocultural context which influenced them.

It is difficult to elicit affect with eating-disordered patients. Anorexics feel empty and have difficulty formulating strong feelings. Bulimics wear a facade and want to protect the therapist from their strong emotions. Obese patients feel shame and subdue their emotional expression. The task of the therapist is the establishment of group norms, including honesty and directiveness, which teach women to trust their own intuitiveness. Therapists need to guard against superficial discussions, rescuing, enabling and isolation. Therapists need to question patients' general statements, confront the facade and reframe critical feedback as caring.

The primary group can replicate the patients' families of origin, and this must be interpreted. Some issues that might arise include family loyalties, sharing family secrets, family communication styles, and patient independence. The core conflict of most eating-disordered patients is separation and individuation. This passage is so difficult for women to negotiate that it causes intimacy problems with peers, competition regarding appearance and rage.

Group is preferable to individual therapy because the group setting facilitates recognition of the commonality of women's problems by exposing their life experiences in the mirror of other women's lives. Menstruation, rape, seduction, physical power and psychological molestation may be shared as the group's intimacy deepens.

A primary issue for group members is the denial of their fear and use of defenses to avoid it. Johnson (1988) documented the eating-disordered woman's struggle with fears of engulfment and abandonment. These fears, traced to the early mother-daughter relationship, may be recapitulated in the group context, where reparative responses can occur. As a result the woman can begin to face her fears and heal those early wounds (Steiner-Adair & Surrey, 1988). Group therapy requires facilitating the ongoing process of merger and separation which vascillate until stabilization of the self. The task becomes finding one's self in all phases of this process and in isolation.

Family Treatment

Families of eating-disordered patients present with a variety of treatment issues. Most families are conflicted about the balance between need for control and personal independence. They also seem to suffer from the perfectionistic need to meet socially prescribed norms. Other common issues include lack of emotional expression, intolerance for conflict and deficits in communication skills. The eating disorder becomes an expression of these unresolved conflicts, both within the family and in the family's response to societal change.

Parents of eating-disordered patients are both frightened and angry. Their anorexic daughter appears to be on the verge of death. Her consistent refusal to eat creates underlying rage, which the parents suppress in fear for her life. Parents of bulimics are often confused about their daughter's behavior. Their emotional expression of fear and rage may result in attempts to control. They may install locks on kitchen cabinets, disturb her privacy in the bathroom or empty their home of food. The parents of compulsive eaters are often ashamed of their daughter's appetite, and may prescribe restrictive diets. They may inadvertently contribute to her sense of shame out of fear that she will grow up unhappy and unloved by others.

Intervention with eating-disordered families requires both education and therapy. Just like the eating-disordered woman herself, the family needs to understand the reality of genetic body types and sizes. Their overprotective controls must be reinterpreted as behavior that surrenders parental control to the adolescent daughter. It is always important to frame the parental controls as originating from concern. Too often families are blamed for the behavior of the eating-disordered person.

Family therapy can be accomplished individually or in multifamily groups. The combining of families in treatment can accelerate the therapeutic response through peer identification, role modeling and support. In conducting family treatment the therapist must switch the focus from the relationship between client and therapist to the relationship between family members. Multigenerational genograms may be used to understand family roles and expectations. The family must be able to understand the helplessness of their attempts to control the patient's behavior and encouraged to develop their own lives. Emotional expression should be facilitated using direct statements. Emotional secrets of the past can be explored. Often the family system may be joined by the therapist whose new family role can be corrective. Both strategic and systemic interventions have been found to be useful with eating-disordered patients (Root, Fallon, & Friedrich, 1986).

SOCIOCOLTURAL THERAPY

Body Image Work

Verbal therapy alone is not enough to bridge the gap between mind and body. It does not and cannot address the estrangement that women feel from their physical selves. Body image work encourages physical awareness through the understanding of body language, breath awareness, movement, voice work and touch (Wooley & Kearney-Cooke, 1986).

Many techniques are available. Encouraging patients to remember their bodies at different ages gives them the background to begin exploration. Drawing or sculpting their most vivid body image helps elucidate distortions. The therapist can encourage a group to explore the meaning of thinness for them by picturing themselves differently (e.g., older, powerful, attractive, etc.). Patients can be asked to draw or role play powerful conflicts about physical transitions in a woman's life such as onset of menses. Videotaping is especially useful, providing the opportunity for patients to observe their body—its language and size. The group of women can create pyramids and art with their bodies to acknowledge flexibility, coordination and grace. The creative activities to enhance body image are unlimited.

Exercise

The use of exercise in eating disorders treatment is essential. This must be combined with the recognition that exercise is a part of the compulsive process and a further demonstration of women's oppression. In health clubs across this country, women work out daily for hours dressed in tight fitting clothing designed to adorn their bodies rather than create comfort. The health club becomes an exhibition place for thinness. In any treatment of eating-disordered women, exercise must be removed from this context. Instead, women are encouraged to perform exercise that is fun, which nourishes the soul instead of depleting the body. Examples include volleyball, horseback riding, bowling and camping.

According to Orbach (1982), "a woman's body . . . is not a very good or safe environment to live inside" (p. 24). Sometimes this alienation can be combated by helping women see their bodies as operational and strong. For women who have been assaulted or molested, basic self-defense classes are sometimes recommended.

Through the use of body image work, enjoyable exercise and self-defense training, the definition of a woman's body can be expanded. Gradually she comes to see that her body can be a friend to be enjoyed rather than an enemy to be subdued.

Grief Work

Overweight individuals need to grieve the loss of the thin person they would have been, in order to allow themselves to stay at their present weight and accept themselves. They need to grieve over abandoning their illness and examine the accompanying losses (Wooley & Wooley, 1981).

Additionally, the women are encouraged to grieve what they did not get from their dysfunctional family of origin by talking about feelings, anticipating a variety of emotions, and identifying stages of grief. Techniques such as bibliotherapy and ritual funerals are also useful.

Anger Work

Therapy with women is truly effective only when each gains access to the full repertoire of her emotions and learns to work with those emotions in healthy ways. Women are entitled to the experience of anger, and they need to use it in ways that do not injure themselves or others. The feminist therapist needs to examine how the patient's personality and the socialized suppression of women's anger interface.

Eating-disordered individuals "stuff" their angry feelings by compulsively eating or starving. They also become self-destructive as opposed to being angry at others. This destructiveness can take the form of self-mutilation or self-abuse. The therapist's greatest tool in combating this inward anger is confrontation. The response to this confrontation is often the patient's outward expression of anger at the therapist. The initiation of this response and its containment by the therapist is the beginning of a new understanding that anger need not destroy. Feminist therapists view women's anger as a potential source of constructive energy for change.

Women's Culture and Herstory

For at least the last 2,000 years, women's herstory and culture have been suppressed. Part of that suppression has always involved patriarchal control of women's bodies. Witness the elongation of necks in Africa, the binding of feet in China, the girdling of hips in the United States and the demands of thinness in today's modern world. Women must realize this herstorical suppression and its result: the loss of alternative role models and archetypes upon which to build their lives.

Weaving the information into the therapeutic process can be difficult. It is primarily an educational endeavor. A group focusing on journal writing is an excellent way to implement this sociocultural heritage.

In a journal group, patients can be instructed to keep a daily account of both conscious and unconscious images. The journal focuses on creative expressions and emotional reactions to them. Material for the journal includes dreams, poetry, music, art, weaving, song writing, movies and literature. Each woman records those creative events to which she responds with strong affect.

Through the process of amplification (Jung, 1966), the images recorded in the woman's journal are expanded to encompass universal image or archetypes. The group educational setting creates an environment where rapid amplification can occur. This labeling of characters and symbols in universal terms or archetypes requires much education. It is in this process of labeling that women's herstory and culture are explored. The final step of journaling is the understanding of the archetypes as they reflect the woman's current life.

During journal group, women can be encouraged to expand upon prevalent images through reading or research. This exploration accomplishes two tasks: expanding the woman's sense of her lost herstory and increasing the archetypal representations available to the developing self.

Spirituality

Feminist therapy with eating-disordered patients also requires the understanding of patients' spiritual needs. A special spirituality group can be established, in some cases led by a female chaplain or minister. Many eating-disordered women suffer from a projection of God as a reflection of the dogmatic and punishing self. They believe that their disorder is created by failure on their part to be holy enough. Challenging this image of God should take place in a group context. Different definitions of God can be explored, alternative religious traditions explained, and the current eradication of a Great Mother by the current patriarchal culture revealed. Alternative uses of prayer and meditation might be shared. The results can be exceptional. As women admonish the punishing God, the punishing self becomes less powerful.

CONCLUSIONS

The feminist therapist confronting the reality of an eating disorder is faced with a multifaceted addiction. Personal, social and family factors create the self-destructive process underlying anorexia, bulima and compulsive eating. Effective therapeutic treatment requires the recognition of eating disorders as illnesses of women that are best healed by the community of women created in group psychotherapy. New advances in developmental theories of women require that rigid treatment approaches be discarded. The feminist therapist replaces trauma with a multilayered approach to treatment encompassing family intervention and creative therapeutic techniques. Body image work, grief and anger management, as well as the introduction of women's herstory, are advantageous in meeting the challenge. The individual development of self will occur as eating-disordered women, under the guidance of feminist therapists, are able to free themselves from the modern-day bondage of thinness.

REFERENCES

Boskind-White, M., & White, W. C. (1983). *Bulimarexia: The binge-purge cycle.* New York: Norton.

Boston Women's Health Book Collective. (1971). *Our bodies, ourselves: A book by and for women* (rev. ed.). New York: Simon & Schuster.

Chernin, K. (1981). *The obsession: Reflections on the tyranny of slenderness.* New York: Harper & Row.

Eichenbaum, L., & Orbach, S. (1983). *Understanding women: A feminist psychoanalytic approach.* New York: Basic Books.

Fairburn, C. (1988, October). *Epidemiology: What we know and don't know.* Paper presented at the National Anorexic Aid Society's Seventh National Conference on Anorexia Nervosa and Bulimia Nervosa, Columbus, OH.

Fedele, N., & Miller, J. B. (1988). *Putting theory into practice: Creating mental health programs for women.* (Work in Progress No. 32). Wellesley, MA: Wellesley College, Stone Center for Developmental Services and Studies.

Gilligan, C. (1982). *In a different voice.* Cambridge: Harvard University Press.

Johnson, C. (1988, October). *Long-term treatment of eating disorder patients with false-self/narcissistic disorders.* Paper presented at the National Anorexic Aid Society's Seventh National Conference on Anorexia Nervosa and Bulimia Nervosa, Columbus, OH.

Jung, C. G. (1966). *Two essays on analytic psychology* (R. F. C. Hull, Trans.) (2nd ed.). Princeton, NJ: Princeton University Press. (Original work published 1943 & 1928).

Kano, S. (1985). *Making peace with food: A step-by-step guide to freedom from diet/weight conflict.* Boston: Amity.

Lerner, H. G. (1985). *The dance of anger.* New York: Harper & Row.

Mitchell, J. (1974). *Psychoanalysis and feminism.* New York: Vintage Books.

Orbach, S. (1979). *Fat is a feminist issue.* New York: Berkeley Books.

Orbach, S. (1982) *Fat is a feminist issue II: A program to conquer compulsive eating.* New York: Berkeley Books.

Price, J. (1988). The importance of understanding the her-story of women. *Women and Therapy, 7,* 37–47.

Root, M. P. P., Fallon, P., & Friedrich, W. N. (1986). *Bulimia: A systems approach to treatment.* New York: Norton.

Steiner-Adair, C. (1987, April 1). Weightism: A new form of prejudice. *National Anorexic Aid Society Newsletter,* (p. 1).

Steiner-Adair, C., & Surrey, J. (1988, October). *Healing the mother-daughter relationship in the treatment of eating disorders.* Paper presented at the National Anorexic Aid Society's Seventh National Conference on Anorexia Nervosa and Bulima Nervosa, Columbus, OH.

Surrey, J. (1984). *Eating patterns as a reflection of women's development* (Work in Progress No. 83–06). Wellesley, MA: Wellesley College, Stone Center for Developmental Services and Studies.

Woodman, M. (1980). *The owl was the baker's daughter: Obesity, anorexia nervosa and the repressed feminine.* Toronto, Canada: Inner City Books.

Wooley, S. C. (1987, October). *Eating disorders: Symbolic meaning of a culture in transition.* Paper presented at Eating Disorders: Myth, Symbol & Reality Conference, Fresno, CA.

Wooley, S. C., & Kearney-Cooke, A. (1986). Intensive treatment of bulimia and body image disturbance. In K. Brownell & J. Foreyt (Eds.), *Handbook of eating disorders: Physiology, psychology and the treatment of obesity, anorexia, and bulimia* (pp. 477–502). New York: Basic Books.

Wooley, S. C., & Wooley, O. W. (1981). Eating disorders: Obesity and anorexia. In A. Brodsky & R. Hare-Mustin (Eds.), *Women and psychotherapy* (pp. 135–158). New York: The Guilford Press.

10

Out of Control and Eating Disordered

Joan C. Chrisler

**THE ROLE OF FEELINGS OF CONTROL
IN DISORDERED EATING**

"I had good self-control at the party—no cake for me." "I lost control and finished all the ice cream." "Can't you control yourself?" "She had such control!" The most common word in women's discussions of eating and dieting is undoubtedly "control." We've all heard it; we've all said it. What is the role of control in women's eating behavior? How do feelings of control relate to women's sense of personal power and their ability to exercise power and control in a sexist society? How can feminist therapists help?

Women who eat or binge/purge compulsively often report doing so because of a "lack of control" or "being out of control." They believe that if they could only establish self-control, they could stop their compulsive behavior. Women who diet and exercise compulsively report doing so out of a need to "be in control." They appear to derive self-esteem from controlling, and exhibiting their control over, temptations to eat.

There is no doubt that gender role learnings are involved in concerns about weight and eating. Women are much more concerned about their weight than men are about theirs. Men who are 100 pounds overweight will say that it doesn't bother them very much; they introspect less about their weight and don't seem embarrassed by it (Millman, 1980). Women, on the other hand, are allowed by our culture's beauty ideal a much smaller range of "acceptable" weight. Nine out of ten participants in weight loss programs are female (Freedman, 1986). Forty percent of college women believe that they are overweight, although only 12 percent of them would meet medical criteria for such a description (Halmi, Falk & Schwartz, 1981).

Many young girls begin their first diet as early as the fourth grade (Guyot, Fairchild & Hill, 1981) and restained eating has now become normative (Rodin, Silberstein & Striegel-Moore, 1985) for adult women.

Food addictions are a "good fit" with the feminine gender role. Food has always been women's responsibility; there is nothing unusual or embarrassing about spending time in grocery stores, bakeries or kitchens. It's difficult for others to tell whether one is obsessed with food or simply carrying out one's duty to nurture others. Food addictions can also fit more easily into women's budgets, as food can be less expensive than alcohol, drugs or gambling. As Lindsay Van Gelder (1987) writes, "Chocolate chips cost lots less than the Las Vegas kind." Since food is a part of women's responsibility, it also seems like something that should be under her control.

WOMEN AND POWER

In a society where women are told that "the hand that rocks the cradle rules the world" and then are simultaneously prevented from exercising power, it is no wonder that issues of control become prominent. Sherif (1982) has defined power as the control of resources and core institutions. Successful wielding of power can be used to satisfy one's desires and contributes to one's self-esteem and confidence (Kipnis, 1976). Women have rarely been successful in exerting societal power and have exerted interpersonal power mainly through helplessness and other forms of indirect, manipulative strategies (Johnson, 1976). Conventional forms of power such as legitimate, coercive, expert or informational have rarely been open to women's use (Frieze, Parsons, Johnson, Ruble, & Zellman, 1978).

Gender role stereotypes make it clear who is powerful and who is not. Women are seen as weak and dependent, while men are seen as strong, dominant, skilled and worldly leaders who are not easily influenced (Kahn, 1984). Because we are not perceived as powerful and have been thwarted in our attempts to exercise power and control in the world, women have tried instead to become powerful in the domestic sphere. This strategy includes exerting control over our weight and eating patterns.

Raven (1965) described six power bases, styles of exercising influence. Reward power is the ability to offer rewards in return for the cooperation of others. Coercion power is the ability to threaten others with punishments if they do not cooperate. Referent power is the ability to influence because of likableness and similarity, often based on a personal relationship ("Do this for me" "Parents should stand together"). Expert power is the ability to influence due to one's special knowledge or skills. Legitimate power is the ability to influence based on one's position. People who cannot help themselves may legitimately influence others, as may those who have done favors ("You owe me one") for the people they are attempting to influence. Informational power is the ability to influence others by explaining to them how cooperation will ultimately benefit them or be their best choice.

Even today, with all the advances made possible by the feminist movement, women complain of not being seen either as experts or as having the legitimate right to issue orders or policy decisions. It is not unusual for men, and other women as well, to doubt information given to them by a woman. Others may doubt that a woman can actually deliver the rewards she has promised and feel certain that she will not carry out her threats. Johnson (1976) found that the participants in her studies believed that coercion, legitimate, expert and informational power were significantly more likely to be used by males than by females. Use of personal rewards like affection or sexuality were seen as significantly more likely to be used by females. Falbo (1977) asked subjects to write an essay entitled "How I Get My Way." The techniques volunteered by the participants were compared with their gender role orientation based on results from the Bem Sex Role Inventory. Feminine persons were significantly more likely to report the use of crying, mood changes and subtle suggestions, and significantly less likely to report the use of assertiveness. It seems that men and women do use different power bases and that more power bases are available for use by men than by women.

It has been suggested (Raven & Kruglanski, 1970, Johnson; 1976) that the way one chooses to wield power also influences how powerful one sees oneself, how powerful others see one and how successful one expects to be in future situations when one attempts to influence others. Influence attempts based on the status given to women by beauty and youth are often successful, but those who use them are usually aware of their temporary nature. The gradual or sudden (facial scarring from burns or accidents) loss of beauty has driven many formerly confident women into psychotherapy (Freedman, 1986); fear of the eventual loss of beauty and youth leads to self-doubt, fear and sometimes drastic measures (cosmetic surgery, severe dieting) to preserve beauty.

The use of indirect and manipulative power strategies by women (Johnson, 1976; Falbo, 1977) is also problematic. These strategies may well be successful in the short-run, but they do not build self-confidence or convey to others the impression of a powerful person. The more successful one is at indirect strategies, the less likely the influenced person is to recognize having been influenced (Frieze et al., 1978), so no credit will go to the influencer. Unsuccessful, obvious attempts at manipulation lead to a backlash against the influencer (Frieze, et al., 1978). No one wants to be manipulated so recognition of the manipulator's tactics puts others on guard to resist future influence attempts.

Why have women so little access to power and so little confidence in our ability to use power successfully? Derived from the legacy of a sexist society in which women have been literally shut out of the corridors of power, women are taught not to try to control our own lives (Lips, 1981), our work and our talents have traditionally been undervalued by society, women's successes have often been attributed to luck rather than to abilities (Deaux & Emswiller, 1974) and we've experienced discrimination on the job. Even programs such as affirmative action, meant to allow women access to power and to the opportunity to develop our abilities, have sometimes resulted in the undermining of self-confidence as newly hired women were treated as tokens who were not talented enough to have been hired otherwise (Lips, 1981; Clance & Imes, 1978). Several writers (Lips, 1981; Friday, 1977) have suggested that because of our reproductive functioning (the menstrual cycle, menopause, pregnancy), women feel that we have less control over our bodies than men do, and that this feeling of loss of control of our bodies may extend to our ability to control or influence other situations.

WOMEN, CONTROL, AND EATING

If power is denied in the public sphere, one must look for opportunities to exercise it in the private sphere, or else surrender to dependence and helplessness. Since the selection and preparation of food is under women's control, and since, barring force-feeding, no one else determines what one puts into one's body, control over food consumption seems a likely battleground. It should not be surprising then to see women setting up rigid habits and elaborate rituals in an attempt to exercise self-control and feel powerful. There is plenty of help available in forming these rigid eating habits from diet programs, women's magazines and the book publishing industry.

Anorexia Nervosa and Control

Anorexic teenagers have been described as helpless (Logue, 1986), inadequate, and ineffective perfectionists (Bell, 1985) who are striving to please others, particularly their controlling parents (Freedman, 1986; Bell, 1985; Boskind-Lodahl, 1976), and who need to control and manipulate their environment (Crisp, 1983). Bruch (1973) writes that the anorexic is in a constant "struggle for control, for a sense of identity, competence and effectiveness." In other words, anorexia can be seen as a desperate attempt by the powerless to gain some control and influence.

Power through starvation should not be seen as a recent phenomenon; it apparently has a long history. Bell (1985) describes the cases of a number of Italian girls whose starvation diets brought them widespread attention in the fourteenth century and who later became saints of the Catholic Church. He suggests that the belief that God was directing them to subsist on such small amounts of food gave these women power over the normally more powerful priests who had no direct line to the deity. Certainly their influence over pious lay people was significant; they were probably as important as it was possible for women to be at that time. America has also had its share of "fasting girls," the most famous of whom was probably Mollie Fancher. In the mid-nineteenth century she became the first American to draw spiritual authority from fasting (Schwartz, 1986). Schwartz describes her fasting as "an assertion of power, a force in and of itself . . . Mollie Fancher was mistress of her world." Refusal to eat has been used more recently by Gandhi, Dick Gregory, suffragists, peace activists and political prisoners to draw the public's attention and to manipulate the powerful. It has frequently been quite successful.

Therefore, one can see in an anorexic's behavior an opportunity to rebel against the powerlessness of femininity (Orbach, 1978) and "to challenge her role as a good girl who should please others" (Freedman, 1986). By refusing to eat, she asserts ownership of her body (Boskind-Lodahl, 1976) and gains a sense of herself as an individual. She gains feelings of competence and effectiveness by setting "for herself a daily, relentless, physically torturing challenge, one over which she alone has control" (Bell, 1985). She gains influence in the family as attention is increasingly focused on her. Bruch (1973) writes of one of her clients, "as she began to lose weight she experienced a great sense of strength and independence." Anorexic girls see themselves becoming self-sufficient and independent (Davis, 1985). In other words, the anorexic girl gains the characteristics we hope that all teenagers will gain, yet her feelings of powerlessness and lack of control lead her down an unusual and dangerous path to individuality and effectiveness.

Bulimia and Control

Like anorexics, bulimics seem to be powerless women trying to bring a sense of order and control to their lives. Bulimic women lack self-confidence (Boskin-Lodahl, 1976; Striegel-Moore, Silberstein, & Rodin, 1986) and report feeling indecisive, incompetent and ineffective (Root, Fallon & Friedrich, 1986). Many bulimics have been victims of traumatic abuse such as rape or battering and others have reported the death of a significant other at critical times in their development (Root, Fallon & Friedrich, 1986). These experiences may have significantly contributed to their feelings of being unable to control their own lives. Bulimic women achieve lower internal locus of control scores than non-bulimic women (Weiss & Ebert, 1983) and ther MMPI scores indicate submissiveness, passivity and lack of assertiveness (Root, et al., 1986).

In addition, bulimic women are highly conforming and dependent for self-definition on the reactions of other people (Boskind-Lodahl, 1976). Binging and purging behavior is often learned from friends (Chiodo & Latimer, 1983; Boskind-White & White, 1983) and may be particularly common where groups of young women live together, (e.g., dorms and sororities). Although many of the bulimics studied are high academic achievers, they tend to see achievement "mainly in terms of what rewards it could provoke from others" (Boskind-Lodahl, 1976), not in terms of self-rewards, self-confidence, or the development of expertise. In fact, the only power base bulimics seem able to develop is beauty/thinness. One of Boskind-Lodahl's clients reported that her bulimia began after being suddenly dropped by her boyfriend without any explanation; "shortly after, I had my nose fixed and began to diet." Feeling powerless, she sought self-control and social influence through beauty and thinness. Bulimic women seem particularly dependent on the admiration of men, while at the same time fearing men's power to reject them (Boskind-Lodahl, 1976).

The establishment of eating plans and rituals helps bulimics to feel in control of their lives. When the rituals are challenged or the plans changed, bulimics may become quite anxious as they are reminded once again of their powerlessness (Root, et al., 1986). When things go as planned, however, the bulimic gains self-confidence and feelings of pride and self-efficacy because she has "the power to do what no one else can do: binge freely and not gain weight" (Freedman, 1986).

Compulsive Eating and Control

Blaming compulsive and binge eating on being out of control is a strategy women have learned from our culture. Several writers (Chernin, 1981; Fursland, 1986) have noticed a connection between women's desires for food and for sex. Society frowns equally on lust and gluttony exhibited by women who are encouraged to "just say no" to any offer of food or sex, no matter how they really feel about it. "Swept away" romantic fantasies lead to the belief that good things are out of one's control and can only be enjoyed when one suspends judgement. Romance novels and television advertising (e.g., the ice cream ad where the woman has just eaten a whole quart in one sitting and the announcer says, "If you don't feel guilty, it wasn't worth it" and the diet pill ad where the woman struggles in vain to resist a wind tunnel sucking her into the refrigerator) reinforces the idea that women should suspend judgement, let go, enjoy themselves and then feel guilty and berate themselves later. Don't decide, just let go and get swept away by powerful forces out of your control.

Bruch (1973) described an obese client who "was completely unable to control her food intake or any other aspect of her life. She experienced herself as controlled from the outside, lacking in initiative and autonomy, without a personality.'' Fat women report that they do not feel free to choose what they want to eat because their choices are dominated by the approval of thin people (Mayer, 1981). Thin people, friends, relatives and even strangers, freely comment on the food choices of fat women, offering unrequested advice on dieting. In theory, it would seem easy to shrug off such rudeness; yet, in practice, fat women know that thin people can expose them to public ridicule and discrimination (Mayer, 1981). Such unsolicited advice further undermines one's sense of self-control.

Of course, fatness has not always been seen as the result of out of control eating. In other cultures, and at other times in our own culture, weight was synonymous with wealth and health. At the turn of the century, with the description of the calorie, the publication of the first nutrition tables, the manufacture of household scales and the appearance of the first insurance company compiled weight charts, the "balanced body" came into vogue. Obesity came to mean overnutrition and dieting was seen as "an act of internal regulation, the balance of control of desire" (Schwartz, 1986). A popular medicinal compound of the time, Slenderine, advertised with the slogan "You at once become the master of your own body. You control your weight ever after" (Schwartz, 1986). By the rise of the flappers in the 1920s, thin was definitely in. Since then, the ideal female body has become progressively thinner.

Compulsive eaters feel the same sense of powerlessness as their anorexic and bulimic sisters. Their approach to dealing with their lack of power is to seek the comfort and self-nourishment that women have always known food provides. The compulsive eater knows, however, that women "should" deny their appetites and that those who do not are unbalanced and out of control. The more she labels herself as out of control, the more she believes that she is out of control, and the more compulsively she eats.

Unlike her anorexic and bulimic sisters who have gained a sense of personal power through self-destructive behavior, the compulsive eater has not won any battles and she knows it. She faces both her failure to exert much influence in the social and business worlds and her failure to exert much influence over her own actions. Constant feelings of failure and powerlessness drive her to the comfort food and eating provide, yet the comfort is temporary. In retrospect, the choice to eat does not seem voluntary and she thinks that she has lost control again. The compulsive eater is trapped in a vicious circle.

FEMINIST THERAPY FOR EMPOWERMENT

Feminist therapists can make an important contribution to the treatment of food obsessions in women by educating their clients about the cultural components of these obsessions. Women clients need help in becoming empowered to make and trust their own decisions, to exercise influence in the world and to gain confidence in their ability to do so. The suggestions that follow are meant to supplement, not replace, standard treatment approaches. The disordered eater may also be in family therapy, supportive group therapy, receiving nutritional counseling or engaged in behavioral monitoring.

A first step in the reduction of helplessness is the active participation of the client in therapy (Bruch, 1973). The client should decide with the therapist which of the following suggestions would be most helpful to her. Conversations about power and influence, food and control, and beauty standards help clients to understand their obsession and their position in society. Therapists should explain that from a young age, girls are taught that exhibiting personal characteristics associated with power and strength is inappropriate and thus adult women are often afraid to exercise power because of a lack of experience in doing so (Burden & Gottlieb, 1987). The therapist can aid the empowerment process for her clients by mentioning times when she, too, has felt unable to exercise power (Greenspan, 1986) and by pointing out powerful women role models. Clients should be encouraged to reject the conventional beauty ideal and decide what their own standard for personal attractiveness will be.

Standard therapy techniques like assertiveness training and the teaching of problem solving skills and interpersonal skills can help instill confidence and self-efficacy (Meichenbaum & Turk, 1987). Katzman, Weiss and Wolchik (1986) believe that inability to assert one's self is a major factor in compulsive eating and bulimic binging and suggest that their clients are eating instead of dealing with what's "eating them." Clients can be taught to use positive self-talk to guide them through their actions and to focus on successes. Attribution patterns must be changed; as clients learn to take credit for their successes, they will feel confident and empowered (Lips, 1981). Coyne (1987) suggests helping clients to see achievement in the fact that their situation is not worse than it is and encouraging them to tap the inner strength and resourcefulness that has kept them from sinking lower and use it to pull themselves up.

Therapists should help clients to reframe their negative cognitions and turn dead-end thinking around. Thoughts like "I have no willpower; I'm out of control" can be replaced with "I'm eating this because I want to" or "I'm making progress all the time, and I can't expect to be rid of lifelong problems in a few weeks" (Brownell, 1983). Therapists should encourage their clients to change their self-image from "victim" to "survivor" (Hartman, 1987).

Clients should learn to temper both their admiration for the excessive self-control of the anorexic and their distaste for the permissiveness of the nonrestrictive eater. They must learn to take for themselves the power to choose what and when to eat. Perfectionists can be encouraged to lower their expectations, thus increasing their opportunities to meet their goals and experience feelings of accomplishment (Katzman, et al., 1986) and empowerment.

To be seen as powerful by others, clients should learn to be more open and direct in their use of power and to take credit when their influence is successful. Remember, "modesty is the enemy of power" (Lips, 1981). To gain increased status, clients can become better educated, develop expertise, apply for promotions or sign up for vocational retraining. The therapist can suggest ways to project confidence and strength nonverbally.

To feel more powerful and confident, clients can develop physical strength (Lips, 1981) and fitness through aerobic exercise and weight training or through learning self-defense skills (Brown, 1985). Acting or voice lessons can give clients the confidence to project themselves into the world and enhance feelings of power and control (Brown, 1985).

Feminist therapy groups are effective empowerment tools for disordered eaters. Meeting with others who share similar problems removes guilt by emphasizing the universality of the problem (Hotelling, 1987); each woman learns that she is not alone. It may be easier in groups to mobilize anger and to build on women's strengths and experiences (Hartman, 1987). Group members can learn from others' successes, which also provide hope (Hartman, 1987; Hotelling, 1987) for those who have not come as far. To avoid reinforcing members' helplessness and dependence, group leaders must foster independence and encourage each woman to take responsibility for herself (Hartman, 1987).

Finally, clients with food obsessions should be encouraged to join a feminist group or to get involved with political activity. Working actively in feminist causes is empowering in itself, as we gain strength from our numbers. It also provides us with the opportunity to achieve increased power and status for all women.

REFERENCES

Bell, R. M. (1985). *Holy anorexia.* Chicago: University of Chicago Press.

Boskind-Lodahl, M. (1976). Cinderella's stepsisters: A feminist perspective on anorexia nervosa and bulimia. *Signs, 2,* 342–356.

Boskind-White, M., & White, W. C. (1983). *Bulimarexia: The binge/purge cycle.* New York: Norton.

Brown, L. (1985). Women, weight and power: Feminist theoretical and therapeutic issues. *Women and Therapy, 4*(1), 61–71.
Brownell, K. D. (1983). Obesity: Treatment effectiveness and adherence to behavioral programs. In R. K. Goodstein (Ed.), *Eating and weight disorders*
   (pp. 71–90). New York: Springer Publishing Company.
Bruch, H. (1973). *Eating disorders: Obesity, anorexia nervosa, and the person
   within.* New York: Basic Books.
Burden, D. S., & Gottlieb, N. (1987). Women's socialization and feminist
   groups. In C. M. Brody (Ed.), *Women's therapy groups: Paradigms of
   feminist treatment* (pp. 24–39). New York: Springer Publishing Company.
Chernin, K. (1981). *The obsession: Reflections on the tyranny of slenderness.* New
   York: Harper & Row.
Chiodo, J., & Latimer, P. R. (1983) Vomiting as a learned weight control tech-
   nique. *Journal of Behavior Therapy and Experimental Psychiatry, 14,* 131–136.
Clance, P. R., & Imes, S. A. (1978). The imposter phenomenon in high
   achieving women: Dynamics and therapeutic intervention. *Psychotherapy:
   Theory, Research and Practice, 15.*
Coyne, J. C. (1987). The concept of empowerment in strategic therapy. *Psy-
   chotherapy, 24,* 539–545.
Crisp, A. H. (1983). Treatment and outcome in anorexia nervosa. In R. K.
   Goodstein (Ed.) *Eating and weight disorders* (pp. 91–104). New York:
   Springer Publishing Company.
Davis, W. N. (1985). Epilogue. In R. M. Bell (Ed.), *Holy anorexia* (pp..
   180–190). Chicago: University of Chicago Press.
Deaux, K., & Emswiller, T. (1974). Explanations of performance on sex-linked
   tasks: What's skill for the male is luck for the female. *Journal of Personality
   and Social Psychology, 29,* 80–85.
Falbo, T. (1977). Relationships between sex, sex-role, and social influence.
   Psychology of Women Quarterly, 2, 62–72.
Freedman, R. (1986). *Beauty bound.* Lexington, MA: Lexington Books.
Friday, N. (1977). *My mother/my self.* New York: Delacorte.
Frieze, I. H., Parsons, J. E., Johnson, P. B., Ruble, D. N., & Zellman, G. L.
   (1978). *Women and sex roles: A social psychological perspective.* New York:
   Norton.
Fursland, A. (1986, March). *Food and sex: Women's desires and women's shame.*
   Paper presented at the meeting of the Association for Women in Psycholo-
   gy, Oakland, CA.
Greenspan, M. (1986). Should therapists be personal? Self-disclosure and ther-
   apeutic distance in feminist therapy. In D. Howard (Ed.), *The dynamics of
   feminist therapy* (pp. 5–17). New York: Haworth.
Guyot, G. W., Fairchild, L., & Hill, M. (1981). Physical fitness, sports participation, body build, and self-concept of elementary school children. *International Journal of Sports Psychology, 12,* 106–116.
Halmi, K., Falk, J., & Schwartz, E. (1981). Binge eating and vomiting: A survey of a college population. *Psychological Medicine, 11,* 697–706.
Hartman, S. (1987). Therapeutic self-help groups: A process of empowerment
   for women in abusive relationships. In C. M. Brody (Ed.), *Women's therapy*

groups: Paradigms of feminist treatment (pp. 67–81). New York: Springer Publishing Company.

Hotelling, K. (1987). Curative factors in groups for women with bulimia. In C. M. Brody (Ed.), *Women's therapy groups: Paradigms of feminist treatment* (pp. 241–251). New York: Springer Publishing Company.

Johnson, P. (1976). Women and power: Toward a theory of effectiveness. *Journal of Social Issues, 32,* 99–110.

Kahn, A. (1984). The power war: Male response to power loss under equality. *Psychology of Women Quarterly, 8,* 234–247.

Katzman, M. A., Weiss, L., & Wolchik, S. A. (1986). Speak, don't eat! Teaching women to express their feelings. In D. Howard (Ed.), *The dynamics of feminist therapy* (pp. 143–157). New York: Haworth.

Kipnis, D. (1976). *The powerholders.* Chicago: University of Chicago Press.

Lips, H. M. (1981). *Women, men, and the psychology of power.* Englewood Cliffs, NJ: Prentice-Hall.

Logue, A. W. (1986). *The psychology of eating and drinking.* New York: Freeman.

Mayer, V. (1981). Why liberated eating? *Women: A Journal of Liberation, 7,* 32–38.

Meichenbaum, D., & Turk, D. C. (1987). *Facilitating treatment adherence: A practitioner's guidebook.* New York: Plenum.

Millman, M. (1980). *Such a pretty face: Being fat in America.* New York: Norton.

Orbach, S. (1978). *Fat is a Feminist Issue.* New York: Berkely Books.

Raven, B. H. (1965). Social influence and power. In I. D. Steiner & M. Fishbein (Eds.), *Current studies in social psychology* (pp. 371–382). New York: Holt, Rinehart & Winston.

Raven, B. H., & Kruglanski, A. W. (1970). Conflict and power. In P. Swingle (Ed.), *The structure of conflict* (pp. 69–109). New York: Academic Press.

Rodin, J., Silberstein, L., & Striegel-Moore, R. (1985). Woman and weight: A normative discontent. In *Nebraska symposium on motivation* (pp. 267–304). Lincoln: University of Nebraska Press.

Root, M. P., Fallon, P., & Friedrich, W. N. (1986). *Bulimia: A systems approach to treatment.* New York: Norton.

Schwartz, H. (1986). *Never satisfied: A cultural history of diets, fantasies, and fat.* New York: Free Press.

Sherif, C. W. (1982). Needed concepts in the study of gender identity. *Psychology of Women Quarterly, 6,* 375–398.

Striegel-Moore, R. H., Silberstein, L. R., & Rodin, J. (1986). Toward an understanding of the risk factors for bulimia. *American Psychologist, 41,* 246–263.

Van Gelder, L. (1987, February). Dependencies of independent women. *Ms.,* pp. 36–38.

Weiss, S. R., & Ebert, M. (1983). Psychological and behavioral characteristics of normal weight bulimics and normal weight controls. *Psychosomatic Medicine, 45,* 293–303.

PART III

Process Dependencies

11

Codependency and Women: Unraveling the Power Behind Learned Helplessness

Patricia O'Gorman

This chapter will attempt to explore why so many women diagnose themselves as codependent. It has been suggested that defining codependency as learned helplessness can empower women since it refutes notions of their "sickness" or second-class status. Empowerment is needed by women who grow up in families offering them little protection from society's sexism towards women, and families which unwittingly replicate the negative attributes ascribed to women by sex role stereotypes. Further, it has been suggested that women joining Twelve Step self-help meetings such as Al-Anon and Adult Children of Alcoholics allows them to nurture each other, as well as to find solace and healing from the often unintended wounds inflicted by both society and their families. Women need the company of like kind, in order to identify and reinforce the strengths needed for their codependence recovery.

INTRODUCTION

What began as a term useful in describing the impact of alcoholism on others, primarily adult children of alcoholics, has now become a movement unto itself. And the codependency movement has expanded to include other groups. Currently many of those attending Adult Children of Alcoholics conferences and the Twelve Step self-help programs such as Al-Anon have no known alcoholic parent or relative. This has led to a plethora of new Twelve Step programs—Codependents Anonymous, Adult Children of Dysfunctional Families, Debtors Anonymous, to name just a few. A common link between all these programs is the high number of attendees who are women and who state that they have the "disease of codependency."

Perhaps the key to understanding the phenomenon of women rushing to diagnose themselves as codependent lies in understanding how alcoholics and other similarly dysfunctional families impact women and serve to reinforce the dominant society's negative stereotypes of women.

UNDERSTANDING CODEPENDENCY

There has been much recent emphasis on understanding the nature and treatment of codependency. While the term has generated many definitions, the simplest and most directional definition of codependence has been developed by O'Gorman and Oliver-Diaz (1987): "Codependency is a form of learned helplessness consisting of family traditions and rituals taught from one generation to the next concerning how the family teaches intimacy and bonding." To this definition has recently been added: "When codependency is viewed within this context, it comprises a type of relationship disorder" (O'Gorman, 1990b).

In viewing codependency it is important to understand that we are dealing with learned behavior and a relationship disorder. Codependent relationships are often characterized by an enmeshed quality that produces a great deal of tension and turmoil. The turmoil is most often generated by each party's unconscious desire to maintain their separateness as a person, and their fear that to own this differentiation will mean that they will be abandoned. In this way abandonment scenarios are enacted recreating childhood crises.

Herein lies an important distinction between "interdependency," which is relationship give and take, and compulsive dependence on another, (i.e., needing to live through someone else). Certainly the goal of therapy and recovery is not to be isolated, nor is it to need another in order to feel complete. Rather, healthy relationships allow individuals to move along a continuum, sometimes being together and sometimes being alone. Codependency is not fluid; instead it is a rigid response to relating with others.

Codependency as a Family Tradition

We learn to be codependent, we are not born that way. Codependence is acquired through our families of origin in the ways in which offspring learn, from observation and experience, how their emotional and physical needs are met. We need to learn how to express our love, to give, to ask for what we need and want, and we need to learn how to receive. We also need to learn how to negotiate, and to share. Our initial source for all of this information is the family. Within families, every new generation teaches the next its beliefs and its rules.

Sometimes these relatively simple lessons of life bring pain and isolation. The source of this difficulty, for the tens of millions affected by alcoholism and other family dysfunctions, is highly dysfunctional family rules, which unwittingly are taught and unconsciously obeyed.

Often these family rules are not perceived as dysfunctional nor as having painful consequences. Usually dysfunctional traditions, such as the use of alcohol to solve a problem, have been incorporated into family norms over a series of generations. Alcohol use may have begun as a specific reaction to a problem and gradually became used for a more general problem solving device. Eventually, in dysfunctional families, the system begins to organize around alcohol use, and develops an identity as a unit where alcohol is used to solve problems. This tendency, combined with a genetic predisposition to develop the disease of alcoholism, sets the stage for development of the typically dysfunctional alcoholic family.

Steinglass, Bennett, Wolin, and Reiss (1987) present a model for an intergenerational approach to understanding this phenomenon. They describe how a family can organize around the use of alcohol in three stages. In the first stage, a new couple creates traditions for their own home and family. If they come from alcoholic backgrounds, they are likely to borrow traditions from their families of origin. As a result, dysfunction has the potential to manifest itself within their newly created family unit. The middle stage is characterized by drinking to solve problems as well as developing problems in the use of alcohol. If the traditions of their family of origin are continued by attempting to stabilize the family through focusing on the alcoholic's volatility, then increasing rigidity in the approach to dealing with stress can be predicted. In the latter stage, the family finalizes its identity and leaves this as a legacy for future generations. If the identity is still as a family that organizes around the alcoholic's drinking or the alcoholic's attempts at sobriety, then this will be a pattern the next generation will borrow (O'Gorman & Oliver-Diaz, 1987).

Alcoholic and other dysfunctional families teach some specific rules concerning caretaking to female children, in particular. Violent intimacy occurring over and over becomes familiar and safe, even though it is painful (O'Gorman & Oliver-Diaz, 1989). The child learns to remain loyal to the family of origin by accepting pain in order to keep away the discomfort of the unknown (Oliver-Diaz & O'Gorman, 1988).

Consequently the child yells or precipitates being yelled at in order to be seen; hits or allows herself to be in a violent situation in order to be touched. It is also learned that intimacy occurs only under the influence of alcohol and drugs or that it is only safe to have intimacy with someone who is under the influence of a chemical. Either way, the cycle of addiction continues as use of a substance, or being with someone who uses, becomes an integral part of achieving intimacy. For the female child this begins to insure the reinforcement of her second class citizenship.

Sexualizing of the home is another problem for the child that sets the stage for codependency and can stem from how the parents model their intimate feelings for each other. If, as a prelude to being intimate, they are sexually provocative in front of the children, if they scream at each other, attack each other's ego, accuse each other of infidelities, name call, threaten bodily injury, and when exhausted finally are sexual, this sets up a pathological model for a child to learn. In this type of family where there is little protection for the children it is not uncommon, when the screaming stops, for a child to check on her parents. In being so concerned she may inadvertently witness them in a coital act, exposing the child to perhaps even greater confusion. Children in this type of family learn to associate being humiliated with being sexual. As a result, a teenager who does well in school may become attracted to someone who has a drug problem, as danger and sexuality seem inextricably linked.

As strident as these teachings are, they tend to remain in place over generations. Dysfunctional families tend to perpetuate themselves because the process of change is full of uncertainty, anxiety and probable pain (Papp, 1983). Consequently, the known seems easier, even if it is more painful. For once there is conscious knowledge of a problem the family can feel compelled to change, and this is frightening. Change is therefore discouraged. To protect its members from the unknown that change brings, a family often sees its rules as the unique, special way that their system relates to the world. To be part of a family, members learn rules. To break a rule is to begin to distance from the family. By learning and practicing what one's family holds to be true, members remain part of the family and its rules are perpetuated to the next generation (O'Gorman & Oliver-Diaz, 1987).

DEVELOPMENTAL ASPECTS OF CODEPENDENCY

We first learn by watching. Our parents, grandparents, aunts and uncles model appropriate behavior within our family. If one or more of our family members are codependent, meaning they assume a powerless stance in times of stress, then this pattern is internalized. We may acquire some of this information through screen memories that are acquired so early that they do not have words attached to them. Such memories include being in a crib, throwing food or playing. They may also be sensations around us that we record as fear or pleasure.

Watching is enhanced when we learn to speak. Now we can watch and listen. We have words to describe what we have experienced. Our ability to understand the world has tripled. In homes with alcoholism, listening can teach that the person who is right yells the loudest, or longest. Observing what goes on around us also teaches the consequences of noncompliance to family rules.

We also learn by imitating what we see around us. Not only can one learn how to perform tasks in this way, but it is also possible to learn how the family expresses feelings. A child may learn to be angry and hit her mother just as she saw her father do. In later life the same child, now a young adult, may seek out abusive relationships hoping someone will feel sorry for her and she will get attention. Children are practical, and they will search out what allows them to get their needs met.

The infant's first need is to master its environment, which is a formidable task in a dysfunctional home. A child's first success in mastery is to cry to relieve hunger pains. Children learn that by crying they can eliminate their distress. By learning how to reduce discomfort they can begin to influence and eventually master their environment.

Dependency is learned as a result of living in a family where a behavior is rewarded one time and punished the next. Children, in general, learn to be dependent on cues from their environment in order to know how to act. If the family teaches them that they should not follow their feelings but rather the actions of another, reacting instead of acting, then the child will grow up to be dependent (Mussen, Conger, & Kagan, 1969).

Codependency develops from an interruption in the learning process. The child's natural tendency to learn how to control and influence her environment is interrupted. The natural tendency to empower herself by validating her feelings and determining what is in her control is stymied by the rigidity of the family's defense structure (O'Gorman & Oliver-Diaz, 1989). This can cause the child to maintain an external locus of control rather than developing an internal locus of control.

Codependency is, on one level, a form of learned helplessness that results from the inconsistent and contradictory messages sent to the child as a result of the alcoholic family's "wet" (when the alcoholic is drinking) and "dry" (when the alcoholic is not drinking) behavior.

In alcoholic families, learning what is the right behavior means being cued into a constantly fluid environment containing rigid rules which demand compliance. The perceptive child grows to learn how to watch the family so that under each changing set of circumstances, such as the alcoholic parent being drunk, hung over or dry, the child will know how to act. When the cues keep changing, and the consequences are severe, the child becomes dependent on these external cues in order to know what to do (O'Gorman, 1976).

The brighter the child and the more in-tune with her or his environment, then the more anxious she or he will become. In a typical alcoholic family scenario, the child may ask if the fighting is over, "Is Mommy all right? Is Daddy still sick?" She will be met by the family's denial that there is or was a problem. The repeated denial of dysfunctional behavior is traumatic for the child. It begins to force her to deny what she has seen, heard and experienced as a way of protecting herself against future violence. This denial also serves the function of bonding the child to the family. As she denies what she knows, she joins other family members who are protecting themselves by the use of denial within the family life.

Gradually the child learns to "discount" her internal perception of what she experiences and begins to rely more on what others say. She learns to be helpless in responses to her world and continues to feel acted upon, as opposed to perceiving herself as powerful and an initiator. Her immature "outer" directedness is maintained by the family. Even when a drinking parent recovers, this "outer directedness" or external locus of control continues. Adolescents from recovering alcoholic homes tend to feel more externally controlled than their peers from nonaddicted families. The dysfunctional family reinforces the child's external locus of control and inhibits the child's natural development of an internal locus of control. In research on children from recovering families, their development of an internal locus of control was found to be significantly delayed. In other words as the child learns to discount her perceptions, she learns to be helpless and dependent on what is outside herself (O'Gorman, 1976).

Codependency results from an adaptation to living within an addicted family. In essence, by living with addiction one needs to learn two sets of rules. There are rules for when a parent is drinking and contact is allowed; but, often it is negative and painful. There are also rules for the dry cycle when contact is not allowed and possibly punished by guilt and total responsibility for what occurs. One result of the codependent coping style is that in order to successfully move from one set of rules to another, one's intuitive feelings have to be discounted.

By learning to trust external cues only, the child learns dependency as well as the belief that feeling good comes from sources external to the self. This explains why many children of alcoholics become dependent on others when in a relationship. It also explains why such children learn to eat, drink, take drugs, work, gamble, spend or have sex compulsively (O'Gorman & Oliver-Diaz, 1987).

The Challenges of Being Female

Miller (1976) speaks about women being society's "carriers" for certain aspects of the human experience. This has to do with their relationship to nurturing, which is essential for human development and the maintenance of relationships. Women represent "connectedness," which requires being vulnerable, able to admit to one's neediness, fears, dependencies, as well as one's strengths and visions.

To venture into this realm is not without its costs. From the dominant culture's perspective, feeling empathetic and compassionate is to suffer from ineffective thought and action, which jeopardizes one's chances for success (Miller, 1976). We have certainly witnessed upwardly mobile women attempting to become successful by the dominant culture's standards. They work excessively; take few if any, vacations; dress nonthreateningly; frequently live hundreds of miles from their significant others, and postpone childbearing.

They evidence none of the passivity in their work life that is the cornerstone of the traditional Freudian concept of femininity, but they also appear to have given up on their capacity for relationships (Johnson, 1988). Many women continue to focus on their similarity to men, particularly in the world of work, instead of allowing themselves to explore their uniqueness, which is part of the special qualities of being a woman. This was certainly true among the early feminists in the sixties and seventies when issues of work and equality were stressed. But women are different than men and it continues to be a difference that can be embraced with success.

Many have been making it by the above standards only to learn, as Schwartz (1989) maintains, that there is a two track system in the corporate world. Career-primary women are those who will not interrupt their career for a family and are on a competitive fast-track with men. Career-secondary women decide to combine professional pursuits with having a family and are on the "Mommy track." This dichotomy is similar to what Ehrenreich and English (1989) call the "breeders" and "strivers." Such a system does little to advance women, and further is reminiscent of earlier attempts to devalue women's capacities and needs.

All of this combines to barrage women with notions of their second class status, which can lead to feelings of powerlessness and low self-esteem. The alcoholic family literally teaches that all family members are secondary to the alcoholic, which reinforces societal views of women as "less than" beings. Consequently elements of codependency strike close to many qualities associated with being a woman. Society's attitudes of women as auxiliary, second class or "less than," combined with dysfunctional family dynamics focusing on the need to control and take care of others, conditions females to be codependent.

Learning to be Helpless

Learned helplessness is a concept that has been used to explain depression (Seligman, 1975) particularly in women (De Lange, 1980). It addresses the fact that due to trauma, one can be conditioned to see that one's actions have little or no impact on resolving problems or providing rewards.

There are four common themes in the concept of learned helplessness: (a) no perceived control of the environment; (b) no task involvement; (c) disrupted normal routines; and (d) the avoidance of social support (Garber and Seligman, 1980). Each one of these themes brings added light to understanding the development of codependence.

The first theme, little control or mastery over the environment, often begins with the child's realization that she or he cannot control parental drinking, arguing, illness or other major and repeated parental behaviors that are consistently detrimental to the child's home life. This has already been discussed under the maintenance of the child's external locus of control by dysfunctional families. This lack of power begins to be generalized from parental behaviors to school, peer and recreational activities, leading the child to develop a more limited range of coping devices than his or her peers (Flannery, 1986).

The second theme of learned helplessness is passivity in the face of disturbing stimuli, while simultaneously worrying, being angry, frightened and thinking about them. At the same time that the child feels powerless to do anything about the problem, it also consumes a great deal of emotional energy which could be going into social and academic development (Flannery, 1986).

Disrupted normal routines are the third theme of "learned helplessness." Here the child has difficulty in knowing what is "normal," for what is expected will change depending on the cycle of the drinking or abuse (O'Gorman, 1990b). This means it is difficult for the child to develop clear expectations and to have a sense of security at home (Flannery, 1986). This lack of feeling secure translates over time to low self-esteem and poor self-concept.

Avoidance of social support is the fourth theme of learned helplessness. The child becomes fearful of what she or he will find at home and gradually begins to disengage socially (Flannery, 1986). The child begins to feel different and to reach out to others less often, as she or he is not sure how to share what is happening at home. Withdrawal also serves to protect the child from being seen by others as disempowered and helpless.

It is interesting to note that neither the passage of time, nor exposure to a traumatic situation with a successful outcome, alters the basic helplessness of the subject's reaction (Garber & Seligman, 1980).

In women from dysfunctional families it may well be that this process is intensified and they are more at risk for developing learned helplessness. Sex role training results in overprotection and reduced opportunity for exploring and gaining environmental mastery (De Lange, 1980), and so increases women's susceptibility to becoming dependent. As a result, the young girl's desire for control and mastery over her environment can be thwarted by the desire of parents who attempt to protect her, rather than allow her to experience pain and help her to resolve it. An outcome of learned helplessness is difficulty in attributing success to one's own efforts (an indicator of an internal locus of control). Because women are prone to learned helplessness, they are less likely to credit themselves with having been successful. When success is achieved, they are more likely to attribute it to chance rather than take credit for the event, which demonstrates a proclivity for an external locus of control (De Lange, 1980). Also, under stress women are more likely to blame themselves and less likely to deflect the responsibility elsewhere. This can lead to a loss of self-esteem due to self-depreciatory and self-critical attitudes in an attempt to reduce isolation (De Lange, 1980).

Being a woman in our society sets the stage of codependency. Three of the four themes of learned helplessness are in evidence in the development of women even before the specific impact of the alcoholic or other dysfunctional family begins. The graphic influence of dysfunctional families tilts the already delicate balance for women towards codependency.

TREATING CODEPENDENCY FROM A FEMINIST PERSPECTIVE

Feminism offers an important tool in understanding codependency. Feminism, in general, is concerned with ending domination and resisting oppression and, as such, is a global view and is not restricted to "women's" issues (Van Den Bergh & Cooper, 1986). The use of power is a central concern for feminists and, as such, a feminist perspective provides an interesting focus for viewing codependence.

For example, feminists have stressed the importance of being able to name one's own reality. This means breaking out of stereotypes as well as breaking the silence of how one has been abused and oppressed. Consequently, renaming oneself as an adult child of an alcoholic or as an incest survivor is important and empowering because it provides personal validation for speaking about one's feelings and experiences. As a result, an internal locus of control can begin to develop for those conditioned to look outside themselves for a sense of meaning and purpose in life. To the extent that a woman can begin to name her own experience and to share that with others, the insidious blame/shame acquired as part of growing up within an alcoholic family can be expunged. Also, by sharing one's experiences in a Twelve Step or treatment group, a woman can see her experience was not idiosyncratic; that many other women have had comparable experiences. This also helps in dissipating the guilt and shame which can undergird codependence. It allows a woman to see that the "personal is political;" that is, similar events occuring to many women bespeak a society permeated with sexist, pejorative beliefs about women.

Basic to feminist thinking is the concept that each woman knows herself best and is her own expert in what she needs (Kaschak, 1981). This concept allows women to be active in redefining their value and worth as persons, the goals they would like to pursue as well as the significance of relationships in their lives.

Codependency leads to a lack of independent action as the person or activity on which the dependency is centered becomes the focus of emotional energy and activity. This is shown in a number of ways including needing to live through the other, taking care of him or her in lieu of caring for oneself, developing dependencies on eating, work, gambling, spending and sex. All of those behaviors are examples of an external locus of control that undergirds codependence. Reaching for something outside of the self is done to both relieve tension and provide enjoyment—but the latter rarely occurs.

The feminist concept of empowerment can be used to treat codependency by giving each woman "permission" to disengage from her enmeshed relationships. This releases psychic energies that can be used to begin a journey toward establishing a separate and complete identity. The very process of beginning disengagement will bring to the surface issues of low self-esteem. However, this process becomes empowering as women realize that their primary mission and purpose in life is not to put caring for others ahead of caring for themselves.

Women who are codependent can be seen as pursuing the archetypal Great Mother in their relationships with others. They seek to be everything to those they love; all nurturing, all powerful, all protective, bestowing blessings, tenderness and benevolence. However, women become impatient or punishing with themselves when the other aspect of the Great Mother appears, the dark side; that of the destroyer, the depriver, the avenger (Carlson, 1989). It is so often a lack of acceptance of these darker feelings that keeps women from disengaging from codependent relationships.

In this sense the treatment of codependence needs to allow women to move from a point of view that only asks "How are they doing?" to a point of view that also asks "How am I doing?" In doing this, an internal balance can be established.

The pain of codependence can be the most helpful tool to use in treating those with the disorder. This pain and turmoil can lead a woman to reevaluate herself, not only as a family member but also as an individual with unique gifts that she needs to accept. Women need to see their affective and intuitive capabilities not as liabilities but as strengths. Women need to be able to define strengths in their own terms and to make allowances for their destructive desires. Strength can be seen as setting limits, boundaries, and assertively saying "no."

Some feminists such as Adrienne Rich, have called for a new language in which to capture and authentically name our experiences (Carlson, 1989). A new language would allow us to reveal more, to risk more in letting others know who we are and to let us know more about ourselves.

CODEPENDENCY TREATMENT GUIDELINES FOR WOMEN

Developing Realistic Treatment Goals

Recovery is not about making all of one's emotional pain go away. Recovery is about resolving trauma by remembering it: understanding both one's own and another's role within the trauma, making peace with what happened and moving on with one's life. The trauma needs to be decentralized as the organizing principle of one's life. Recovery is about resolving trauma and making room in one's life for other events (Oliver-Diaz & O'Gorman, 1988).

Owning the aspects of the Goddess and of the Great Mother that are seen in each woman, can allow women to move beyond the past to creating a new role for themselves in a life built around their truly feminine aspirations.

Encouraging Social Support by Encouraging Attendance at Twelve Step Recovery Groups

Women are more vulnerable to stress when they are deprived of intimate conversations, affection and attachment. Our society has certainly witnessed the alienation of women from each other. This was particularly true when the "stay-at-home-Mom" was the norm. However, with the significant entrance of women into the workforce, it may become easier for women to find "bonding spaces." Women need to be encouraged to seek out the support of others, and this may account for why so many women are found in Adult Child of Alcoholics meetings. Here, in a predominantly female setting, women can experience the nurturance of woman to woman healing in the sisterhood of a recovering community.

Feminist therapy encourages group experiences where women can hear other women's experiences. "The personal is political" comes into play as they see their individual experiences as similar to that of many other women. New meanings occur for old hurts when risks are taken with one's peers; personal pain can be healing when shared with other women and it can create feelings of validation and empowerment.

Redefining the Concept of Codependency

Women should not be told that they are "sick" because they are codependent. With such labeling women may act accordingly because of poor self-esteem. Defining the concept of codependency as "learned helplessness" is empowering because it allows women to know what to do with their codependence (i.e., to learn to help themselves so as to become empowered).

Using Empowering Concepts such as Self-Parenting

Women are the traditional caretakers of society but they need to learn how to take care of themselves. Self-parenting implies that one has the capacity to nurture oneself.

Emphasizing Strengths and Accomplishments

What has been found in anecdotal treatment reports is that when women believe that they have been damaged, they also believe their children have similarly been damaged. This fear of contagion needs to be directly dealt with by talking about one's parenting behaviors and roles. It is crucial to focus on their strengths and accomplishments as mothers, in addition to providing practical information on parenting effectiveness techniques. Additionally, information about when and how to explain codependency to children, in age appropriate terms and concepts, should be shared with clients.

Focusing on Growth

Treatment should build up women's self-esteem by honing their ego strengths. Same-sex groups can be very effective with women as they allow the experience of validation by peers. Retreats that allow women a "time out" from their commitment to work and personal life can also be important. Additionally, individual work that allows women to make peace with their human neediness can be empowering. It is ultimately debilitating to try to be perfect, a goal for many with codependency. Women need to understand and make peace with their vulnerabilities, yearnings and needs, in order to move beyond codependent relationships.

Encouraging a Spiritual Exploration

Transcendence is an important human need, a crucially important female need. Transcendence over immediate and past trauma is facilitated by developing a sense of spirituality. Acquiring a belief system of inherent purposefulness can solidify a sense of personal worth, value and esteem, and can help to develop an internal locus of control.

The very development of spirituality is consistent with feminist theory and principles; both are holistic perspectives and concern the interrelatedness of one's mind, body and spirit. Concepts found in readings on the Goddess and Great Mother, as well as the Virgin Mary, the Old Testament story of Ruth and Native American Mother Earth, provide a rich network for beginning a feminist spiritual dimension. In fact, the earliest religions were based on feminine deities and embodied truths that can be nurturing to those struggling with codependency. The old religion stressed life as essentially a process, a "becoming," instead of a "being" (Carlson, 1989). Such concepts can empower women to free themselves from self-definitions based only on their past, while allowing them to be in the present, "becoming" who they are.

SUMMARY

This chapter has attempted to explore why women are at risk for codependence. It has suggested that codependency, viewed as learned helplessness, can be viewed as an inevitable outcome of sex role stereotyping and women's second class status. Empowerment is needed by women who grow up in families that offer them little protection from the negativity of the dominent society toward women, and familes that echo and amplify many of the negative attributes ascribed to women by sex role stereotypes. Further, it has been suggested that women joining Twelve Step self-help meetings, such as Al-Anon and Adult Children of Alcoholics, can nurture each other by finding solace and healing for the wounds inflicted by both society and their families.

This fact should be kept in mind when working with women. They need the company of like kind with whom they can identify and reinforce the strengths they need in order to recover.

REFERENCES

Carlson, K. (1989). *In her image: The unhealed daughters search for her mother*. Boston: Shambhala Books.

De Lange, J. (1980). Depression in women: Explanations and prevention. In A. Weick & S. T. Vandiver (Eds.), *Women, power and change*. First NASW Conference on Social Work Practice with Women.

Ehrenreich, B., & English, D. (1989). Blowing the whistle on the "mommy track." *Ms.*, Vol. xviii, Nos. 1 & 2, pp. 56–63.

Flannery, R. B. (1986), The adult children of alcoholics: Are they trauma victims with learned helplessness? *Journal of Social Behavior and Personality*, Volume 1, No. 4, pp. 497–504).

Garber, J., & Seligman, M. E. D. (Eds.). (1980). *Human helplessness: Theory and application.* New York: Academic Press.

Johnson, M. (1988). *Strong mothers, weak wives: The search for gender equality.* Berkeley: University of California.

Kaschak, E., (1981). Feminist psychotherapy: The first decade. In S. Cox (Ed.), (2nd ed.), *Female psychology: The emerging self.* New York: St. Martin's Press.

Miller, J. B. (1976). *Toward a new psychology of women.* Boston: Beacon Press.

Mussen, P., Conger, J., Kagon, J. (1969). *Child development and personality.* 3rd edition. New York: Harper & Row.

Oakley, A. (1981). *Subject women.* New York: Pantheon Books.

O'Gorman, P. (1976). Self-concepts, locus of control and perception of father in adolescents from homes with and without severe drinking problems. Doctoral Dissertation, Fordham University.

O'Gorman, P. (1990a, January-February). Teaching parenting skills. *Counselor Magazine,* pp. 20–21, 45.

O'Gorman, P. (1990b, March-April). Developmental aspects of codependency. *Counselor Magazine,* pp. 14–16.

O'Gorman, P., & Oliver-Diaz, P. (1987). *Breaking the cycle of addiction for adult children of alcoholics.* Deerfield Beach, FL: Health Communications.

O'Gorman, P., & Oliver-Diaz, P. (1989). *Creating healthy families!* (audio tape). Boulder, CO: Sounds True.

Oliver-Diaz, P. & O'Gorman, P. (1988). *12 steps to self parenting for adult children.* Deerfield Beach, FL: Health Communications.

Papp, P. (1983). The process of change. New York: The Guilford Press.

Schwartz, F. (1989, January-February). Management women and the new facts of life. *Harvard Business Review,* pp. 67–74.

Seligman, M. E. D. (1975). *Helplessness: On depression, development, and death.* San Francisco: Freeman.

Steinglass, P., Bennett, L., Wolin, S., & Reiss, D. (1987). *The alcoholic family.* New York: Basic Books.

Van Den Bergh, N., & Cooper, L, B. (Eds.). *Feminist visions for social work.* Silver Springs, MD: National Association of Social Workers.

12

Looking for Love in All the Wrong Places

Jed Diamond

OVERCOMING ROMANTIC AND SEXUAL ADDICTIONS

When people find that their romantic relationships are a series of disappointments yet continue to pursue them, they are looking for love in all the wrong places. When they are overwhelmed by their physical attraction to a new person, when the chemistry feels "fantastic," and they are sure that this time they have found someone who will make them whole, they are looking for love in all the wrong places. When they are in committed relationships but find themselves constantly attracted to others, they are looking for love in all the wrong places. When their desire for "more sex and romance" interferes with their family or professional lives, they are looking for love in all the wrong places. When they are as preoccupied with not having sex as others are with having it, they are looking for love in all the wrong places.

Clinicians and researchers have only recently recognized that hidden below the surface of this endless search for love and romance is a deadly addiction. Stanton Peele (1975), one of the first serious researchers to focus on relationship addictions says:

> Many of us are addicts, only we don't know it. We turn to each other out of the same needs that drive some people to drink and others to heroin. Interpersonal addiction—love addiction—is just about the most common yet least recognized form of addiction we know (p. 1).

Peele makes clear that love is an ideal vehicle for addiction because it can so exclusively claim a person's consciousness. Addictive relationships are patterned, predictable and isolated. When a person goes to another with the aim of filling an inner void, the relationship quickly becomes the center of his or her life. The core of addiction comes from the void we feel inside that continually calls out to be filled.

There is still controversy and confusion over definitions in this relatively new, emerging field of study (Coleman, 1987). However, the following is offered as a working definition of sexual or romantic addiction: Pursuing sexual or romantic behavior in an attempt to relieve emotional pain and fill a perceived inner void. This behavior is compulsive, out of control and continues in spite of adverse effects on one's life.

One of the major programs designed for relationship addicts, Sex and Love Addicts Anonymous (SLAA), describe the people who are its members as suffering from a compulsive need for sex, and/or a desperate attachment to one person. What all members have in common are obsessive/compulsive patterns, either sexual, emotional or both, in which relationships or activities have become increasingly destructive to all areas of their lives—career, family and sense of self-respect (Augustine Fellowship Sex and Love Addicts Anonymous, 1985, p. 2).

Clinically, there are two types of sex and romance addicts. One type is hooked on *attachment*. They become dependent on one person and remain in bad relationships. Robin Norwood (1985) called them "women who love too much," though men can just as easily become hooked on attachment. The other type of sex romance addict is hooked on *attraction*. He or she thrives on romantic intrigue and has difficulty committing to a single relationship.

Experts estimate that one in 12 adults is sexually addicted (Carnes, 1988) and many more are romantically addicted. Although the two types can overlap, those hooked on romance are looking to "be in love," while those addicted to sex seek the excitement of a purely sexual encounter.

Relationship addictions have become so pervasive that they are almost normative. Peele (1975, p. 6) says of our compulsive search for sex and love, "Addiction is not an abnormality in our society. It is not an aberration from the norm; it is itself the norm." My own clinical experience suggests that the core of this addictive search arises from childhood abuse and neglect. Feeling damaged by a lack of trusting and accepting nurturance as youths, addicts go on an endless search for intimacy. By finding that "perfect relationship" they believe that the inner void can be filled and self-completeness can be restored.

Since people can never find their missing selves in others, their relationship inevitably become excessive. An examination of the life of Janis Joplin, a rock/blues sixties music legend, can help us understand the behavior of addicts.

Her biographer, David Dalton (1971), described Joplin in a way that personifies the way many sex romance addicts see "love:"

Janis insisted on following the bright, colorblind, toenail party of love. Like the fantasy worlds of Gothic Romances and Coke commercials, her notion of love was of such excessive proportions, so extreme and absurd, that it transcended not just the real world but also any real possibility of satisfaction. Janis wanted to make up for the pain of a lifetime in one love affair (p. 52).

Sex and romance addicts seem always to be moving toward that magical something and away from where they are. They are like confused homing pigeons, flying faster and faster, but in the wrong direction.

What are some of the commonalities in life experience that predispose people to sex and romance addiction? Wounded as children, many become afraid to risk developing intimate attachments to others as adults. One man in recovery from addictive relationships, reflecting on his childhood, had this to say. "Looking back today with the help of therapy, I can see that I was a physically and emotionally abused child. When I discovered sexuality, I fell in love with it." He acknowledged two themes in his adult life that are common for those addicted to sex or romance, fear and desire. "I looked for situations where I could experience sexual contact without emotional entanglements—sex without commitment." Yet as addicts run faster and faster to get away from their childhood fears, they get farther and farther away from their only true source of love—themselves.

What's the relationship between sexual and romantic addictions and other addictions? Carnes (1983), draws a parallel between sex and romance addictions and chemical dependencies. Like an alcoholic, sex and romance addicts substitute a sick relationship with something outside themselves for a healthy relationship with others. Carnes notes that "For the addict, the sexual experience is the source of nurturing, focus of energy, and origin of excitement" (p. 16). The addict's relationship with a mood-altering experience becomes central to his or her life.

Dr. Eli Coleman (1987), Associate Director of the Human Sexuality Program, University of Minnesota Medical School, points out the pattern of excesses, the lack of control, the amount of preoccupation and the disruption of their lives that is characteristic of people who are having problems with their sexual and romantic relationships. The same patterns are present for other addictions.

Coleman goes on to make an important distinction between healthy expressions of sexuality and unhealthy or destructive sexuality. He makes no value judgement about any particular expression of sexual or romantic interest. He points out that pornography, prostitution, masturbation, homosexual or heterosexual intercourse, affairs, anonymous sex or sexual fetishes may be either addictive or nonaddictive. It is the pattern of the sexual behavior, it's motivation and the resultant outcomes that determine whether it is addictive or nonaddictive.

Peele (1975) says that an addiction exists when someone's attachment to a person or sensation lessens their ability to deal with other things in the environment or with personal needs. The sex or romantic addict becomes increasingly dependent on sexual behavior as their only source of gratification. It is a sterile, ingrown dependency relationship with another person who serves as the object of one's need for security (p. 1). The "addiction" doesn't come from the "thing," be it a drug or another person, but from the internal void that continually calls out to be filled.

Anne Wilson Schaef (1987) says that more and more people are using sex and romance as way of getting a fix, rather than as a means of relating. For many couples she sees in therapy, "getting enough sex" translates into avoiding tensions and feelings. They use lovemaking to keep from dealing with themselves. When a sex and romance addict gets a fix, it serves the same purpose as a drink or a drug, and the personality dynamics that develop are essentially the same.

In sum, sexual and romantic addiction is an unhealthy relationship characterized by compulsion, loss of control, cutting off from self and others and continued involvement despite problems that it causes in a person's life.

Who Are Sex and Romance Addicts?

We may think of sex and romance addicts as "those people," yet they are more likely to be individuals pursuing "normal lives," just like ourselves. Let's meet some of the people who have become hooked on sex and romance. Diamond (1988) introduced a number of such people in his book *Looking for Love in All the Wrong Places: Overcoming Romantic and Sexual Addictions:*

Richard, age 32, licensed psychologist, married with two children:

I became a psychologist because I wanted to help people and I'm sure, on some level, to work out some of my own hangups from childhood. I've always had a strong desire to have a family. I met my wife when we were both students in college. We married young and had two children in succession.

When the kids were small she stayed home and I rapidly rose in my field of community mental health treatment. Things seemed to go well between us until the kids went off to school and Dorothy wanted to get a job. I was all for it, and still am, but she seemed to lose interest in me in her excitement to get herself established.

As a psychotherapist, patients are always falling in love with their "doctor." Although I've been tempted a few times in the past, I could always restrain myself. I'd remind myself about my professional ethics, the needs of the patient, and my own happy home. Lately I can't keep my eyes, and sometimes my hands, off women who come to see me. I'm elated when a new client is an attractive woman and disappointed when it's a man. I look for ways to hold on to her hand a little longer when we touch to say goodbye. God, I even find myself losing track of what a particularly attractive patient is saying. I find I'm thinking about what she would be like with her dress pulled up and me making love to her on the couch.

I haven't acted on these fantasies, but I can't seem to stop them. I know many other people in the helping professions—psychiatrists, psychologists, social workers, clergy—who are having the same problem. Some I know have slept with their clients. Some justify it as "therapeutic," while others candidly admit that is is wrong, but they can't control themselves.

Sometimes I think it wouldn't be so bad to go all the way. Maybe I would get it out of my system. Yet I know what I'm doing is dangerous and I feel terribly guilty about taking money from clients while I'm lusting after them in my mind. I got into this field to help people and now I think it's me who needs help.

Jennifer, age 30, buyer for a large department store, single:

Most men think I am pretty and I never have had a problem getting dates. Yet I still feel like the "chubby girl with glasses" I remember from my fourth grade picture. I could go out every night if I wanted to accept all the invitations I get, but the problem is the kind of men I attract.

They always look good, at first. They are handsome, well dressed, intelligent, and successful. But invariably we get involved in some kind of dangerous romantic activity. I have been going out with this one guy, Tom, for about a year and he seems like a really nice, "normal" kind of man. We like each other's company and enjoy making love. Yet he often wants to tie me up, which really turns him on, and our love making always seems to have an edge of suppressed violence. I don't like it, but I can't seem to say "no" to him. I've threatened to leave, but I never get the courage to go through with it. Whenever I hint about our relationship not being right, he showers me with tenderness and love. He brings me presents, treats me like a queen, and once again I am swept off my feet. But, underneath his smile I sometimes detect a frightening look in his eyes, like if I ever did leave he might do something to harm me. I'm never sure whether I'm attracted to his gentleness or the violence that seems to be just below the surface. I don't know why I keep attracting men like this, but its beginning to worry me.

What do these two cases point out about the dynamics of sex and romantic addiction? First, both of these individuals seem to feel that there is something missing at the center of their being. Second, both display a level of sadness and depression that is dealt with by seeking excitement and thrills in their sexual and romantic lives. They both live "on the edge" and run the risk of physical and emotional injury. Finally, they both seem external in their locus of control. That is, a great deal of their self-worth is derived by how other people see them. It is not necessarily a problem to allow for the development of identity and esteem by seeking connection with others. But it is a problem when the primary emphasis for self-worth is placed on pleasing others.

Mental health literature indicates that healthy individuals have a balance between their internal and external locus of control. To be internal means to believe that you can be the prime mover in determing what happens in your life; that your identity rests on your own validation. Persons with an external locus do not believe that they are "captains of their ship;" they believe others determine the course of their life. It has been empirically validated that individuals who are depressed have an external sense of control. This seems to mean that they have a pervasive sense of loss, believing there is something essential missing in them.

It would seem that an overly external locus of control would be predictive of relationship addiction. If one believes that he or she is missing something essential for survival and that the core of their being is bad, they are drawn on a search outside themselves. If these beliefs are coupled with the feelings that people cannot be trusted and that sex and romance are essential for survival, relationship addictions are very likely to result.

In summary, both Richard and Jennifer personify relationship addicts. They have begun to sacrifice their true selves for the illusion of sexual and romantic fulfillment.

Feminist Perspective on Sex and Romance Addicts

How does the prior explanation relate to a feminist perspective on relationship addiction? Women, particularly, are socialized to believe that it is their responsibility to ensure that relationships in their life are positive. Additionally, caring for others' needs is considered to be a female mandate, even when that behavior involves self-sacrifice. Martyrdom is almost a *sine qua non* of traditional feminine sex role socialization. Women are socialized to become "attachment" addicts, deriving their experience of aliveness from their connection with another.

This is not to suggest that men are immune from being pathologically external in their locus of control. However, there has been some empirical evidence that as a rule, men are more internal than external in locus. It may be that men who have subscribed to the "cult of machismo," which emphasizes conquest of others as a test of true masculinity, are most "at risk" for developing addictions to "attraction." Particularly for adolescent males, much value seems to be placed on being able to share stories with buddies of "how much they got" from female dates.

A feminist perspective on relationship addiction, then, suggests that the etiology of the phenomenon may emmanate from oversubscription to traditional sex role stereotypes of what it is to be a male and female in society. Women who fall prey to this syndrome will tend to abandon themselves in order to receive the attention and approval of others. Men, on the other hand, will tend to focus on conquering others, through sex, in order to prove their virility.

A feminist perspective on sex and romance addiction can also assist us in understanding the roots of addiction traceable to early childhood experience. Research reported by Carnes (1988), indicates a high level of child abuse in those experiencing problems with sexually addictive behavior. In a sample of 351 addicts, 72 percent indicated they had been abused physically, 83 percent reported being abused sexually, and 97 percent said they had been abused emotionally. Although females report more child abuse than do males, Carnes believes that males have less conscious memory of abuse and more often see sexual experiences between a male youth and female adult as "scoring early" rather than as child abuse.

Abused children develop feelings of shame that many feel is at the center of the addict's belief system, driving his or her addictive search away from self and toward others. (Fossum & Mason, 1987; Kaufman, 1980; & Kurtz, 1981). The core of shame that drives sex and romance addicts is the same for males and females. Both feel damaged and believe that something essential is missing within them. However, there are differences in the way our sexist culture conditions males and females to understand that damage and look for their missing self. The qualities men are taught they *cannot* be are the exact qualities women are taught they *must* be and vice versa (Neitlich, 1985). For example, men *cannot* be and women *must* be: loving, nurturing, tender, feeling, domestic, beautiful, soft, curvey, thin, passive, receptive, nice, sweet, quiet, giving, apologetic. Additionally, men *must* be and women *cannot* be: economically powerful, physically strong, courageous, cool, stoic, protective, responsible, logical, active, aggressive, hairy, athletic, muscular, outspoken, rugged, tough.

It isn't surprising to find that men are more often hooked on *attraction*—the compulsive search for new and exciting sexual and romantic interest. Women, on the other hand, are more often hooked on *attachment*—the compulsive need to hold onto a single relationship no matter how bad it gets. Those who are dependent on their attraction to a succession of relationships have an exaggerated need for *space*. Their irrational fear is of being *trapped* or *engulfed*. However, for those dependent on attachment, their primary need is for *connection*. They have irrational fears of *loss* or *abandonment*.

A feminist approach to treating sex and romance addicts would begin with recognizing that the damage to the individual caused by childhood abuse is compounded by sex role stereotypes. Rigid beliefs about masculinity and femininity deter the development of psychic balance by suggesting that we can only be complete by attaching ourselves to "an other." Effective treatment must deal with both the individual manifestations of addiction as well as the social conditioning that fuels it.

Treating Sex and Romance Addicts: How It Works

Most effective recovery programs have, at their core, a close tie between client involvement in a Twelve Step program such as Sex and Love Addicts Anonymous (SLAA) as well as effective psychotherapy.

In the initial ''checking out'' period, the professional can help a client recognize their addiction, understand it, and prepare them for involvement in SLAA. The Twelve Step group can provide peer support and guidance in the early stages of recovery. At this therapeutic stage, involvement in SLAA and beginning to ''work the steps'' should be given greater emphasis than psychotherapy. In the latter stages of recovery, a therapist once again becomes vital in connecting individuals with the lost parts of themselves and with their social environment. The client can be helped in recognizing that ''the personal is political'' in the sense that their addiction relates to imbalances within the social structure. A therapist can encourage clients to challenge sex role stereotypes and gender-mandated behaviors that could be precursors for addictive episodes.

It is also crucial for psychotherapists to recognize their own addictions. Addiction doesn't occur to a few unfortunates, and having acquired professional credentials doesn't make one immune. Therapists who recognize this view and have been actively involved in their own recovery can be considered ''two-hatters.'' They understand recovery from the inside out and can use their own experience in helping clients. By recovering themselves, therapists can eliminate an artificial separation and false dichotomy of being ''different'' from their clients.

As a result of my own experience as a recovering sex and romance addict, and as a therapist treating others with that addiction, I have developed the following treatment steps that can be used with clients.

(1) Exploring the Addictive Process
(2) Finding a Guide
(3) Understanding Different Types of Addictions
(4) Evaluating the Pros and Cons of Addiction
(5) Admitting the Need for Help
(6) Deciding on a Program
(7) Developing Safety, Support and Abstinence
(8) Dealing with Grief, Defenses and the Meaning of Being an Addict
(9) Accepting a New Life Based on Self Valuing and Love

Steps one through four are the ''readiness'' steps. They help a person explore his or her own life, looking for addictive patterns without demanding an admission of addiction. Steps five, six, and seven, are the ''recovery'' steps and can best be done within the context of a Twelve Step program. Steps eight and nine are the "growth" steps and help a person expand his or her base of recovery back into the larger environment.

1. Exploring the addictive process.

Long before an addiction is recognized, sex and romance addicts focus on their intimate relationships as an important barometer of life quality. They alternate between hope, as a new relationship gets started, and despair when the inevitable ending is experienced. This step may go on for years, is usually done alone and is a time for self-observation of behavior. Personal insights often come in small flashes and there will be self-directed questions about one's sexual and romantic life. Feelings alternate between "something isn't right here" and blind faith that "things will be better tomorrow." The sex and romance addict becomes increasingly confused. The end of step one is reached when an individual accepts the fact that he or she is not sure they have a problem, but guidance is needed in order to help sort things out.

2. Finding a guide.

Finding a guide is crucial to recovery from sexual and romantic addictions. Everyone who has an addiction also has a great fear of people. Addicts are survivors and believe they have gotten by, thus far, by being wary of people. Although one may have experienced superficial closeness, one's innermost self was protected. At the point that a decision is made to find a guide, the addict feels caught in a dilemma. Although the individual knows that he or she can't continue to deal with their sexual and romantic behavior independently, there is a fear of allowing anyone to get close enough to help them. This includes fear of reaching out to God or a Higher Power. Individuals who can't relate to spirituality frequently felt abandoned by God as children, experienced religion as oppressive or simply have found the concept of spirituality alien to their experience.

Reaching out for a guide is a step toward accepting powerlessness, as an individual, in solving one's problems independently. A guide is simply a source of wisdom that can help us gain clarity on our problem and could be:

(1) the knowledge in books;
(2) the beauty in music;
(3) a friend;
(4) one's inner self;
(5) one's higher power;
(6) a sponsor in one of the Twelve Step programs;
(7) a professional counselor or therapist.

Searching for guidance is an ongoing process and can logically lead us to the next step.

3. Understanding different types of addictions.

When an understanding of addictions is expanded, it is possible to have a better chance to find the "hook" that will enable one to get the help that is needed. Many people who are blind, at first, to their sex and romance addiction might recognize that their cocaine use is getting out of hand. Others are able to recognize their problem with compulsive spending or with food, long before they recognize their problems with people. Most activities such as compulsive eating, excessive spending and out-of-control sexual and romantic activities have not been looked at as addictions. Misunderstanding the nature of addiction delays one's ability to find solutions to his or her problems.

By expanding one's understanding of addictions it is possible to recognize that being hooked on one thing predisposes a person to being hooked on others. If the edifice of denial is cracked for one addiction, then a domino-like effect can occur in acknowledging dependence on other things.

4. Evaluating the pros and cons of addiction.

Examining the positive as well as the negative consequences of addiction is essential if recovery is to be based on a solid foundation. Often neglected, the hidden benefits of addictive behavior can be probed by asking these four simple questions:

1. What are the specific problems you are having as a result of your sexual and romantic addictions?
2. If you were not addicted to sex and romance, how would your life be better?
3. In what ways do your sex and romance addictions serve you?
4. In you gave up your addiction to sex and romance, how would your life be worse?

Asking these questions allows us to generate a balance sheet on the advantages and disadvantages of our addiction. This kind of self-audit can help an individual get clear about their motivation for acknowledging powerlessness over an addiction. Only by looking honestly at both the pluses and minuses of an addiction can one begin to deal effectively with his or her sexual or romantic addiction.

5. Admitting the need for help.

Admitting to having an addiction requires an act of total surrender. Some describe it as "being sick and tired of being sick and tired." An internal voice may say, "Maybe, just maybe, surrendering and admitting that I have a problem might help me." Deciding to ask for help is like jumping off into the unknown, a place of suspended animation between life and death. The interesting paradox of admitting powerlessness is that it provides a feeling of freedom from bondage to an external object. Taking this step simply requires saying: "My sexual and romantic life is out of control. I can't do it myself. Please help me."

6. Deciding on a program.

There are three types of recovery programs one can choose from, depending on his or her needs and the resources available. The first is a residential program which typically varies in length from one to three months. The second type is an outpatient program where one meets regularly with a counselor trained in treating sexual and romantic addictions. Usually this treatment approach includes group therapy with others who are also sexually and romantically addicted.

The third program approach includes total involvement in a Twelve Step program such as Sex and Love Addicts Anonymous, Sexaholics Anonymous, or Sex Addicts Anonymous.[1] It is often recommended, in the early stages of recovery, that one attend a meeting every day.

The best program for most individuals combines both professional and self-help approaches. Some people begin seeing a professional, then later get involved in a self-help group. Others begin in a Twelve Step group and find later they can get additional help from a professional.

7. Developing safety, support and abstinence.

Because sex and romance addicts often have been abused as children, addressing the issue of safety is crucial. They need to know that the people whom they come to trust can be relied on not to touch them sexually or to be provocative. Secondly, one needs to feel safety in being accepted as one is, without judgement. Third, human imperfection must be accepted, which means accepting that even those we feel are most loving and nurturing are not perfect. An addict needs to use vigilance in choosing who will be in his or her support system. Perhaps the best indicator of trustworthiness is the consistency of behavior which another person demonstrates.

Abstinence for sex and romance addicts means defining the behaviors that they must give up in order to be in recovery. For some, abstinence might be as rigorous as deciding to give up all sexual activity for awhile. Others may need to give up pornography and focus on sexual relationships with only one partner.

It is important to note that behaviors aren't given up because they are "bad," as moral judgement isn't involved. Behaviors are given up that cause an individual to act out addictively. Also, one's "bottom-line" abstinence behaviors may change over time. For example, as one moves through recovery, it may be necessary to give up a behavior we previously thought was innocuous. Or, certain activities may be subsequently engaged in that one originally gave up, without triggering a relapse. Each person must decide for themselves what constitutes "abstinence."

Often an addict fears that giving up so many behaviors which had been highly valued will lead to even more obsession. They reason that doing just a little bit of acting out will take the edge off their compulsive desire. However, the reality is that when an addict gets clear about those activities he or she must abstain from, and sticks with that resolve, preoccupation lessens and the addict finds life quite manageable.

This whole process may take some time and a strong program with good support will enable movement to the next step.

8. Dealing with grief, defenses and the meaning of being an addict.

Initially, when beginning a program of recovery, relief can be experienced in having gotten rid of the addictive behavior. However, as we move on in recovery, a sense of loss can be experienced, since our addiction was like an "old friend." It may feel like something has died and there is a need to grieve. In order to move ahead with recovery it is necessary to go through the same process as if a loved one had died. Additionally, psychological defenses previously used in order to survive can interfere now with continued recovery and they, too, must be given up or modified to be consistent with the recovering addicts emerging strength.

The final task of this stage is to come to terms with what it means for one to be an addict. Addicts often judge themselves in extreme terms. Either they are totally right or they feel totally worthless. Accepting addiction means accepting that we are fallible and human. To accept one's addiction and the development of a recovery program can lead to more than being "normal." It can lead to a life of value and worth, including being of real service to others.

9. Accepting a new life based on self valuing and love.

In many ways the journey ends where it began. We came into the world as loving and complete human beings. Damaged as children, we felt an inner void that we went searching to fill. Having looked in all the wrong places for a solution through sex and romance, it became apparent that the answer was to become self-loving.

At this stage it is possible to believe that our Higher Power is really in us and the love that we had sought is also within us. Having arrived at the understanding, it was also possible to believe that when people hurt or rejected us, it was because of their own fear and pain, not because we are bad or they are evil.

Accepting that we are not victims, but survivors, it is possible to forgive those who have hurt us, including our parents, by seeing that they too were damaged children and passed on their own pain to us.

The process continues and the steps continue. It is not like climbing a ladder. You don't stop at the top and look down. It's more like going around and around a continuously evolving spiral. Just when it appears we have learned all the lessons there are, new ones emerge.

Perhaps one of the gifts of life is that the journey never ends. We can never have too much love and we can never stop learning how to love more deeply.

NOTES

1. The major Twelve Step programs that deal with sexual and romantic addictions are based on the program of recovery developed by Alcoholics Anonymous and each is unique in its approach. The Augustine Fellowship, Sex and Love Addicts Anonymous (SLAA), is for those who desire to stop living out a pattern of sex and love addiction, obsessive/compulsive sexual behavior or emotional attachment. Sexaholics Anonymous (SA), is an international program of recovery for those who want to stop sexually destructive thinking and behaviors by seeking mutual support to achieve and maintain sexual sobriety. Sex Addicts Anonymous (SAA) is a fellowship of men and women who share their experience, strength, and hope with one another so that they may solve their common problem and gain freedom from compulsive sexual behavior. Address and phone numbers for each of those groups are noted below:

SLAA
PO Box 119
New Town Branch
Boston, MA 02258   (617) 332-1845

SA
PO Box 300
Simi Valley, CA 93062   (818) 704-9854

SAA
PO Box 3038
Minneapolis, MN 55403   (612) 339-0217

REFERENCES

The Augustine Fellowship Sex and Love Addicts Anonymous. (1985). *An introduction to sex and love addicts anonymous.* Boston: The Augustine Fellowship Sex and Love Addicts Anonymous.

Carnes, P. (1983). *Out of the shadows.* Minneapolis: CompCare Publications.

Carnes, P. (1988, September 20). (Interview with P. Carnes, author of *Out of the shadows.)*

Coleman, E. (1987). Sexual compulsivity: Definition, etiology, and treatment considerations. *The Journal of Chemical Dependency Treatment, 1*(1), 1–7.

Dalton, D. (1971). *Piece of my heart.* New York: St. Martin's Press.

Diamond, J. (1988). *Looking for love in all the wrong places: Overcoming romantic and sexual addictions.* New York: G. P. Putnam's Sons.

Fossum, M. A., & Mason, M. J. (1987). *Facing shame: Families in recovery.* New York, W. W. Norton.

Kaufman, G. (1980). *Shame, the power of caring.* Cambridge, MA: Schenkman Publishing Company.

Kurtz, E. (1981). *Shame and guilt: Characteristics of the dependency cycle (an historical perspective for professionals).* Minneapolis: Hazelden Foundation.

Neitlich, A. (1985). *Building bridges: Women's and men's liberation.* Cambridge: Building Bridges Foundation.

Norwood, R. (1985). *Women who love too much.* New York: Pocket Books.

Peele, S., with A. Brodsky. (1975) *Love and addiction.* New York: New American Library.

Schaef, A. W. (1987). *When society becomes an addict.* San Francisco: Harper & Row.

13

When Lady Luck Loses: Women and Compulsive Gambling

Henry R. Lesieur,
Sheila B. Blume

Martha (all names used here are fictitious although the stories are true) sits in a Gamblers Anonymous meeting recounting how she held a gun in her hand but couldn't kill herself. She didn't want her daughter to find her dead when she got home from school. Karen lost her job and is facing possible prosecution for embezzling over four million dollars to finance her addiction to stock options. Helen says she is ashamed to say that she owes her 17-year-old son $3,000, which she borrowed $100 at a time. It all went into the slot machines. Judy, who used her college loan to pay for poker losses, went from job to job with little employment stability. She is now starting a civil service job with a city agency as a clerk. She just can't seem to quit gambling. Her life is a mess.

These women all have a common problem; they are compulsive (pathological) gamblers. In 1980 the American Psychiatric Association first included pathological gambling in its Diagnostic and Statistical Manual as a disorder of impulse control (1980, pp. 291–293). Pathological gamblers are persons who have a chronic and progressive failure to resist impulses to gamble, a failure that compromises, disrupts and damages personal, family and/or vocational pursuits. The principal features are emotional dependence on gambling, loss of control and interference with normal functioning.

Pathological gambling has been conceptualized in a variety of ways over the years, but the most recent and productive model has been that of addictive disease (Blume, 1987). Just as a chemically dependent person becomes addicted to alcohol or drugs, the pathological gambler becomes addicted to the "high" feeling produced by the "action" of gambling. In 1987, the American Psychiatric Association recognized that pathological gambling shares many features with alcoholism and other forms of psychoactive substance dependence. The diagnostic criteria for pathological gambling were modeled after those for psychoactive substance dependence (Blume, 1987). They include: (a) frequent preoccupation with gambling or with the activity needed to obtain money to gamble; (b) frequently gambling with more money or for a longer period of time than intended; (c) a factor similar to tolerance—the need to gamble with increasingly larger stakes or with greater frequency to achieve the desired excitement: (d) a withdrawal-like factor—restlessness or irritability when the individual is prevented from gambling; (e) repeatedly chases losses—gambling with the intent of winning one's money back; (f) attempts to control the problem by efforts to cut down or quit; (g) gambling instead of fulfilling social, educational or occupational obligations; (h) giving up some important activities in order to gamble; (i) persistence at gambling in spite of knowledge that mounting debts or other significant problems are exacerbated by gambling. Four or more of these criteria are needed to diagnose pathological gambling (see APA, 1987, pp. 324–325). With the exception of criterion (e), the criteria are parallel to those for psychoactive substance dependence. In additon, recently established inpatient and outpatient programs have followed an addictions treatment model, including the use of Twelve Step programs (see Blume, 1986).

EPIDEMIOLOGICAL SURVEYS

According to the Commission on the Review of the National Policy Towards Gambling there were approximately 1.1 million "probable compulsive gamblers" and another 2.2 million "potential compulsive gamblers" in the US in 1974 (1976, p. 74). About one third of "probable" and "potential" compulsive gamblers in the US are female (1976, p. 74). More recently, statewide surveys have been conducted in Ohio, New Jersey and New York. These studies estimate that between 1.4 percent and 3.4 percent of the adult population are "probable pathological gamblers" (Culleton, 1985; Volberg & Steadman, 1988). Again, they have found that one third of these probable pathological gamblers are female. In contrast to this community male to female ratio, between 93 percent and 98 percent of those in treatment in Gamblers Anonymous (GA) are male (Lesieur, 1988a). Thus women who have gambling problems are a chronically underserved group.

Part of the reason for the underrepresentation of women in treatment and self-help is society's stereotype of the gambler. The Damon Runyon figure of the "gambler" is a male image. He is the big shot, big spender with a big ego. He is the man about town who wears an extensive amount of jewelry, brags when he wins (and claims to win when he loses) and thinks of himself as smarter than the average sucker. The female who gambles heavily does not fit this colorful image. She carries a stigma.

One consequence of the perceived stigma is that female compulsive gamblers are more likely to gamble alone and to be closet gamblers than their male counterparts. In addition, the women in Gamblers Anonymous are more likely to be single, separated or divorced than men in GA. They have fewer significant others who are likely to complain and pressure them into treatment. Unfortunately, this also translates into fewer social supports during recovery. These factors in combination produce the scarcity of females in GA and compulsive gambling treatment facilities.

Other categories of individuals who are overrepresented in community surveys of compulsive gamblers include those under 35, lower income groups, Blacks and Hispanics, as well as Catholics (Culleton, 1985; Volberg & Steadman, 1988). Each of these categories, with the exception of Catholics, is also underrepresented in Gamblers Anonymous (Lesieur, 1988a). Quite obviously, there is a need for outreach to all of these underserved populations, but there is a particularly acute need to reach women.

BACKGROUND CHARACTERISTICS

This section reviews the findings of Lesieur's study of 50 women pathological gamblers (Lesieur, 1988b). The study, partially funded by the New York State Office of Mental Health, was based on intensive interviews with female GA members from across the US. Subjects were questioned about their life histories. Lesieur probed for information about their gambling histories, the intersection of gambling with family, work, financial, emotional and other factors, and the relation between compulsive gambling and other addictions. Their treatment histories were also stressed. It is understood that these women may not be representative of female pathological gamblers as a whole. However, they are the largest sample systematically studied to date.

The stories of the lives of these women often reveal problem childhoods, troubled marriages and troubled adult lives. Although the women's reports of their childhood experiences range from happy and healthy to severely disturbed, well over half had difficult early years. Table 1 indicates their statements about disorders in their parents.

Alcoholism in parents was more common than compulsive gambling. Included among ''other serious problems'' were parents who were mentally ill or who subjected them to physical or sexual abuse. As a result of these childhood experiences, several mentioned getting married in order to escape the family. The marital status of these women is shown in Table 2.

TABLE 1. Parental Pathology

Type of family pathology	Number	Percent
Father alcoholic	14	28
Mother alcoholic	5	10
Father compulsive gambler or probable compulsive gambler	10	20
Mother compulsive gambler	2	4
Other serious problems	6	12

Source: Survey of 50 female pathological gamblers.

In addition, four women's childhoods were disrupted by World War II. Two lost their parents in the Nazi holocaust, the father of a third was imprisoned in a concentration camp, and the fourth survived the bombing of London.

It is clear that the marriages of these women were severely troubled by factors in addition to the subject's gambling. Sixty-two percent married troubled husbands who were pathological gamblers themselves, alcoholics, drug abusers or had other problems. These problems are listed in Table 3. A common factor in many of the marriages was the husband's frequent absence from home. Forty-four percent were absent either because of evening or night shift work, or jobs that involved travel. This gave rise to chronic loneliness. Twenty-nine percent had physically abusive husbands, most of whom were alcoholics.

More than half of the women stated that they initially looked upon their gambling as a means of escape from overwhelming problems, including traumas of the past, troublesome marital relationships and loneliness. What attracted all of the women to gambling was the ''action,'' which will be discussed in the next section.

TABLE 2. Marital Status of Female GA Members (N = 50)

Marital status	Number	Percent
Never married	8	16
Currently divorced/separated	15	30
Currently married	26	52
Widowed	1	2
Total	50	100%

Source: Survey of 50 female pathological gamblers.

TABLE 3. Problem Husbands of Female Pathological Gamblers (N = 42)

Type of problem	Number	Percent
Married to pathological gambler	8	19
Married to alcoholic	14	32
Married to other drug abuser	4	10
Married to mentally ill husband	4	10
Married to "womanizer"	5	12
Married to "workaholic"	9	21
Married to any of above	26	62
Husband has none of problems above	16	38
Total ever married	42	100%

Source: Survey of 50 female pathological gamblers.

PHASES IN THE CAREER OF THE FEMALE PATHOLOGICAL GAMBLER

Robert Custer describes three phases in the career of the compulsive gambler: the winning, losing and desperation phases (1984; 1985). These adequately describe the male gambling pattern but need to be revised when discussing women.

Gambling starts as a recreational activity for all who gamble. Compulsive gamblers are no exception to this rule. Like others, they win, lose and break even; win, lose and break even. For about one half, an upsurge in gambling activity begins with a big win or a winning streak, frequently resulting in the equivalent of half a year's income or more. They become convinced that they can win a fortune by gambling, and simultaneously feel the thrill of being "in action." They are "smarter than the average sucker" out there. While some women experience this early pattern, it is more common among male compulsive gamblers than females, many of whom never have a big win at all. More than half of the women stated that they initially looked upon gambling as a means of escaping from overwhelming problems.

The women also differ from male GA members in their preferred types of gambling; they opted for legal gambling, with card games, slot and poker machines, horse racing and lotteries the most frequent choices. Male compulsive gamblers' preferences have been found to be horse racing, sports betting and dice games, with far less emphasis on legal betting.

For all heavy gamblers, "action" is also sought in addition to money or escape. Action is an aroused, euphoric state comparable to the "high" derived from cocaine or other drugs. "Action" means excitement, thrill, and tension. In short, the "adrenalin" is flowing:

I'd need one number, the adrenalin would pick up, I'd get all numb, hoping and praying that number would be called. [Hope B.—talking about bingo]

I was a maniac in the casino . . . My adrenalin starts to go. Meaning, I start gettin' high, start gettin' nervous, looking forward, rushing compulsively. Ah, going up to the first table where I could get a spot right in the middle so I would have enough room to place my bets wherever I felt hot on a number. [Sue M.—a roulette player]

The desire to keep the action going is so great in later stages of compulsive gambling that many women discussed going without sleep for days, not eating, and not getting up from a seat until there was a desperate need to go. Being in action pushes out other concerns for these women.

Those who are escaping from some problem comment on gambling as an "anesthetic" which "hypnotizes." Durand Jacobs calls these phenomena, which many gamblers experience, "dissociative states" (1988). They include "memory blackouts," "trances," "out of body experiences" and the feeling of taking on another identity while gambling. Regular gamblers discuss these experiences as being "on tilt" (Browne, in press). Gamblers who are escaping troubles come to appreciate these feelings, particularly since they are combined with the euphoria of the action.

Those with a winning phase derive an increasing proportion of their self-esteem from their handicapping abilities. They spend more and more time in an effort to produce a winning system to beat the horses, sports, stock options or numbers. When they experience a "bad beat," an unexplainable loss or losing streak produced by bizarre circumstances (see Rosecrance, 1986), many will "chase" their losses in an attempt to get even. They will try to get their money back and frequently become obsessed with doing so. The losses represent a serious blow to their self-esteem. The consequent chasing produces irrational gambling and further losses (Lesieur, 1979).

Those who escape gradually come to rely more and more on the action for "time out" from their troubles. This "time out," however, is expensive. As costs rise, they also borrow and stretch their expenses to the limit. When they gamble on borrowed money, they chase their losses in an attempt to pay back the borrowed money. Now, not only do they have their original troubles to escape from, they have problems produced by their gambling that compound these troubles.

For both the "adventurer" and the "escapist," there is a gradual deterioration in the home, job and financial realm as the gambling progresses in the losing phase. Relationships suffer as family members and friends are borrowed from, and lies are told. The job is exploited for what it can bring: time to gamble and money to pay for it. Eighty-six percent of the women were or had been employed. Only four women described themselves as "housewives," two were disabled and one was a student. Compulsive gambling leads eventually to financial problems. All of the women used both their own and their family's money to finance their gambling, typically delaying payment of household bills, exhausting bank accounts, borrowing from friends and family (including their own children), taking out small loans (sometimes forging their husband's signature), and spending their unemployment or welfare checks. Family possessions, savings and legitimate sources of funding are exhausted. Eventually, these no longer bring in the needed resources and family members are asked for a "bailout" (a sum of money sufficient to pay outstanding debts), complete with promises that "I will never gamble again." Alternatively, two-thirds eventually engage in illegal activity that further exacerbates their troubles. Table 4 compares the gambling-related illegal activities reported by the female GA members with those reported in a study of 190 GA members, only four of whom were female (Nora, 1985).

The most common forms of crime these women committed included check forgery, embezzlement and running illegal gambling operations (typically operating a small-time card game and "cutting the pot"). When compared with male compulsive gamblers, the females were more likely to have passed bad checks and engaged in prostitution (although most of these were prostitutes before they became compulsive gamblers). They were less likely than males to have been involved in loan fraud, tax evasion, tax fraud, larceny, burglary, selling drugs, hustling at gambling games and fencing stolen goods.

Both legal and illegal sources of money are treated as a "big win" in that they enable the gambler to continue and possibly escalate the gambling. Yet, the gambling now takes on a desperate quality. Gambling is still exciting but the negatives outweigh the positives. Obsession with getting out of trouble overtakes a desire for excitement as the principal motive for gambling. When this fails, as it often does, serious bouts of depression are experienced. Suicide attempts are common, with rates of 17 percent to 24 percent reported in surveys of GA members and individuals in treatment. Arrest and imprisonment are also a possibility. While only two of the 50 women interviewed were arrested and jailed for gambling-related offenses (another was under federal investigation for a multimillion-dollar stock fraud), other research has indicated a high incidence of pathological gambling (up to 30 percent) among female prison populations (see Lesieur, 1987).

HELP SEEKING BEHAVIOR

Many of the female pathological gamblers interviewed had sought help. Fully 70 percent had received treatment from a mental health profession-

TABLE 4. Illegal Activities and Civil Fraud Engaged in by Female Pathological
Gamblers and a Comparison of (Primarily Male) GA Members.

Type of illegal activity	Female GA N=50	Nora study N=190
Loan fraud (civil)	44%	41%
White-collar crime		
Check forgery	40%	33%
Systematic loan fraud	2%	13%
Forgery	18%	18%
Embezzelment and employee theft	24%	38%
Tax evasion	12%	28%
Tax fraud	4%	18%
Commonplace crime		
Larceny	14%	21%
Burglary	2%	15%
Armed robbery	2%	4%
Pimping	0%	2%
Prostitution	10%	0%
Selling drugs	0%	9%
Gambling system connected bookmaking or working in an illegal game	26%	23%
Hustling at pool, golf, bowling, or other sport	10%	19%
Hustling at cards or dice	6%	21%
Run a ''con game;'' Swindle suckers	12%	9%
Fencing stolen goods	4%	14%
Engaged in any of the illegal activites above	68%	n/a

n/a—information not available.
Note: offenses listed in the table were engaged in as a consequence of gambling only. Table
values indicate the percentage of repondents within each group who participated in the activity.
Sources: Survey of 50 female pathological gamblers and survey of 186 males and 4 females
conducted by Rena Nora, M.D., in New Jersey (1985).

al. More than half of them had such treatment before reaching GA. This compares with 24 percent of the largely male population studied by Nora (1985). Knowledgeable professionals have a real opportunity to intervene with these suffering patients, and several did so by recommending GA along with other sources of help. Unfortunately, the vast majority of therapists either failed to recognize the gambling problem or failed to intervene effectively.

The women in the study suffered from a variety of disorders in addition to their pathological gambling. Twenty-six percent of the women stated that they suffered serious depression (12 percent made suicide attempts) prior to any gambling problems. Their depression was made worse by gambling-related problems. Substance abuse problems are also fairly extensive. Table 5 lists self-reported problems with psychoactive substances. These rates of alcohol and substance abuse are two to three times higher than those for the adult female population (Robins, et al., 1984). They are comparable to the rates found for hospitalized male compulsive gamblers (Ramirez, McCormick, Russo, & Taber, 1983).

Other addictions also intruded into the lives of the women interviewed, primarily compulsive overspending and compulsive overeating. Since compulsive gambling may be confused with overspending, the women were asked about indebtedness apart from their gambling. Twenty-four percent went through spending sprees which cost them thousands of dollars. This

TABLE 5. Psychoactive Substance Dependence and Abuse, Self-Reported by Female GA Members (N = 50)

Substance abused	Dependence[a]		Abuse only	
	Number	Percent	Number	Percent
Alcohol	7	14	9	18
Amphetamines	5	10	4	8
Cocaine	—	—	2	4
Tranquilizers/Valium	5	10	7	14
Heroin	1	2	1	2
Marijuana	2	4	2	4
Hallucinogens	—	—	1	2
Any psychoactive substance	11	22		
Abuse without dependence on any other drug			13	26
Dependence and abuse combined			24	48

[a]DSM-III-R criteria used for Psychoactive Substance Dependence and Abuse (APA, 1987).
Source: Survey of 50 female pathological gamblers.

seemed to occur most frequently after quitting gambling. Twenty percent called themselves compulsive overeaters. An additional 12 percent were possibly sexually addicted. Each mentioned multiple sexual forays and affairs and also had used sex to obtain money for gambling.

A number of women (26 percent) had experienced hallucinations, mostly due to drugs, but one in the context of sleep deprivation after several days of continuous casino gambling. Twenty-six percent of the women (some overlap with those reporting hallucinations) reported feelings that might be considered paranoid. However, it is difficult to separate paranoid symptoms from real fears of loan sharks and other creditors. In five cases the paranoid symptoms appeared to be related to amphetamine abuse.

FEMINIST PERSPECTIVES ON
WOMEN AND COMPULSIVE GAMBLING

The careers of female pathological gamblers ring with some of the same themes as those for female alcoholics and drug addicts. Like their alcoholic counterparts (see Blume, 1982; 1985), the women compulsive gamblers are often victims of the social stereotypes and limitations imposed upon women. Although often trapped by economic pressures and social role prescriptions in unhappy and abusive families, these women expect themselves to fulfill the functions of homemaking and childrearing along with their work responsibilities. Intense guilt accompanies their failure to succeed. Gambling, to them, begins as a temporary way to escape life problems. In becoming a problem itself, compulsive gambling further interferes with their ability to function in these socially prescribed feminine roles. These women are acutely aware of the stigma applied by society to a woman who fails to meet the high moral standards expected of women placed ''on a pedestal.'' They feel both deeply ashamed and deeply resentful over the double stigma of not only being a compulsive gambler but of not having fulfilled their roles as moral models for society. The higher the pedestal, the greater the fall.

> She should be a mother and she doesn't have time to think about gambling. She should be thinking about raising a family. [Marsha—off-track bettor]

> It's ok for a man to go in and screw up and lose the money and steal and this and that and, he's going to GA and he's wonderful and he literally wallows in the gutter and comes out smelling like a rose. But yet, there's this double standard where a woman is a gambler and steals or commits a crime or whatever, she's a goddamn bum. [JoAnn—card player]

> We have the nurturing stigma and all that. That a nurturer should have more control over these types of things. [Pat R.—race track gambler]

Not surprisingly there is a high incidence of depression among female compulsive gamblers. Available research on the general population points to the higher incidence of depression among women than among men. The ratio is about two to one (Guttentag, Salasin & Belle, 1980; Weissman & Klerman, 1977). Studies also point to the fact that women demonstrate a greater sense of responsibility for the well-being of others (Gilligan, 1982); this is reflected in life-stress scores on tests (Miller, 1976). When members of the family or friends have problems, women are more likely to evidence distress and concern than men (Carmen, Russo, & Miller, 1981). It is not surprising then that one effect of stressful life events in the lives of the female pathological gamblers studied was to resort to some means of escape as a method of coping. Distress over relationships with others appears to be a common precipitating factor. Traditional sex role socialization suggests that one's value as a female is highly related to acting in a "caretaking" role as a wife and mother by attending to others' needs. Writers on problems among female alcohol and drug abusers point to a similar theme (See Camberwell Council on Alcoholism, 1980; Marsh, Colten & Tucker, 1982).

For some women, gambling also acts as a means whereby they can become empowered through competition in a male dominated world. This was particularly true for middle class career women but was not limited to them.

> I'm finally on level with the men. Cause I would sit down and play level to level with them. And I matched them bet for bet. [Delores—casino gambler and corporate executive]

> I play like a man I think. I play rough, you know . . . It is hard to bluff me out because I'll stay in. . . . I heard across the table, someone cursed me. And I looked at her. I gave her the filthiest look. I gave the gruff exterior. I wanted to be a man maybe, I don't know. [Judy—card player and secretary]

It is possible that a sense of inadequacy in being traditionally female (produced by poor socialization experiences and failed relationships) may have propelled these women to compete in a stereotypically male domain—gambling. If a female could be successful in this male turf, then she might acquire a sense of personal power that would counteract a poor self-esteem. This seems to be true for the competitive types of gambling like cards, the race track, the stock market and sports. However, slots, bingo and the lottery are not stereotypically male pursuits. For these domains, the desire to escape into another world where problems can be forgotten appears to be the dominant theme. In either case, however, external events seem to be more important for female than male compulsive gamblers.

The risk taking eventually has its toll. Because of the structure of gender stratification, women come to experience pressures that are different from those of their male counterparts. The female pathological gamblers interviewed were predominantly in secretarial, clerical and other pink collar positions. This produced low pay and consequently, lower indebtedness. The average debt for the women interviewed was $14,979 in contrast with over $53,000 for the average male in treatment (Lesieur, 1988a). One result of the lower debt was less pressure to engage in illegal activity to support their addiction. Another was a proportionately greater raiding of the family budget for food and necessities. In addition, crimes women did commit were less serious (and more stereotypically ''female'') than that of their male counterparts.

Another consequence of the occupational segregation women experience is that they are less likely to be noticed by employee assistance programs. In one study of 86 EAPs and service providers, only 8 percent of the compulsive gambler clients screened by the responding organizations were female (Lesieur, in press). At present, we cannot tell whether these referral agents accept the stereotypes of females as not ''really'' gamblers or have other reasons for not recognizing gambling problems among women.

SCREENING THE FEMALE PATHOLOGICAL GAMBLER

The population of female compulsive gamblers is being underserved by Gamblers Anonymous and existing treatment facilities. This can be partially rectified by actively screening current populations in treatment for other emotional and addictive disorders. At South Oaks Hospital, a screening instrument was devised using both female and male subjects (Lesieur & Blume, 1987). This South Oaks Gambling Screen was used in a recent statewide epidemiological survey (Volberg & Steadman, 1988). One third of the ''probable pathological gamblers'' found in the survey were women. The South Oaks Gambling Screen (the SOGS) is a valid, reliable instrument that does not require extensive instruction to administer or code. The instrument is currently used in numerous treatment facilities in the US and abroad. For example, of 133 female inpatients admitted to South Oaks Hospital for alcoholism and/or drug dependence, 6 percent were found to have significant gambling problems using the SOGS (Lesieur, Blume & Zoppa, 1986). Those interested in the SOCS should contact the authors.

TREATMENT OF COMPULSIVE GAMBLING IN WOMEN

Once a gambling problem has been identified, treatment must focus on helping the patient achieve abstinence from gambling. This process involves a combination of supportive acceptance and confrontation of the defenses of denial and rationalization. Although the process is similar for both sexes, the depth of guilt and shame in the female patient requires special attention. Motivation may be shaky at this stage of treatment and must be carefully nurtured. Often, treatment is initiated in response to external pressure such as being caught in a criminal act or defaulting on debts. It is important to build strong internal motivation from the beginning so that the patient does not drop out of treatment and eventually relapse once the initial crisis is resolved. The female patient must be helped to establish enough self-esteem to feel worthy of recovery, and to care enough about the future to expend the necessary effort.

Gamblers Anonymous is helpful in this process, although the female compulsive gambler may feel uncomfortable if there are no other women at the first meeting she attends. It is therefore important that the mental health professional making the referral be sufficiently acquainted with the local GA groups to help the newly identified problem gambler make initial contact with a woman in the program. Ideally, "adventurers" would be paired with other "adventurers" and "escapists" with other escapists. Although there are more than 600 GA groups in the United States (and over 1,000 worldwide), there are areas of the country where GA is unavailable. Compulsive gamblers in these areas may find it helpful to send for GA literature at the address given in the next section.

In addition to GA referral and treatment of her compulsive gambling and additional disorders, attention to the female gambler's family members and significant others is important. Parents and children as well as spouses are very much affected by this illness and need help in their own right. In addition, family members who have accepted compulsive gambling as a disease can be realistically supportive of the gambler's recovery. They can also be helped to accept the changes in family structure that emerge as the recovering gambler develops a new self-concept and revises her goals. Both family counseling sessions and referral to Gam-Anon, a self-help group for families of compulsive gamblers, are helpful adjuncts to the individual or group psychotherapy that is provided to the gambler.

Once initial abstinence is attained and the immediate urgent problems have been attended to, the female compulsive gambler will begin to confront the realities of her life without being able to use gambling as a convenient, if destructive, escape. The therapist must try to help her rebuild her self-esteem, which often in the women patient has been severely affected by sexism and traditional societal ideas of women's place in the world. Those who are living with abusive spouses will need help to become both emotionally and financially independent of these relationships. Those who have histories of alcohol and drug abuse must be helped to avoid relapse into these behaviors. In all cases, the patient can be greatly aided by an understanding of the addictive process, so that a substitute addictive behavior such as spree spending or overeating can be avoided. The long and painful process of building a satisfying and productive life can be helped by psychotherapy, either individual or in a group. A women's group may be particularly helpful as therapy proceeds. At the present stage of development of treatment services, few if any agencies carry a sufficient number of female compulsive gamblers in their caseloads to support all-female compulsive gamblers' therapy groups. However, it is feasible to treat such women in groups with women who suffer from other addictive disorders and simultaneously attend Alcoholics Anonymous, Women for Sobriety, Narcotics Anonymous, or other self-help groups while the gambler attends Gamblers Anonymous. The compulsive gambling outpatient program at South Oaks Hospital has used this approach successfully. However, it is important that the group leader be familiar with the similarities and differences between compulsive gambling and other addictions. It is not therapeutic to regard differences as unimportant or to instruct a patient to attend self help for another addiction and merely substitute the word "bet" for "drink" or "drug" in her own mind.

For the compulsive gambler, slow and gradual repayment of her debts, at whatever rate she can afford, helps to improve self-esteem. Self-esteem is also founded on a rethinking of her concept of herself as a woman and her role in society. She can be helped to see herself as a valuable individual in her own right rather than merely value herself for how much she is able to do for others. She can be helped to take control of her life, usually for the first time. Since recurrence of depression may precipitate a relapse in those patients who have a history of depression, the therapist and patient should remain alert to changes in mood, appetite and sleep, and other symptoms. Self-esteem and early recovery can be damaged by a relapse into gambling. A female compulsive gambler needs a great deal of support and encouragement to re-establish abstinence following a slip, but can be encouraged to look upon her relapse as a learning experience and a step toward permanent recovery.

Little is known about the outcome of various types of treatment for compulsive gamblers in general. One study of inpatient treatment in the Veteran's Administration system found that 55 percent of respondents to a follow-up questionnaire were abstinent for at least one year since discharge and 92 percent reported less gambling than before (Russo, Taber, McCormick, & Ramirez, 1984). There are no studies of treatment for women. Clinical experience leads us to the conclusion that women can and do recover, but they need the help of sensitive concerned professionals who can identify the nature of their problems and provide appropriate intervention.

OTHER INFORMATIONAL RESOURCES

The National Council on Compulsive Gambling is an organization that was established in 1972 for education, information and referral. It distributes fact sheets and literature for those interested in the disorder. The council also operates a national hotline (800) 522-4700. It can be contacted by phone at (212) 765-3833 and is located at 445 West 59th Street, New York NY 10019. The NCCG sponsors the *Journal of Gambling Behavior*, the only scientific journal devoted to the study of this disorder. The journal is published by Human Sciences Press. Gamblers Anonymous can be contacted by phone at (213) 386-8789 or through the World Service Office, PO Box 17173, Los Angeles, CA 90017. Gam-Anon has its International Service Office at PO Box 157, Whitestone, NY 11357 and is reached at (718) 352-1671. Gamblers Anonymous and Gam-Anon hold periodic conclaves at which workshops are held for members and interested parties. These are ideal settings for professionals to learn about the organizations. Nearly all workshops are open to interested professionals. Workshop topics include things like running step meetings, "pressure" groups, expressing feelings, the dual addict and communication. In addition, at some conclaves professionals have been invited to speak, be members of panels or conduct workshops themselves.

REFERENCES

American Psychiatric Association. (1980). *Diagnostic and statistical manual* (3rd ed.). Washington, DC: Author.

American Psychiatric Association. (1987). *Diagnostic and statistical manual.* (3rd ed. rev.). Washington, D.C.: Author.

Blume, S. B. (1982). Psychiatric problems of alcoholic women. In J. Solomon (Ed.), *Alcoholism and clinical psychiatry* (pp. 179–193). New York: Plenum Publishing.

Blume, S. B. (1985). Women and alcohol. In T. E. Bratter & G. G. Forrest (Eds.), *Alcoholism and substance abuse: Strategies for clinical intervention* (pp. 623–638). New York: The Free Press.

Blume, S. B. (1986). Treatment for compulsive gambling: An overview. In S. J. Levy & S. B. Blume (Eds.), *Addictions in the Jewish community* (pp. 371–379). New York: Federation of Jewish Philanthropies.

Blume, S. B. (1987). Compulsive gambling and the medical model. *Journal of Gambling Behavior, 3,* 237–247.

Browne, B. (in press). Going on tilt: Frequent poker players and control. *Journal of Gambling Behavior, 5.*

Camberwell Council on Alcoholism. (1980). *Women & alcohol.* London: Tavistock.

Carmen, E. H., Russo, N. F., & Miller, J. B. (1981). Inequality and women's mental health: An overview. *American Journal of Psychiatry, 138,* 1319–1330.

Commission on the Review of National Policy Towards Gambling. (1976). *Gambling in America.* Washington, DC: US Government Printing Office.

Culleton, R. P. (1985). *A survey of pathological gamblers in the state of Ohio.* Philadelphia: Transition Planning Associates.

Custer, R. L. (1984). Profile of the pathological gambler. *Journal of Clinical Psychiatry, 45,* 35–38.

Custer, R. L. with H. Milt (1985). *When luck runs out.* New York: Facts on File Publications.

Gilligan, C. (1982). *In a different voice.* Cambridge: Harvard University Press.

Guttentag, M., Salasin, S., & Belle, D. (Eds.). (1980). *The mental health of women.* New York: Academic Press.

Jacobs, D. F. (1988). Evidence for a common dissociative-like reaction among addicts. *Journal of Gambling Behavior, 4,* 27–37.

Lesieur, H. R. (1979). The compulsive gambler's spiral of options and involvement. *Psychiatry: Journal for the Study of Interpersonal Processes, 42,* 79–87.

Lesieur, H. R. (1987). Gambling, pathological gambling and crime. In T. Galski (Ed.), *Handbook on pathological gambling* (pp. 89–110). Springfield, IL: Charles C. Thomas.

Lesieur, H. R. (1988a). Report on pathological gambling. In Governor's Advisory Commission on Gambling, *Report and recommendations of the Governor's Advisory Commission on Gambling* (pp. 104–165). Trenton, NJ: Governor's Advisory Commission on Gambling.

Lesieur, H. R. (1988b). The female pathological gambler. In W. R. Eadington (Ed.), *Gambling research: Proceedings of the seventh international conference on gambling and risk taking* (pp. 230–258). Bureau of Business and Economic Research, University of Nevada, Reno.

Lesieur, H. R. (in press). Experiences of employee assistance programs with pathological gamblers. In H. Trice & W. Sonnenstuhl (Eds.), special issue of *Journal of Drug Issues.*

Lesieur, H. R., & Blume, S. B. (1987). The South Oaks Gambling Screen (The SOGS): A new instrument for the identification of pathological gamblers. *American Journal of Psychiatry, 144,* 1184–1188.

Lesieur, H. R., Blume, S. B. & Zoppa, R. M. (1986). Alcoholism, drug abuse, and gambling. *Alcoholism: Clinical and Experimental Research, 10,* 33–38.

Marsh, J. C., Colten, M. E., & Tucker, M. B. (Eds.). (1982). Women's use of drugs and alcohol: New perspectives. Special issue of *Journal of Social Issues, 38.*

Miller, J. B. (1976) *Toward a psychology of women.* Boston: Beacon Press.

Nora, R. (1985). *Overview of compulsive gambling.* Paper presented at the First National Conference on Gambling of the National Council on Compulsive Gambling, New York.

Ramirez, L. F., McCormick, R. A., Russo, A.M., & Taber, J. I. (1983). Patterns of substance abuse in pathological gamblers undergoing treatment. *Addictive Behaviors, 8,* 425–428.

Robins, L. N., Helzer, J. E., Weissman, M. M., Orvaschel, H., Gruenberg, E.

Burke, J. D., & Regier, D. (1984). Lifetime prevalence of specific psychiatric disorders in three sites. *Archives of General Psychiatry, 41,* 949–958.

Rosecrance, J. (1986). Attributions and the origins of problem gambling. *The Sociological Quarterly, 27,* 463–477.

Russo, A. M., Taber, J. I., McCormick, R. A., & Ramirez, L. F. (1984). An outcome study of an inpatient treatment program for pathological gamblers. *Hospital and Community Psychiatry, 35,* 823–827.

Volberg, R., & Steadman, H. (1988). Refining prevalence estimates of pathological gambling. *American Journal of Psychiatry, 146.*

Weissman, M. M. & Klerman, G. L. (1977). Sex differences and the epidemiology of depression. *Archives of General Psychiatry, 34,* 98–111.

14

A Feminist Perspective on Work Addiction

Diane Fassel
Anne Wilson Schaef

FEMINISM AT A TURNING POINT

The past 15 years have been rocky and confusing for the feminist move-ment and for individual feminists in the United States. Who would have thought that the gains made in the 1970s in equal pay for equal work and reproductive rights would slowly be eroded in the eighties and nineties? Who could have imagined that women who had once proudly identified themselves as feminist would fear having "that word" applied to them? Or that young women would eagerly accept the gains achieved by earlier feminists but eschew being labeled as feminists? What accounts for such a change among women? Is it solely the cumulative results of a conserva-tive tide in the country or has feminism itself precipitated some of the backlash?

We believe there has been a sizeable backlash against the gains women have achieved. More troublesome, however, is the fact that the feminist movement has been in danger of being coopted into the white male sys-tem and subsequently into the addictive system as well.

Unfortunately, some schools or groups of feminists have continued in the white male system by their insistence upon full incorporation into that system. As a result, some women mistakenly believe that opportunities to enter the work force and to seek education result in equality with men and the benefits of the system. A feminist-addictions perspective questions the illusion that full incorporation into the dominant system is possible or desired and it also questions whether such incorporation is healthy. Is this "success" even helpful for those who "make it?" The opportunity to "suit-up" and join the team has inched some women to the top of the white male system, but it has not proved beneficial to women-at-large, for massive numbers of women are left out: women of color, aging women, single parents, women in the home, women who are disabled or needing special services.

The cooptation of the feminist movement has occurred, we believe, because there has been a lack of awareness and understanding of the power and pervasiveness of addiction in the individual and in the society. Addictions numb us and adjust us to the craziness of the dominant system. Addictions make us more malleable and less capable of feeling our rage at the inequities of the system. Ultimately, addictions rob us of our lives.

The addictive system is described as "cunning, baffling, powerful and patient." We should not miss the fact that whenever feminists participate in either system we participate in a nonliving process which ultimately ends in physical, mental and spiritual death. Nor should we avoid seeing that when certain schools of feminist thought (e.g., cultural feminism), advocate total immersion into this white male system/addictive system, it is more difficult for all women to survive economically and personally, for in buying into the dominant culture we buy into the culture's pervasive addiction—workaholism. Inevitably when feminists support full participation in the society as it is, we unwittingly support work addiction because work addiction is integrated into every aspect of the society. It is in our families, our organization and in the society at large.

THE SOCIETY IS WORKAHOLIC AND THE ORGANIZATION IS WORKAHOLIC

It is apparent to us that work addiction is only one of many process addictions that are rampant in the society. It is a manifestation of a larger addictive process. The society itself actually fosters individual addictions because the best adjusted persons in the society are those who are numb. When we are numb we are more malleable. When we are numb we are not in touch with feelings of outrage, sadness and despair at the processes of the society. The pollution of the air and water, the danger of nuclear holocaust and the pain of sexism, racism, classism and so forth are not felt when we are numb. Of course, every addiction numbs us to what we know and feel. It puts a buffer, takes the edge off our awareness and keeps us busy. When we are in our addictions we cannot take care of ourselves, much less be concerned about the society.

The addictive process has the same characteristics in the individual, the organization and in the society. The characteristics may manifest differently, yet at root they are the same. These characteristics are denial, dishonesty, control, thinking processes that are obsessive, dualistic, and confused, self-centeredness, perfectionism, judgmentalism, grandiosity, scarcity, crises, confusion and progressive moral deterioration. These characteristics comprise the underlying addictive process regardless of the specific addiction. Consequently, the individual addict may lie to herself about the unmanageability of her life in relation to food or a relationship while working for an organization that is perfectionistic in its expectations of employees. This organization exists in a society in which the political process is based on dishonesty and control. The addictive process permeates these layers from individual to society. Our individual addictions accommodate us to the addictive process of the society and the organization. Because we meet the addictive process everywhere, we begin to believe it is normal. Thus, the illusory addictive system becomes our reality. We believe that this process, which is actually a disease, is "just the way things are."

This problem of believing that the addictive process is normal is especially true in relation to work addiction. The addiction to work is a particularly cunning addiction because it is the only addiction in which part of the denial consists in boasting about the addiction. One never hears an overeater proclaim: "I binged on an entire chocolate cake and I'm proud of it." Yet work addicts frequently boast about their long hours and their overinvolvement. The media places before us articles about entrepreneurs who declare themselves "proud workaholics." These people are presented as models to be imitated, not as examples of a disease that is progressive and fatal. Work addiction is the cleanest of all the addictions and therefore extremely dangerous. It is socially acceptable because it is thought to be socially productive. Nothing could be farther from the truth.

Feminists have long maintained that we must see the connection between things personal and global. The phrase "the personal is political" originated in the feminist movement. The reality of this connection is obvious in the workaholic society. According to a 1985 study by Weitzman, many women become workaholic just to survive in the society. At this time, 60 percent of all women are employed—most in jobs at the lower end of the economic scale. Fifty percent of all marriages end in divorce and, contrary to popular media myths about fathers being sole parents, women receive custody of children in 90 percent of all divorces. Wages have not kept up with inflation and after divorce, women's income drops 73 percent, while men's income increases by 42 percent. In many cases, sheer survival in this social context means that women are working two jobs while doing second and third shifts at home. To compound the problem, much of women's work is performed in the workaholic organization. These organizations are thoroughly immersed in the addictive process and are a marked contrast to a feminist perspective, which espouses wholeness in all areas of life.

The workaholic organization is the context within which most of us learn to be work addicts. It is structured to hook our disease. These organizations operate out of identifiable characteristics. They are the norm for organizational life yet they are a different world from a feminist perspective on work. (For a fuller description of these characteristics, see Diane Fassel. 1990. *Working Ourselves To Death*, San Francisco: Harper & Row.)

Characteristics of a Workaholic Organization

In the workaholic organization the mission of the organization is denied, ignored or forgotten. People forget why the organization exists, they are so busy pursuing their own goals. They use "busyness" to avoid seeing that the organization no longer does its mission. This problem has been evident in the health care profession where many people joined the profession to do the mission of healing only to find themselves in a big business where profit ruled all decisions.

By contrast, a feminist perspective takes the organizational mission seriously. Mission is central. When the mission is no longer appropriate for the times, there is not a frantic rushing around to replace the old mission with a new one. Instead, there is a letting go and a willingness to wait with the process.

The workaholic organization believes in corporate survival above all. Consequently, people are commodities to be used up, then discarded. This is one reason why many organizations offer stress management to their employees. The stress management enables the workaholic pace to be more bearable while keeping the focus off the systems of the organization that are causing the stress in the first place. A feminist perspective is not wedded to the perpetuation of any organization. It is especially wary of organizations that survive at the expense of the environment and the planet.

Profit is the driving force in the workaholic organization. As a result, the organization seeks short-term solutions and short-term results. The organization is greedy. It wants immediate gratification. For feminists the financial bottom line is not the sole focus of the organization, the mission and people are. The bottom line of profit is a by-product of producing a good product and staying in integrity with the mission.

The individual addict is highly self-centered. Workaholics will do anything to maintain their stash, which could be their busyness, their jobs, the excessive rushing and caretaking. *The workaholic organization is also self-centered. It has no boundaries and no respect.* An addictive organization flows over into worker's lives. It does this through excessive demands for more time. Electronic mail and voice mail as well as beepers and cellular phones are modern developments that enable the organization to contact workers at any hour. The workaholic organization makes itself primary in the employees' lives. It creates dependencies through perks and benefits.

We know many employees who say, "I hate my job; yet, I can't afford to leave it." Their addiction is to their benefits, they have no interest in the job. In contrast, a feminist perspective establishes boundaries and respects them. There is the clear distinction between the "me" and the "not me" and the knowledge that it is inappropriate to take over another's life. The existence of boundaries results in priorities so that organizations are governed by things that are important, not by every crisis that comes along.

A company president reflected the effect of appropriate boundaries when she discovered a worker who was putting in 12-hour days. She warned the employee that the organization did not support work addiction and she asked the employee to stop work after 8 hours. The employee refused, so the president took the employee's keys and locked her out at five o'clock every evening. The employee was furious until she saw that her productivity was higher in her 8-hour days than in her 12-hour days. Said the president, "I know I have no control over this employee's work addiction; however, I can set boundaries for my company and I will not be a company which encourages and fosters work addiction in our system."

Crisis management is the norm in the workaholic organization. The function of crisis is to keep everyone off balance and emotionally "pumped up." Crisis shifts our focus to solving the crisis and away from our own needs and feelings. While we are busy with crisis we are not aware of our own pain with the organizational system. During crisis the members of the organization have the impression that something significant is happening. But this is rarely true, for the workaholic organization gives the illusion that something is happening when, in reality, it is becoming a static, closed system.

A feminist approach is suspicious of constant crisis, for constant crisis is nothing more than a sustained high, which itself becomes addictive. Feminists see the need for living a day at a time as well as long range planning. There is the awareness that unless each person is taking self-responsibility, organizational planning is irrelevant. Unfortunately, in the workaholic organization, the focus is external and people feel driven. Therefore, enlightened planning is nearly impossible.

Finally, *there is no intimacy in the workaholic organization.* There is no intimacy with the self, with co-workers or with the work itself. The organization is structured to prevent intimacy, for if we were to really know ourselves and our work we might not be able to support an addictive organization. Or conversely, we might experience our power and the organization would be blasted out of its complacency and become successful, which for some organizations is more fearful than death. People are cogs in the workaholic organization. They are easily used up through burnout. Because there is a ready source of new workers, the workaholic organization does not feel responsible for examining its own internal structure and because it abhors intimacy, workers rarely protest their treatment and rebel.

The feminist perspective is relational and therefore assumes intimacy. Relationships are important—first with the self, then others and then society. If any characteristic describes feminism, it is the longing to connect with the universe at every level of experience. Without relationships, life is nothing. It is here that the feminist perspective is dramatically different from the workaholic organization. By definition, intimacy does not occur in the workaholic organization because the disease process keeps us from being present to our own experience and encourages isolation. Thus, relating to self, others and work is not possible. There is only the numbing effect of the addictive process and the progressive disengagement from feelings when one functions as a workaholic.

Workaholism in Women's Organizations

Unfortunately, all of the foregoing characteristics are often the norm for many organizations. The workaholic organization's denial rests on the fact that it is hooked on these organizational myths. Unfortunately, many feminist organizations have bought into the process of the workaholic organization. If one were to read the mission and goals of most feminist organizations, one would think them to be a radical departure from the white male system, addictive organization. In fact, often their theory has changed but their processes have stayed the same.

One example of feminists staying in the addictive system is seen in the battered women's shelters. Battered women's shelters are characteristically places where staff work long hours under extreme stress for very poor wages. The nature of the work is a setup for burnout. Staff kill themselves in the service of a good work, not stopping to examine the model of self-abuse they portray to residents. Many staffs of these shelters have reacted with horror when confronted about their workaholism, declaring that the measure of one's dedication to the cause is the willingness to work hard with little or no remuneration. The message is "if you are not workaholic, you are not dedicated." The theory underlying treatment in the battered women's shelters is that women are victims. Unwittingly, the shelters perpetuate women's victim status. They do this by counseling battered women to fight the system that abuses them. Yet we have found that the process of fighting the system or going along with it are one in the same. This is a dualism that keeps battered women stuck in the system because both ends of the dualism of "going along" and "fighting" keep the focus "out there" on the white male, addictive system, and away from focusing on the needs of women. The workaholism of the staff perpetuates this dualism because their burnout, busyness and rescuing prevents them from taking responsibility for themselves. It is easier to focus on the victim and the white male system that batters women than to begin their own recovery and to facilitate that in the clients. Workaholism keeps the shelters hooked into the very system they despise.

Battered women's shelters are not alone in this problem of becoming part of the system that they oppose. Many women's organizations (church groups, clubs and agencies) and feminist organizations are workaholic in their organizational processes. Perhaps this is one reason why there is a pervasive disillusionment in the feminist community: Women feel the disparity between their theory and their behavior but do not know what to do about it. Feminist organizations are often characterized by such issues as control, perfectionism, power plays and ideological battles. These addictive processes have become the norm in the organization. To the extent that we believe that such processes are normal in feminist organizations, the feminist organizations have become part of the very disease they claim to abhor.

It has become obvious to us that organizational recovery is not possible without individual recovery. Individual workaholics love the workaholic organization because it feels familiar and the disease feeds the disease. Let us turn now to the individual woman and work addiction to understand why this is so.

WOMEN AND WORK ADDICTION

A work addict is a person whose life has become unmanageable in relation to work, busyness, rescuing and caring. Like other addictions, work addiction is chronic, progressive and fatal if not intervened upon. Surprisingly, our research has shown that work addicts tend to die sooner than alcoholics. This is due to the fact that many work addicts look good on the outside because they are careful about diet and exercise. However, their seeming health habits are actually in the service of "protecting their supply" because if their bodies give out, the work addict cannot work. Thus, work addicts often die rapidly from such catastrophic diseases as brain hemorrhages and massive coronaries. In the middle stage of work addiction, there are other physical symptoms such as ulcers, backaches, chronic fatigue, migraine headaches and hypertension. A nonrecovering work addict who teaches at an Eastern women's college confided that she was hospitalized every 5 years for ailments related to excessive rushing and busyness. Periodically, her body "takes her out." It reacts by getting the rest it needs through acute disease. This is common among work addicts who will stop for nothing. Their bodies force them out.

As feminists we have perpetuated certain myths about work addiction.

One myth is that workaholics are always actively working. This is not true. Sometimes workaholics are sitting comatose in front of the TV or they may be socializing; yet in their minds, they are working. They are rehearsing meetings, planning budgets, mentally reviewing personal issues. One is not necessarily physically active when one is work addicted. Also, not all work addicts are compulsively working. Some are work anorexics, which means they obsessively procrastinate about work, waiting until the last minute to complete projects. Work anorexics are as addicted as compulsive workers only their focus takes the form of avoiding work rather than doing work.

Another myth is that work addicts are usually high-powered male and female executives. Although the media's favorite work addicts are the Lee Iacocca's of the world, it is simply not the case that this disease only affects executives. There are many homemaker addicts, volunteer work addicts, professional caretaker work addicts, in addition to the typical executive woman workaholic.

A woman whose workaholism took the form of constant rushing was a whirling dervish of activity. She went to aerobics before her children awoke, got them dressed and ready for school, drove them to school, visited relatives, ran (emphasis on *ran*) errands, picked the children up at school, delivered them to after-school activities, prepared supper or dashed into a fast food outlet and attended evening meetings. None of these activities related to wage labor. She was addicted to rushing. The result of the addiction was that she never slowed down enough to feel her feelings, nor to acknowledge her pain in her marriage. Constant motion gave her and her family the illusion they were a "family." In reality they were robots. Their frantic activity kept them in stasis and allowed them to maintain a closed system.

Among women, workaholism is the addiction of choice of the unworthy. In *Women's Reality* Schaef (1981), described the original sin of being born female, (i.e., that women are seen as innately inferior). Women carry a void or inner chasm that we have attempted to fill or close from the outside. We believe that some outside intermediary (a relationship, a cause, our work) could help us fill this void; yet all attempts to fill the void externally prove futile.

Many women work addicts believe they are no one unless they are doing. "To be" is not allowed, for why should an innately inferior being be allowed to exist? They have to prove themselves. A colleague said as much when she disclosed that her rampant work addiction kept her from dealing with a feeling she had carried since childhood: "I have no right to exist if I am not doing something productive."

The busyness-unworthiness link is particularly insidious for women for throughout history and even today, in some cultures women are mutilated or killed because they are seen as flawed or unwanted by the society. By remaining in work addiction, women internalize this misogyny into self-hatred and oppress themselves. In reality, our excessive busyness keeps us powerless to claim ourselves while under the illusion we are getting somewhere in the white male system.

Link Between Work and Relationship Addiction

Work addictions and relationship addictions often operate together in women's lives. These two addictions keep women in the addictive process. A woman whose relationship with her husband was psychologically abusive could not bring herself to terminate the relationship. She could not conceive of life without him. She felt lonely and terrified of living on her own without his support and without her identity as part of a couple. Her relationship addiction was apparent in her inability to live without this particular man. She had no life separate from him. Her work addiction entered the picture when she began putting in 16-hour days on the job and being the perfect homemaker/cook the rest of the time. Her work addiction numbed the pain of the unsatisfactory relationship as well as made her indispensable to her husband.

Many women, in their effort to please others, rescue them, or to be liked and affirmed by them (relationship addiction), have worked like dogs. We believe that without our efforts we will be abandoned, as indeed we are when those around us despair of ever having a relationship with us because we cannot be present or intimate when we are in our addiction.

Our focus on serving others to the detriment of attending to our own needs has been a deadly process for women. Typically, we have denied our need for nurturance early in our lives. Then we have tended to choose characteristically women's work like nursing, teaching, social work, etcetera. These professions are setups for our work and relationship addictions because they are jobs where the demands are great and salaries are low. We are supported in our caretaking roles by our children, partners, the society and the church. Against this barrage of support we refuse to attend to our physical needs for rest and our psychological needs for solitude and nurturance. Soon we are projecting onto our loved ones the perfectionistic expectations we have for ourselves. We continue to increase the stressors in our lives while becoming less capable of judging the effects. Many workaholic women have almost died because they refused to endanger a relationship by saying "no" to excessive demands.

Several other characteristics mark women's work addiction. A chief one is denial. We referred earlier to the fact that boasting about work is a unique aspect of work addiction. The denial is subtle in that few workaholics will vehemently deny that they overwork. Instead we compare. We say, "Working is a lot better than other things I could be doing, for example, drinking, drugging, etcetera. The next ploy of denial is to look at trade-offs. We say, "I know I'm a work addict but look at the benefits I've received." Finally we reach the most dangerous level of denial, we say, "Of course I am a workaholic but I do not see it as dangerous for me." This is the most frightening aspect of the denial process because, as every alcoholic knows, a drink makes one feel good temporarily. So, too, with work addiction, the temporary high and sense of well-being only portends an imminent disaster. In the service of staying in our denial we are dishonest about how much our work and our busyness affect us. Unfortunately, work addiction medicates our feelings so that in the latter stages of the disease we no longer monitor our bodies. Thus, stopping is less likely to be an option the farther down the scale we go.

External referrenting is another aspect of our work addiction. This characteristic relates to our lack of self-esteem. We look outside ourselves for proof that we are okay and we provide that proof by our busyness. We attempt to convince ourselves and others through our accomplishments.

Workaholics are list makers. The list serves as an external referent. We can no longer manage our own lives—the list tells us where to go and what to do. Many women workaholics have said that without their list they would have no idea as to their own priorities. Rather than a flexible guide, the list becomes a tight girdle. One woman allots a certain amount of time each day to spend with her children. If the children are not willing or available between three o'clock and five o'clock, they get no time with their mother. The list is a link to our stash. It tells us what we have accomplished and what is left to be done. The problem, for the work addict, is that the list is never done. There is always another list.

Workaholics are unable to relax. The inability to relax is a process of the disease as well as a physical reality. Work addicts usually schedule too many activities, projects or involvements. Consequently, they are rushing from one engagement to another. The net effect of rushing is that one is not present to the activity at hand. Of course, having "just a few more tasks" is part of the stash of the workaholic.

The physical aspect is that work addicts get an adrenaline high from their rushing and busyness. Some workaholics feel their addictions may be to the rush of adrenaline which keeps them on a perpetual high and enables them to accomplish unusual feats. Without the adrenaline high, normal life feels very dull indeed. The problem with incessant adrenaline production is that it is almost impossible to relax and eventually the adrenal glands give out. Severe exhaustion and burn-out are frequently the exhaustion of the adrenal glands. Conversely, for the work anorexic the inability to relax is the result of the constant inner turmoil and blaming associated with the avoidance of work. In both the compulsive and the anorexic workaholic there is a sad dilemma: They are exhausted but unable to relax.

As women it is important that we reflect on the similarities of oppression of our work addiction and oppression by the white male system. The above example is a case in point. Work addiction is, at root, self abusive. We choose conditions that result in our leaving our female system process to seek affirmation by the addictive white male system. Our excessive pleasing, busyness and overworking exhaust us, yet the very process prevents us from reflecting on our own lives and on the society itself. The inability to relax, which is a result of the work addiction, keeps us in the cycle of addiction and seeking ways to numb our pain. We are either too busy or too tired to notice that the values we sought in our emerging female systems have given way to the old dysfunctional system. All around us we are told that the addictive system, especially overworking, is normal because everyone does it. Before long, we are back in the white male system that knows and understands everything, and which is the only reality there is, we believe.

RECOVERY FROM WORKAHOLISM

After years of working with women, organizations and the addictive process, it is clear to us that the way out of the addictive system and the white male system lies first and foremost in women beginning their own recovery. Too often feminists have been seduced into social analysis and social experiments without having done their own recovery. It is very appealing to try to reform the society before healing as individuals. Unfortunately, with the addictive system, it never works. As long as we remain focused "out there," we remain mired in the society's addictive disease and work addiction is especially good at keeping us externally oriented.

The individual, the organization and the society are all immersed in the same disease process. The shift out of this disease process is not found in a technique, a mantra, or an exercise program. The white male addictive system is a paradigm. We may believe it has come to the end of its usefulness but it is all-pervasive even as it becomes progressively dysfunctional, even fatal. It is imperative that as feminists we remember that reclaiming our lives is found in our willingness to make a profound paradigm shift. It is a shift out of the white male, addictive system and into an emerging living process system. Paradoxically, this shift is both absolute and done a day at a time and a step at a time through such well-tested programs as the Twelve Steps of Alcoholics Anonymous now used in all the Twelve Step based programs. Recently, Workaholics Anonymous groups have been springing up in several major cities in the United States. They offer a program for healing and a way into an alternative paradigm.

The one thing that we know works effectively with addictive diseases, that has a solid track record, and that is used successfully by millions of addicts, is the Twelve Step program originially begun by Alcoholics Anonymous. Continuing in this tradition, Workaholics Anonymous groups are spreading across the United States. They apply processes which have worked for 50 years with other addictions to the disease of workaholism.

Workaholics Anonymous offers such processes as: attendance at Workaholics Anonymous meetings where workaholics share their stories, strength and support with one another in an environment of acceptance and confidentiality; working with sponsors, who are people with longer recovery from work addiction who assist others in their recovery program and are available for counsel, reality checking and guidance with the steps; identification of bottom-line behaviors that trigger us into our addiction; developing a work inventory and a program of sane working; and the Twelve Steps of Workaholics Anonymous as an overall framework for recovery.

Workaholics, like overeaters, have an especially challenging road to recovery. Unlike alcoholics or drug addicts, who abstain completely from the addictive substance, the workaholic must develop a sane relationship to the addictive process of work from the first day of recovery. While society frowns upon alcohol and drug addiction, work addiction is actively supported. Consequently, we believe that work addicts need to pay careful attention to supporting themselves with solid recovery programs.

Finally, a word about the place of stress management in recovery from workaholism. For many years, addictive organizations have offered stress management programs to employees as a way to cope with the excessive demands of the job. Although stress management can be helpful in reducing the physical and psychological effects on the person, stress management alone is not an effective antidote for work addiction. Moreover, when workaholic organizations are in denial about their workaholic systems and expectations, they provide stress management to employees in order to make the addictive organization more tolerable to them. In actuality, the organization itself is the source of the stress. Stress management offered to individual employees keeps the focus off these dysfunctional organizations. Thus, we should not assume that stress management programs will address the underlying addictive process in either the organization or in ourselves. As an adjunct to recovery, these programs are fine. Used by themselves, they only prolong the addictive disease.

CONCLUSION

Workaholism is known as the "addiction of choice of the unworthy." As women, we live in a culture that defines us as unworthy. Unfortunately, many of us still hold the belief deep inside of us that if we just do it right, if we just do enough, and if we just put others, our work, or anything besides ourselves first, we will be legitimate and we will be accepted.

In an addictive society, no one is unaffected by addiction, whether we are female or male. Women, too, have been affected by addictions, especially workaholism and it is up to us to heal ourselves with support from others. We did not cause these addictive diseases and we can heal from them, but first, we must name them, then we must notice how they affect our lives, and then we must begin our recovery.

REFERENCES

Fassel, D. (1990). *Working ourselves to death.* San Francisco: Harper & Row.

Schaef, A. W. (1981). *Women's reality: An emerging female system in the white male society.* San Francisco: Harper & Row.

Weitzman, L. J. (1985). *The divorce revolution: The unexpected social and economic consequences for women and children in America.* New York: Free Press.

Index

Springer Publishing Company

FEMINIST ETHICS
IN PSYCHOTHERAPY

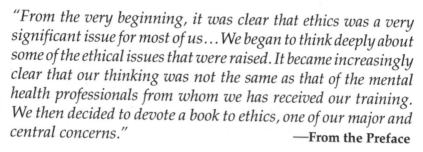

Hannah Lerman, PhD,
Clinical Psychologist, Los Angeles
Natalie Porter, PhD,
University of New Mexico School of Medicine, Editors

"From the very beginning, it was clear that ethics was a very significant issue for most of us... We began to think deeply about some of the ethical issues that were raised. It became increasingly clear that our thinking was not the same as that of the mental health professionals from whom we has received our training. We then decided to devote a book to ethics, one of our major and central concerns." —**From the Preface**

Focusing on the Feminist Therapy Institute's Code of Ethics, this important volume addresses a variety of issues—including ethics of power differentials • therapist accountability • specific cultural diversities and oppressions • the therapist-society relationship.

PARTIAL CONTENTS: The Contribution of Feminism to Ethics in Psychotherapy, *H. Lerman and N. Porter*. The Need for an integrated Analysis of Opression in Feminist Therapy Ethics, *V. Kanuha*. Empowerment as an Ethical Imperative, *A.J. Smith and M.A. Douglas*. Boundary Violations: Misuse of the Power of the Therapist, *H. Lerman and D.N. Rigby*. How To Be a Failure as a Family Therapist: A Feminist Perspective, *E. Kaschak*. Working Within the Lesbian Community: The Dilemma of Overlapping Relationships, *A.J. Smith*. On Being an "Only One," *V.L. Sears*. The Self-Care and Wellness of Feminist Therapists, *P.S. Faunce*. Women in Poverty: Ethical Dimensions in Therapy, *P.S. Faunce*. Therapy, Feminist Ethics and the Community of Color with Particular Emphasis on the Treatment of Black Women, *E.K. Childs*. Feminist Ethics with Victims of Violence, *L.E.A. Walker*. Public Advocacy, *L.B. Rosewater*. Feminist Therapy Ethics in the Media, *K. E. Peres*.

1990 267pp 0-8261-6290-8 hard